Antique
WOODWIND INSTRUMENTS

An Identification and Price Guide

Peter H. Adams

D1608948

Schiffer Publishing Ltd

4880 Lower Valley Road, Atglen, PA 19310 USA

Library of Congress Cataloging-in-Publication Data

Adams, Peter H.
  Antique woodwind instruments : an identification and
price guide / Peter H. Adams.
      p. cm.
  ISBN 0-7643-2224-9 (pbk.)
1. Woodwind instruments—Identification. 2. Woodwind
instruments—Prices. 3. Woodwind instruments—Collectors
and collecting. I. Title.

ML931.A33 2005
788.2'19'075—dc22

                          2005012798

Designed by "Sue"
Type set in Zurich Blk BT/Souvenir Lt BT

ISBN: 0-7643-2224-9
Printed in China

Published by Schiffer Publishing Ltd.
4880 Lower Valley Road
Atglen, PA 19310
Phone: (610) 593-1777; Fax: (610) 593-2002
E-mail: Info@schifferbooks.com

For the largest selection of fine reference books on this and
related subjects, please visit our web site at
www.schifferbooks.com
We are always looking for people to write books on new and
related subjects. If you have an idea for a book please
contact us at the above address.

This book may be purchased from the publisher.
Include $3.95 for shipping.
Please try your bookstore first.
You may write for a free catalog.

In Europe, Schiffer books are distributed by
Bushwood Books
6 Marksbury Ave.
Kew Gardens
Surrey TW9 4JF England
Phone: 44 (0) 20 8392-8585; Fax: 44 (0) 20 8392-9876
E-mail: info@bushwoodbooks.co.uk
Free postage in the U.K., Europe; air mail at cost.

Contents

Acknowledgements

The Library of Congress, Dayton C. Miller Collection within the Music Division, has kindly provided the color photographs that appear on the covers of this book. I wish to thank the Music Division, and especially Carol Lynn Bamford, Music Specialist, Library of Congress, Dayton C. Miller Flute Collection, for taking the time to provide images of the following instruments in the Collection: DCM 0158 Hendrik Richters/Oboe in C, and DCM 0945: Johann Benedikt Gahn/Treble (Alto) recorder in F. I also wish to thank the Library of Congress, Music Division for providing me access to the musical instrument trade catalogs that form such a large body of this book. These images are the property of the Library of Congress, and have been kindly provided for this book.

The following people have been invaluable in answering questions during the preparation of this book. Dr. Al Rice, curator at the Fiske Museum, Claremont College, answered technical questions about musical instrument history, and read the manuscript. Andreas Strieve of Half Moon Bay, California, greatly helped by translating much of the Heckel catalog. While not a musical instrument expert, Mr. Strieve is a native speaker of German. I also wish to thank Peter Schiffer of Schiffer Publishing for suggesting and publishing this book.

I also wish to extend a special thank you to Tony Bingham, the publisher of *The New Langwill Index*, for allowing me to abstract information from this invaluable reference book.

Preface

This book is designed as an identification guide for people who are unfamiliar with European-style woodwind instruments. It is not designed to provide new information; rather, it relies upon research in *The New Langwill Index (NLI)*, trade catalogs printed before 1932, *The New Grove Dictionary of Music and Musicians (NGDMM)*, and other works cited in the bibliography. As woodwind instruments have existed since at least 10,000 BC, this book must be introductory in nature. Specifically, this book is designed to help identify and value some of the more common instrument types that were manufactured for the U.S. market between about 1800 and prior to about 1932, along with a few earlier instrument types. The scope of this book is therefore to bring together information as a finding aid for beginning collectors and anyone who encounters a European-style woodwind instrument that needs to be identified.

The year 1800 is offered here as a beginning point for this book, simply because this was when technological, aesthetic, and political developments began to reshape the U.S. and imported goods arriving here. A more in-depth explanation of this statement will be found later in the book. This date is more or less the beginning of the Industrial Age.

While 1932 is a subjective cut off point, this decade experienced significant changes. Pitch in Europe and North America finally standardized. Newer musical styles replaced older styles. Makers went out of business due to the Great Depression, while others fought to stay profitable. Europe suffered from the afteraffects of World War I, eventually leading to World War II, when the geopolitical world was greatly remade. Community bands and orchestras began a decline in the U.S., partly for financial reasons. The recording and radio industries finally began to make significant inroads in music listening habits. Because of these and other events, U.S. musical instrument manufacturers began a slow decline that led to companies buying out other companies. This has had an important effect upon recently-made instruments. One must be careful to find out if an instrument was made by a company before it was acquired or after it was acquired. Often, but not always, quality suffered after the acquisition.

The structure of this book follows that of my first book *Antique Brass Wind Instruments*. In both books, musical instrument trade catalogs from makers and dealers have provided an acceptable amount of images and information. Both of my books are organized around specific instrument makers, beginning with a gallery of illustrations of various basic instru-

ment types for quick identification. The second part of this book consists of the makers' sections. The book concludes with various appendices designed to help value instruments and find additional information. All images of musical instruments that appear in this book are extensively redrawn, and are therefore copyrighted by this author. No reuse is allowed without written permission of this author.

The reader is advised that because musical instrument catalogs rarely provided complete information or provided information in a less-than-standardized manner, some inconsistencies will appear in the descriptive lists. I have tried as much as possible to standardize information, and have ignored information about types of cases, accessories, and their prices. Missing information about makers and catalog numbers are not of my making. Because images are repeatedly reused, the reader will encounter images of instruments that are not listed in the price lists.

Because of space limitations within this book, some musical instrument trade catalogs examined in preparation for writing this book have not received the same coverage as others. Though unfortunate, this situation is unavoidable in order to keep down the size of the book. Also, while I would have preferred to use only catalogs from manufacturers, trade catalogs are not always available. Readers are advised to consult the Index as well as pages 7 and 8, which include brief comments to help identify differences between instruments, and especially key systems. Readers are also advised that some catalogs reused catalog numbers, omitted numbers and full descriptions, etc. Every effort has been made to retain the original order of these catalogs.

As this book is designed to help identify woodwind instruments sold in the United States, some countries will not be well represented here, especially Eastern European countries. For the most part, Germany, France, and England were the major exporters of all forms of non-keyboard musical instruments during the 19th century. Musical instrument makers are known to have worked in Eastern Europe, Italy, Spain, Scandinavia, and Japan. Yet, only after Japan emerged from its devastation of World War II did it begin to export musical instruments to the United States. Not discussed at all in this book are exports of musical instruments from the United States. The reader is therefore advised to be aware of the unavoidable Euro-centric bias of this book

Introduction to Identifying and Valuing Musical Instruments

The most difficult feature in writing this book has been providing values for musical instruments. The value of historical and even used musical instruments is highly subjective. An instrument has value for the following reasons: a famous person might once have owned the instrument (its history); the company that made the instrument might have been important; the material that was used to make the instrument (such as ivory, glass, ceramic, wood, metal, etc.) might have value; the instrument's key system might be highly desired; the instrument's condition might be exceptional; the instrument's tone and ease of playing might be highly desired; and the construction technique might be significant. Rarity of an instrument is a question that simply cannot be answered with any degree of certainty. While a company may have offered an instrument, records rarely exist that document how many of a specific instrument were actually made. For museum-quality instruments, musical quality and condition are often less significant than for instruments meant to be played.

Identifying a previous owner is a task often best done by an expert. All too often, family stories, such as "Grandfather used it during the Civil War," are faulty. If, however, authentic documents exist that can attest to an instrument's history, the value generally increases. Yet, this area of valuing instruments is fraught with chicanery, especially by unscrupulous antique dealers.

Identifying instrument makers can be a challenge. Quality instruments are often marked by the maker. Some instruments are marked with the name of the company that sold the instrument, but did not actually make the instrument, especially beginning in the Industrial Age. During the Renaissance and even into the Baroque period, some makers used symbols rather than names to identify their instruments. A very few instruments are marked with the name of an owner. Most instruments of unexceptional quality were/are never signed. So, instruments with names on them (engraved, burned, stamped, etc.) command more interest but not necessarily higher value than unmarked instruments. *The New Langwill Index* (hereafter *NLI*) is the single most useful book to sort out this complex situation. As a caution, information can be stamped onto an instrument at any time, thus making fakery very easy. Additionally, information can easily be removed from woodwind instruments. Yet, due to the relatively low value of woodwind instruments, fakery is not endemic.

Within the last one hundred years or so, antique instruments have been reproduced in both quantity and quality (and lack of quality too!). So, even though an instrument may have been correctly identified as being a Renaissance-type instru-

ment, one must be careful not to assume that the instrument dates from the Renaissance. In fact, only a handful of Renaissance-era instruments exist outside of institutional collections, and they tend to be well documented. Therefore, this book does not discuss at length any of the various woodwind instruments then in use. For that, readers are directed to Anthony Baines' *Woodwind Instruments and their History.*

Identifying an instrument's age and value by what it is made of can be problematic. Prior to the introduction of material from the tropics, maple, boxwood, fruitwood, silver, bone, and animal horn were used almost exclusively to make woodwind instruments. For example, most bassoons were made of maple because of its strength, relative lightness, and availability. A few bassoons were made of boxwood, or walnut. Today, quality bassoons are still made of maple. Boxwood was the preferred wood for making flutes, piccolos, clarinets, oboes, etc. during the Classical and early Romantic periods. It was used well into the 19th century, increasingly on student grade instruments. The cream-colored wood is relatively free of knots, is not prone to splitting, and generally does not grow large enough to make bassoons. Mounts were made of horn or bone for average quality instruments during the Renaissance and Baroque periods, but increasingly were used on inexpensive instruments at the end of the 19th century. Brass was used as early as the Renaissance to make most keys. Carse states that clarinets made of brass were made as early as 1818 (p. 161). Brass persisted into the 19th century, often plated with German silver (G.S.), and late in the 19th century plated with pure silver. Prior to the 19th century, G.S. was not used, and then only after about 1840. Pure silver was used on rare occasions to make mounts as early as the Renaissance and is still used today on better-quality instruments. Such examples always command attention by serious buyers. Very few solid silver woodwind instruments date from before about 1850. Gold was very rarely used to make keys during the Baroque era. By itself, gold is too soft to make keys. So, gold must be plated over a base metal. Instruments with gold keys were intended for only the wealthiest people, such as nobility, and always command attention by serious collectors. When gold was used during this time, it was most often used as a gold wash, or gold plate on keys or bells, and even then only offered as a special order item. During the later part of the 19th century, both the increased availability of gold and silver (partly due to discoveries in California, Nevada, and elsewhere) and the rising socio-economic level in Europe and the U.S. allowed instrument makers to construct instruments made of silver or gold. Even then, only a few flutes were made of gold. Aluminum came into use toward the end of the

19th century, but enjoyed only minimal success in making musical instruments. One flute is mentioned in this book that has an aluminum head joint. Platinum also came into use during the end of the 19th century, but was too expensive to use on woodwind instruments. Only later in the 20th century, flutists began to use platinum head joints on silver flutes. A flute made entirely out of platinum would be prohibitively expensive, even today.

Ebony, ivory, and other exotic tropical materials came into Europe in sufficient quantity to be made into musical instruments during the Age of Discovery. While ivory woodwind instruments were made in the Renaissance, most of the early woodwind instruments made of ebony evidently date from the Baroque period. The end of the 19th century saw extensive use of these materials. Their use declined in the early 20th century, partly due to World War I and World War II, but also due to decreased supply. Crystal, glass, and ceramic evidently came into very limited use during the middle of the 19th century. The earliest use of ebonite, a vulcanized rubber/sulfur compound, was by A.G. Badger to make a flute dated 1859. Celluloid was used for a limited time to make student-grade recorders around the beginning of the 20th century. True plastic was used to make woodwind instruments around 1939, according to a patent for the predecessor of the Tonette. Late in the 20th century, companies began developing plastic that looked like ivory. Some makers of historic flutes and harpsichords have found these plastics to be quite usable.

Identifying and Valuing Flutes and Clarinets

Identifying flute key systems can be very difficult, as so much innovation has been lavished upon these two instruments. Nancy Toff's book documents in detail how many key systems have been invented for the flute (see page 130 for a list of some key systems). Toff, like many other writers cited in the bibliography of this book, uses schematics of key systems that at first look bewildering. A competent flute player can often help explain some of the basics of these schematics. These diagrams can be more valuable for identifying variant key systems than a good quality photograph, if one has the level of knowledge to use the schematics. Another important resource is found on pages 42-43, Vol. 9 of *NGDMM*, which includes illustrations of thirteen flutes with various key systems, including a few rare types on p. 42 (examples E and F), and p. 43 (examples B and C).

Various types of key systems have been used to make flutes. The earliest key system used a simple lever with a touch piece at one end and a keypad at another. The earliest pads were simply pieces of leather. The key itself was a flat piece of brass. Evidence is sketchy, but the fulcrum and lever key was evidently invented in the later part of the Renaissance, if surviving instruments are any indication. This key type persisted into the early 20th century on one-key flutes and on clarinets until about 1840. However, by that time, flat sheets of brass (or bars for long keys) were no longer used, except on clarinets. This older key type appeared on Albert system clarinets, and was only used on the long clarinet keys that covered the lowest notes. The newer, mass produced keys have a uniformly round, and often oversized keypad. The touch piece also had evolved from a flat wide end of the key into an organic, almost tear drop

shape. During the 1810s, Iwan Müller invented the first stuffed pad, and this pad was quickly adopted by most woodwind makers.

Around 1780, Mr. Tromlitz invented a key that was basically a fulcrum system, except that the key was secured at one end to a fulcrum. In the middle of the key was a touch plate. At the end of the key was the keypad. This invention was an improvement above the previous key. It could span distances (though not as long as a two-part fulcrum key), and was considerably quieter, easier to maintain, more elegant, and most importantly, more reliably covered the tone hole. It was, however, more expensive, if only because of all the handwork needed to make this key. This key was used not just on flutes and clarinets. It even can be found on large recorders made in the 20th century.

Early in the 19th century, some flute makers began adding keys to play below D. These key arrangements varied in quality of workmanship. About 1820, makers developed a more refined nearly dome-shaped key flap. These keys have been called salt spoon keys, as they very closely resemble the small salt spoon then in vogue in Europe.

With the advent of mass production, key designs became more uniform. Gone were the flat keys in common use from the Renaissance through to the Classical period. Gone were the salt spoon keys that persisted into the middle of the 19th century. Gone was the Tromlitz key. Gone was the pewter plug key favored by the English. Gone too was the use of wood blocks in favor of posts. As such, any flute that contains any of these features is surely pre-1850s, and probably earlier. With the exception of student grade flutes, the fewer the number of keys a flute has, the greater the likelihood that the flute was made before 1800 (or is a copy of an early flute).

The most common key system for flutes today is the Boehm system, named for its inventor Theobold Boehm. His last design (1847) is the basis for the modern flute and can be identified by having rods and pillars to which keys and pads are attached. For this type of flute, three types of touches can be found. The first touch (and the oldest) is called a key ring. Though not found on modern Boehm-system flutes, ring keys are still found on clarinets. The second type is also called a covered key. The touch is a complete disk without a hole. A third touch at first looks like a covered key, but has a small hole in it. Late in the 19th century, flute makers began using the plateau key (a form of covered keys). The key stands above the instrument on metal extensions, as is found on all saxophones. Previously, the simple system (also called the Meyer system for flutes, made mainly during the 19th and early 20th centuries) used a toggle or lever type of key system. Meyer flutes could have as few as one or as many as 17 keys. They generally had touches that were either ring keys or covered keys. A few makers, such as the company Rudall, Carte & Co., made a flute that had plateau keys, but was fingered like a simple system flute. These flutes were called Pratton model. See the illustrations on pages 12-15 to help better understand these keys. Another feature that can help distinguish Boehm system flutes from Meyer system flutes is that Boehm system flutes have roller keys for the little finger of the right hand. Meyer system flutes did not have roller keys, except as a special order item.

The key system of a woodwind instrument can greatly determine its value. For example, a Boehm-system flute made in 1890 originally sold for as much as $300, while a new simple system flute of the same time rarely sold for more than $30. So, it is in the interest of the owner to identify the key system of an instrument. The addition of a single key or the repositioning of a single key can signify a different key system. Also, Boehm system flutes can have either an open G sharp or closed G sharp key. Knowing the difference is something that only a flutist can verify.

Identifying the key system for a clarinet is only slightly less complex than for a flute. Albert Rice's book *The Clarinet in the Classical Period* will be of help. *The Development of Woodwind Fingering Systems in the Nineteenth and Twentieth Centuries* by Jerry L. Voorhees is a second book that can assist in identifying a variety of key systems for woodwind instruments. The clarinet was invented in the Classical period by the Denner family. In its earliest form, it looked much like a baroque recorder, but with a single reed tied to the mouthpiece with waxed thread. The earliest surviving clarinets have as few as two keys made of sheet brass. By the end of the Romantic era, clarinets usually had 5 or 6 keys. In 1812, Ivan Müller introduced the 13-key clarinet, later developed by the Albert firm, now called the Albert system. The keys were brass. The two keys for the left little finger were long lever keys that were made of thin square brass bars. Müller also made other improvements to the clarinet. One example is around 1845, when he joined with Heckel to apply ring keys to the lower joint of the clarinet. Later, Carl Baermann and Georg Ottensteiner together applied ring keys to the upper joint. As with the flute, many makers developed variations in order to overcome some problem. Other makers simply wanted to avoid paying royalties to others. The Klosé-Boehm 17-key clarinet became the dominant clarinet during the middle 19th century. Klosé was a clarinet teacher at the French Conservatory who worked with Auguste Buffet to develop this clarinet. It shares the Boehm name because it uses keyworks developed along the lines of research conducted by Boehm on the flute. Boehm had no hand in developing the Boehm system clarinet. Even this clarinet was subjected to developments. Late in the 19th century, makers developed a hybrid called the half Boehm, in which the upper joint had the Albert system and the lower joint had the Boehm system. This hybrid was not widely accepted, and examples are possibly rather rare today. One feature that can help differentiate Albert system clarinets from Boehm system clarinets is that Boehm system clarinets rarely have roller on the keys for the little fingers. Beginning in 1821, César Janssen introduced these rollers. The Fiske museum owns a circa 1825 13-key Baumann clarinet with such keys. Roller keys eventually were placed upon many types of woodwinds. Boehm system clarinets also have between 2 and 5 spatula-shaped keys for each little finger.

Pitch of an instrument can also help date the instrument. Prior to about 1900, pitch in Europe and the U.S. was not standardized. Pitch was locally controlled. Piano makers, and later American reed organ makers, banded together around 1890 to create a standard pitch that would help them more easily sell their instruments. Pitch began to be standardized shortly thereafter into high pitch (A=440) and low pitch (A=435). Instruments with either H.P. or L.P. were surely made between about 1880 and 1930. As a caution, in its undated catalog (circa 1895), *Musikinstrumente und Saiten*, p. 140, G. and A. Klemm offered tuning forks that were either pitched in A=870 or A=888. The first pitch is often given as low pitch (A=435). In the catalog, however, the low pitch tuning fork is

stamped "International Pitch." High pitch (A=444) is described as Vienna pitch. Pitch began to be standardized shortly thereafter in high pitch (A=452) and low pitch (A=439). In England, Rudall, Carte & Co.'s 1931 catalog specifies on its cover: "Note, Please state whether high Pitch A=452.4 or Low Pitch A=439 is required." Thus, even during the time that H.P. and L.P. were being stamped onto instruments, some variations in pitch still existed. As late as 1930, a few makers were still offering high and low pitch instruments in the U.S. Buegeleisen (and surely others) even offered to remake low pitch instruments into high pitch instruments by cutting them down. One wonders how satisfactory this operation really was.

Identifying the age and key system of all other woodwind instruments is nowhere as complex as for flutes and clarinets. Although the oboe and bassoon were invented in the 17th century in France, all such examples are surely in museums by now. 18th century oboes can be found rarely, and are much like their 17th century ancestors. The oboe of this time was made in three pieces, sometimes with corps de recharge. Boxwood, ebony, or maple were the dominant woods. Ivory ferrules and brass keys dominated. Silver keys and ferrules are found on a few instruments, and generally are of superior construction, or the earlier keys and ferrules were replaced at a later date. The earliest oboes had 3 keys allowing for 2 low notes. Because some players preferred to play with the left hand below the right hand, a duplicate D sharp key was offered. Some oboes of this time have this duplicate key removed, and the tone hole plugged. The non-duplicate key had a touch for either hand, and is often called a swallow-tail key. This same type of key can be found on large Renaissance recorders. During the first quarter of the 19th century, the oboe began to be fitted with more keys, following somewhat the developments of the Boehm system flute. Even pre-19th century oboes were occasionally retrofitted with modern contrivances. In 1825, Joseph Sellner with the assistance of the maker Koch, developed an oboe with 10 keys. In France, Trièbert, Barret, and later Lorée developed the modern French oboe. Ebony, cocus, pear wood, and grenadilla eventually replaced boxwood. For a short time, metal oboes were made during this period, but their tone was found objectionable. The French Conservatoire Model developed around 1880, and Carse states (p. 140) that this was the final development of the modern French oboe. Today, the French oboe is widely used in the U.S. The German oboe with its more robust tone and a tuning hole in the bell joint is still used in Germany and Austria. Variations in profiles can sometimes help identify the region where an 18th century instrument was made. Bells are less flared. The finial at the top of the oboe (also called an onion shape) can be either bulbous (found throughout Europe, mainly in Germanic regions) or might not exist at all (exclusively English). Oberlender was known for making his finials almost oval. French finials are some of the more elegant onion shaped finials. By the 19th century, the finial had been reduced to only a small turning, and is even less indicative of a region. Bell shape can also help determine age. For example, late in the 18th century, some instruments were made with a bell that flared out, then changed direction, and again flared out, resulting in a bell with a stepped look. This type of bell persisted throughout the 19th century.

The history of the bassoon is rather complex, given the many different bass double reed instruments that preceded the bassoon's rise to supremacy. Few if any 16th or 17th century bassoons survive outside of museums. A fair number of 18th century bassoons still exist in private collections and can be easily identified by their profile and key systems. Variations in profiles can sometimes help identify the region where an instrument was made. Bassoons were and still are made in five sections: the metal crook, the wing joint, the butt joint, the long joint, and the bell joint. Two thumb keys and one additional key on the butt joint are common on late 18th century bassoons. These keys are flat brass lever keys. Early 18th century bassoons often had elegant turnings on the tubes. The flared bell developed evidently late in the 18th century. Bassoons of the 19th century generally were still made of maple, often stained black, but increasingly also included German silver mounts. One easy way to tell if a bassoon is old is to examine the butt joint for worm holes. Most of the 18th century instruments that survive have suffered this damage, and therefore should never be played. Those of the 19th century quickly developed more keys to accommodate increased range and chromatic notes. During this time, two bassoon systems developed: German and French. In the U.S., the German system is more common than the French system. The German bassoon, based upon the work of Almenräder and later by Heckel, is robust and rich. The French bassoon is more elegant, yet less robust.

Identifying the value of an instrument based upon its condition is critical. For example, a flute made of ivory, glass, ceramic, ebonite, or stone with a crack in the body can sometimes be repaired satisfactorily but only by an expert. However, a poorly repaired instrument will have less value than an unrepaired instrument. So, if in doubt, don't repair. Cracks in wooden instruments can be repaired successfully, especially ebony. An instrument made of metal with a crack in it can often be repaired. Missing keys, though problematic for pre-1800 instruments, can be remade without significantly decreasing the value of an instrument. Broken joints, missing keys, or missing joints greatly reduce the value of an instrument. However, any pre-1800 instrument or otherwise historically significant instrument even with major damage should never be discarded, but should be examined by a professional. Missing ferrules do not significantly decrease the value of an instrument, unless the other ferrules are highly ornamented.

Identifying the value of an instrument based upon its playability is a question best left to a musician who is expert at playing a given instrument. Generally, historic instruments are not valued based upon their playability. Only relatively modern instruments are so identified, and are outside the time frame of this book. As a warning: any woodwind instrument that has not been played for any great length of time should not be played until it has been properly reconditioned. This often means oiling the instrument to prevent cracking. Such a process should be left to professionals.

Identifying the value and date of an instrument based upon its construction technique involves many aspects. The construction technique might show experimentation in developing a new key system, or solving some critical problem like intonation. However, construction techniques are better at dating an instrument than providing value. Consider the following seven examples.

First, prior to the 19th century, quality flutes, clarinets, piccolos, and oboes were made with rings of wood surrounding the tube. These rings were often carved away, leaving a knob into which a lever-type key could be placed, or were left for ornamentation. Early 19th century clarinets often retained the entire ring. Some late 19th century D and E flat clarinets still retain the entire rings.

Second, prior to the adoption of cork joints in the late 19th century, wax impregnated thread was lapped over the male tenon, and inserted into the other joint. This and the preceding features can be found on instruments of modest value that were made late into the 19th century. Cork tenons seem to have been introduced in Teobaldo Monzani's patent of 1812. Tenons were covered with cork or cloth and had chamfered or beveled ends on the ends of the tenons for use on flutes and clarinets. Also, period instruments have occasionally been fitted with cork joints.

Third, prior to the complete adoption of post-and-pillars (early in the 20th century) to which the keys were mounted, a few makers made brass saddles that were screwed into the body of the instrument. This U-shaped structure (see page 19), found especially on late 18th century bassoons, would then be the support into which the lever-type key would be fastened.

Fourth, partially or fully metal-lined wood and ivory flute head joints came into use during the late 19th century to prevent the joint from splitting on quality instruments. This feature is not generally found on quality flutes before at least the middle of the century. Late 19th and early 20th century wood flutes without lined metal head joints are generally of inferior quality.

Fifth, ornamentation, if found, may appear on keys, ferrules, bell, and rarely on the tube itself. As examples, clam shell-shaped keys exist on rare instruments of high quality. Highly decorated ferrules exist. Some makers heavily engraved the bells of clarinets, especially on high-quality instruments, instruments intended for trade fairs, or on presentation instruments. Also, a few makers of clarinets, oboes, and recorders carved the body of the instrument, sometimes very elaborately. Laurant even went so far as to mount gemstones on a few of his flutes that were made of solid crystal. Highly ornamented instruments are usually museum pieces. Even incomplete examples are of value because of their rarity.

Sixth, on English clarinets of the late 1700s, makers seemed unique in constructing the mouthpiece and barrel out of the same piece of wood. By 1785, English makers gave up this practice. An example is pictured on page 903, Vol. 5 in *NGDMM*.

Seventh, page 281, Vol. 18 in *NGDMM* includes illustrations of seven oboes of the 18th and 19th centuries. One of the rarest examples on this page is the Vox humana that at first looks like a plain English oboe without ornamental wooden rings. However, the instrument's bell is very much wider than an English oboe. The vox humana is a tenor oboe in the key of F. Surviving examples of the vox humana are mainly English, but southern Italian examples might exist. The vox humana enjoyed some success mainly during the 18th century. Two bass oboes are also shown. Bass oboes often are made with a butt joint similar to a bassoon. The easiest way to tell the difference between a bass oboe and a bassoon is that the bass oboe's bell ends about a quarter of the way up the instrument. The bassoon's bell extends well above the rest of the instrument. Neither of these instruments is depicted in this book.

Patent numbers, dates, and serial numbers can greatly help to date instruments. The earliest woodwind instruments that have patent numbers were made by the Monzani Co. of London about 1809. The date, however, only means that an instrument was made after the date that the patent was applied for. So, an instrument with a patent date of 1884 was made no earlier than that year. Serial numbers only came into wide use toward the middle or end of the 19th century. Because so many factories burned down at that time, reconstructing a working list of serial numbers for even the largest makers is an on-going task, and dating an instrument in this manner is sadly still not without problems.

As can be seen from the above discussions, small features that one might miss at first glance can often greatly help in identification. Instruments that have been significantly altered or damaged might therefore be most difficult to properly identify and value. In such cases, an expert appraiser will be required.

For this book, I have used the definition of antique as being anything made over one hundred years ago. Instruments made less than fifty years ago are semi antiques, and are not discussed here in any length. Anything made before 1800 is, however, considered by many experts to be an antique. So, some care is needed when using this term. Also, any instrument that a non-expert identifies as being from the U.S. Civil War could have been made anytime between about 1830 and 1920. Thus, unless proof exists that an instrument was actually used during a given time, the reader is advised to be very skeptical of such claims. Instruments used during the Civil War all too often command prices higher than instruments made before or after that event (even identical examples!), even when the quality or condition of the instrument would indicate otherwise. I have spent so much time discussing the dating of instruments because woodwind instruments made before 1800, in good condition, and well made always command special attention by serious collectors.

Instruments that do not appear in this book should not be considered as rare. Many non-Western woodwind instruments have value. Some instruments have absolutely no musical value, such as tourist-grade instruments like the dvoynice pictured on page 10. Sadly, most non-European instruments are tourist grade and are of no significant value. Other instruments, especially those brought to the U.S. as war loot, might have considerable value. If an instrument is not found in this book, the reader is instructed to consult the chapter on "Societies, Museums, Auction Houses, and Websites" (pages 157-158), and the Bibliography. The most important beginning point in identifying a musical instrument is the *NGDMM* or *The New Grove Dictionary of Musical Instruments*. The first dictionary is owned by many large libraries, and is worth the time to find and learn to use. The second dictionary basically includes articles from the first publication in a shorter format. Few libraries also have a copy of this dictionary. Both dictionaries contain scholarly articles of the highest quality. New information, however, is always being discovered. For that, one must turn to scholarly journals, such as are listed on page 157 of this book.

Musical Instruments and the Internet

One feature of this book that is not found in my first book is a concentration upon instruments offered via online auctions. The development of online auctions has dramatically changed the buying, selling, collecting, and researching of instruments since the publication of my first book, *Antique Brass Wind Instruments*. Considerable misinformation and misspelling of names abound online, limiting one's ability to efficiently locate instruments. Additionally, during any given day, as a conservative estimate, at least half of the antique musical instruments offered on auction boards are of questionable value and/or ownership! With the advent of the Internet and specifically online auction services, I have spent considerable time examining these websites to determine what types of identification errors sellers are making. I have therefore included a few remarks about how best to post instruments to maximize sales, and how best to avoid paying too much for instruments offered online.

Prices for woodwind instruments vary considerably, but generally sell for well less than violins. Only the rarest woodwind instruments sell for more than a few thousand dollars. Bassoons are something of an exception, and can sell for upwards of $20,000 for new, professional-quality instruments. New, professional-quality instruments are best purchased only after playing the instrument. This is a feature not always available via Internet sales. Prices for antique bassoons can be found in the Price List of Instruments (pages 143-156). The maker's name will help in valuing the instrument. Readers are advised to consult experts when questions arise. The American Musical Instrument Society and the Galpin Society (U.K) are the two premiere societies whose members include specialists that can help identify and value instruments. I have made a point of not including websites in this book due to their ephemeral nature. However, any powerful search engine can prove most useful in obtaining website addresses. Information found on websites operated by societies dedicated to specific instruments are always to be considered more trustworthy than websites operated by individuals. Websites operated by companies can often be of value, but tend to concentrate on recent history and selling of modern instruments. A recent trend has been for college students to publish research papers on the Internet rather than publish them in peer-reviewed journals. While some of these websites can be very informative, their contents must be viewed carefully. The articles also tend to be ephemeral. Presently, no means exists for preserving or reviewing these articles.

As so many instruments appear on these Internet boards, proper spelling is essential in posting and locating instruments. For example, saxophone never appears in any scholarly publication as saxaphone. Some people seem to think that using a misspelled word will call attention to itself. However, listing an instrument with a misspelling means that it will not be found if a prospective buyer uses a search engine to locate the instrument using the proper spelling. Fair warning: use spell check prior to listing instruments online, and consult this and other books to verify spelling and identification. Merely stating "flute for sale" is almost pointless. "Wooden horn" is almost laughable, but actually appeared as a description for a clarinet on eBay. Clearly, more information is needed in the description. "Boehm system flute?" is acceptable when the flute appears to be a Boehm system flute. Antique should be used only for instruments that are clearly one hundred years old or more. If in doubt, simply use words such as "old" or "possibly 19th century" to help give an idea of age.

An additional caution is offered here. All too often, general dealers in antiques do not take the time to determine what they are offering for sale, and value instruments far too high. Rarely do they value them too low. The following comments have been made before, but need to be repeated. As an example, any woodwind instrument that has a crack in the body of the instrument (especially ivory joints) will rarely command even modest interest by a serious collector, unless the instrument was made by an important maker or has a rare key system. Repairing cracked ivory is problematic and will result in a color difference. New head joints can be made of synthetic ivory, but will be costly. Missing keys or parts also lower an instrument's value. The reason here is simple. Damaged instruments rarely can be put back into playing condition, and the repair costs can exceed the value of the instrument. Missing cases, though annoying, do not lower the value of a woodwind instrument. "Mint in box" is a phrase that should never be used to describe an antique instrument, but has actually appeared on eBay.

Here are offered a few pointers about photographing instruments. Always post photographs of instruments, especially if the seller is uncertain what is being offered. Never post a blurred or overly dark image. A pixel count of 300 or higher is critical for providing an acceptable digitized photograph. Black and white photographs are acceptable. Two photographs per instrument (front and back) are acceptable, unless the instrument has some special feature that requires a close up. Don't post too many images as doing so greatly slows down retrieval of the page. Photograph instruments out of doors on a slightly overcast day to obtain a diffuse light. Avoid photographing in direct sunlight. Photograph instruments indoors only if properly lighted. Truly important instruments should be photographed against a neutral background, like an ironed bed sheet or a white sheet of thick paper, and preferably by a competent photographer. Never use the digital zoom feature on a digital camera.

With the influence of the Internet, and the increasing rarity of truly important instruments, providing a price guide in this book has been most challenging. The reader is advised to use the price guide on pages 143-156 only as a way of identifying instruments that are inexpensive, moderately priced, expensive, or extremely valuable. This appendix consists of a list of prices from various auction houses. For instruments listed in the makers sections, a very general guide is to multiply the price by between 7 and 10. Thus, a flute that sold new for $30 in 1890 might, and I strongly emphasize the word "might", sell for as much as $300 if in perfect condition, with a well-established history. $200 is a much more likely price. A Boehm system flute that originally sold for $300 in 1890 will rarely sell for $3,000 because new, semi-professional-quality Boehm system flutes can be purchased for less than $3,000.

Gallery of Instruments

Late 19th Century flutes

Simple system

flutes on this page are not to scale

Zeigler system flute, with reform head; note the extra keys and ring keys
for the right hand. See also the next flute for non-Zeigler flute

Simple system flute with reform head, extending to low B natural;
note different type of keys for right index finger with above flute

Half Boehm system, also called Pratton system

Boehm system flutes

Boehm system flute, 1847 model; note that post and pillers
are on only one side of the flute, note also the G sharp key

Alto flute, also called Bass flute and Flute d'Amour

Albisiphone; note the T-shaped head joint

Various types of fifes common during the late 19th century and 20th century

Military fife, metal, raised embouchure plate and finger holes

Fife; note tapering profile, 1 piece body, and no keys. Larger fifes were made in 2 pieces

Military flute, or Band flute

The above examples are not as common as the following examples

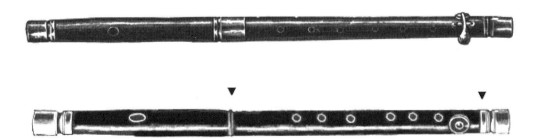

Note that band flutes are about the size of piccolos, are made in 2 pieces, might have one key, and do not have a tapering profile

A comparison of flute types

Late 1700s flutes

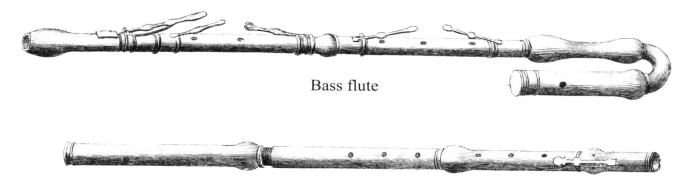

Bass flute

1 key flute, 4 piece body

Rare 1800s flutes

Ward flute, no head joint shown;
note small keys for left index finger
are not post and piller type

Boehm flute system of 1832, based
upon the simple system flute;
note ring keys mounted on pillers

Gordon flute; note unique key design

Flute family

Instruments are not to scale

Non-Boehm system piccolos

Piccolo, 2 pieces, 1 key, note bulge at end of head joint, not characteristic
of fifes

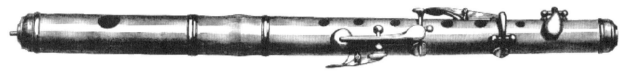

Piccolo, 2 piece, 6 keys, tuning slide

Piccolo, 2 piece, 6 keys, tuning slide, metal-lined embouchure hole
and finger holes

Note that the rods are on both sides of the piccolo's body. Not characteristic of
Boehm system. From Meinl catalog No. 403

Boehm system piccolo

Plateau keys and post and pillar, though characteristic of
Boehm system instruments, are not unique to this system

Flageolets in C

3006, 3012, 3014, 3015

Piccolo-Flageolet

3016, 3017, 3018

Penny whistles

2998, 2999

3002, 3004

Late 1700s oboe finials,
also called cotton spool
finials

Oberlender
finial

Anonymous
finial found
in much of
Western Europe

19th century single and
double reed instruments

Instruments are not to scale

Bassoon

English horn

Oboe

Albert and Boehm
system clarinets

Metal Boehm
system clarinet

Sarrousophone

Musette

Octavin

Saxophone

Examples of 18th century wood wind instruments

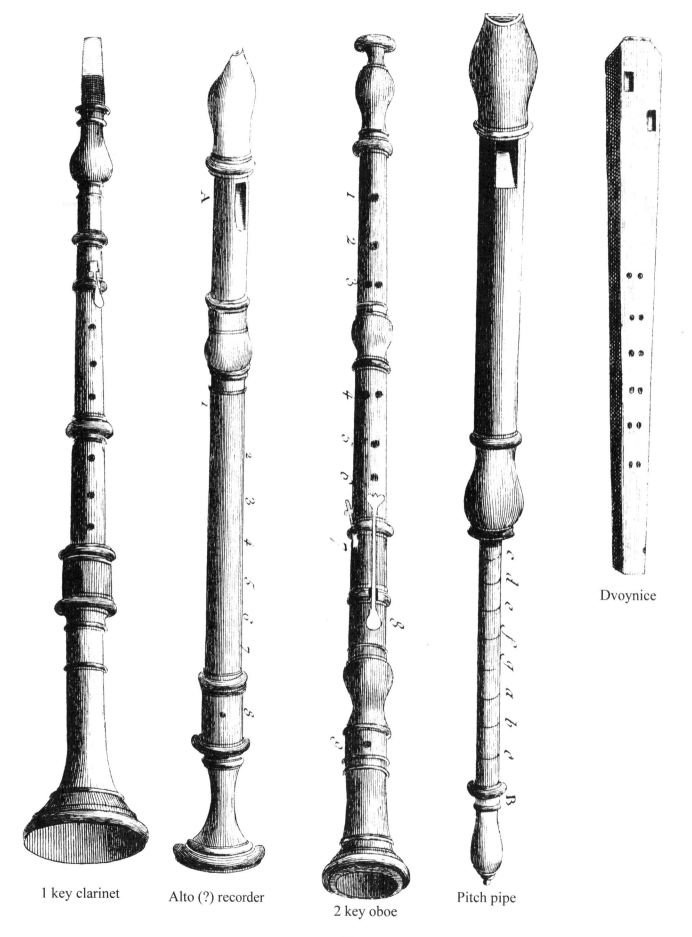

1 key clarinet   Alto (?) recorder   Pitch pipe   Dvoynice

2 key oboe

Example of 18th century bassoon and keys

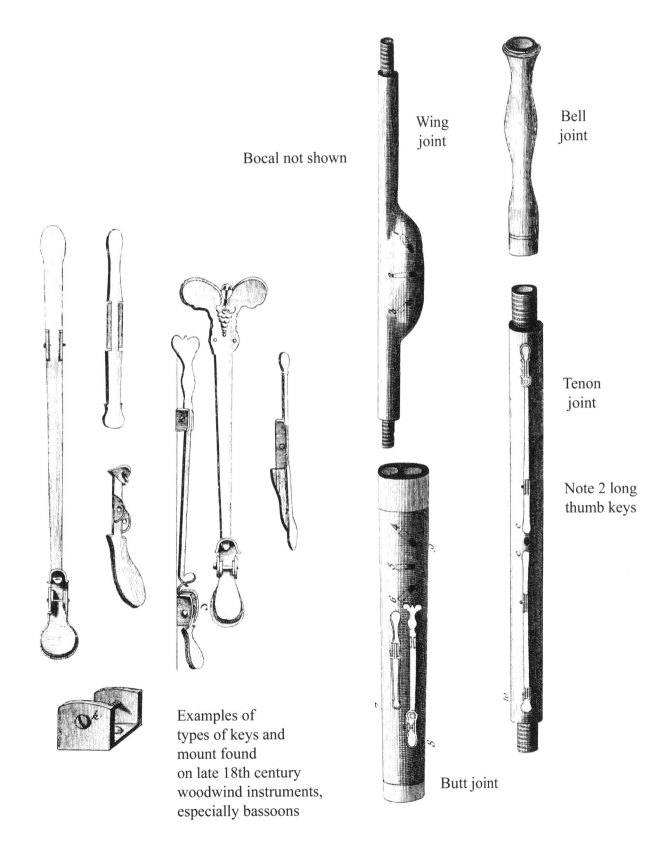

Bocal not shown

Wing joint

Bell joint

Tenon joint

Note 2 long thumb keys

Examples of
types of keys and
mount found
on late 18th century
woodwind instruments,
especially bassoons

Butt joint

Types of key designs found on wood wind instruments from the Renaissance to the present day

C   C   D   E   F   F

A. Bassoon open key. B. Basoon closed key. C. Flute closed key.
D. Oboe closed key. E. Oboe open key. F. Clarinet closed key.
Designs of the touch can indicate a region and maker

B

A

Key designs found frequently in the 19th century to present

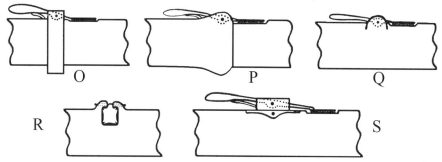

G   H   I   J   K   L

M   N

G, H, I. Flute. I. Invented by Potter. J, K, L. Woodwinds, examples of early padded keys. M, N. Woodwinds, padded keys often mass produced in France, found on late 19th century instruments, keys still in production today

Key mounts found on 18th and 19th century woodwinds

O   P   Q

R   S

O. Wood ring. P. Sculpted wood ring. Q. Key in block.
R. Curved key in blocks. S. Key in brass saddle

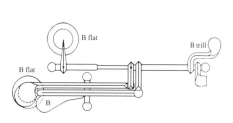

B flat
B flat
B trill
B flat
B

Briccialdi B flat thumb lever,
redrawn from Dayton C. Miller

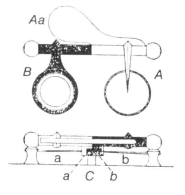

Aa
B   A

a   b
a'   C   b

Dorus G sharp key
from Rockstro,
Treatise

These last keys are found on late 19th century flutes only. The
other keys can be found on early woodwinds, especially flutes.

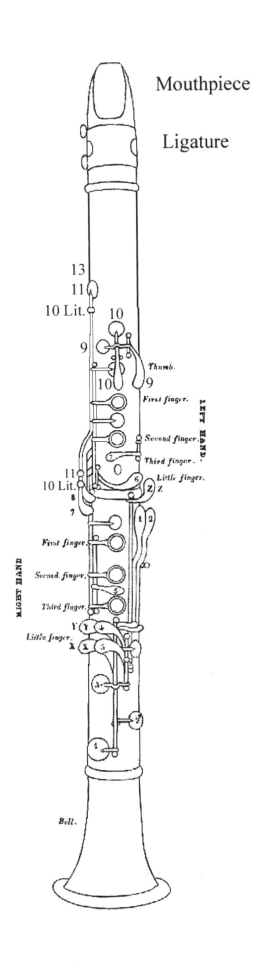

Mouthpiece

Ligature

13
11
10 Lit.
10
9
Thumb.
10
9
First finger.
Second finger.
Third finger.
Little finger.
11
10 Lit.
Z Z
8
7
1 2
First finger.
Second. finger.
Third finger.
5
Little finger.
Y Y 4
X X 3
3
2
4
Bell.

LEFT HAND.

RIGHT HAND

George Bauer

George Bauer was based in Philadelphia, and was mainly an importer and evidently a maker of plucked stringed instruments, such as mandolins. The company is not listed in *NLI*, strongly suggesting that this company did not make wind instruments. However, in an undated catalog (c.1900), the company offered its own line of instruments called Renab (not proof in itself). Many retailers often stamped their name on instruments made by other companies. The company also offered kinder instruments (see Glossary).

Bassoon, Buffet, Crampon & Co.

Rosewood, 15 keys	$102.90

Clarinets, Albert system

1	Key of A, B flat, C, or E flat, ebony, 13 G.S. keys, 2 rings, extra B flat and D sharp keys	$13.20
2	Key of A, B flat, C, or E flat, ebony, 15 G.S. keys, 2 rings, extra B flat and C sharp keys	$16.80
3	Key of A, B flat, C, or E flat, ebony, 15 G.S. keys, 4 rings	$27.00
4	Key of A, B flat, C, or E flat, 13 G.S. keys, 2 rings, extra B flat and C natural keys	$18.00
5	Key of A, B flat, C, or E flat, ebony, 15 G.S. keys, 2 rings	$27.00

Clarinets, stamped Renab

6	Key of A, B flat, C, or E flat, grenadilla, 13 G.S. keys, 2 rings, extra B flat and C sharp keys	$30.00
7	Key of A, B flat, C, or E flat, grenadilla, 15 G.S. keys, 2 rings, extra B flat and C sharp keys	$36.00
8	Key of A, B flat, C, or E flat, grenadilla, 15 keys, 4 rings, extra B flat and C sharp keys	$40.50
9	Key of A, B flat, or E flat, grenadilla $16 G.S. keys, roller keys, 4 rings, professional quality, extra B flat and C sharp keys	$48.00

Clarinets, Buffet

10	Key of A, B flat, C, or E flat, ebony, 15 G.S. keys, 2 rings, extra B flat and C sharp keys	$39.00
11	Key of A, B flat, C, or E flat, ebony	$15.00
	G.S. keys, 4 rings, extra B flat and C sharp keys	$45.00
12	Key of A, B flat, C, or E flat, ebony, 17 [G.S.?] keys, 6 rings, Boehm system	

In ordering clarinets state whether low or high pitch is wanted.

Flutes, 1 key

1	Key of D, maple, bone mounts	$0.66
2	Key of D, boxwood black, G.S. mounts	$1.35
3	Key of D, cocus, G.S. mounts, American, Renab	$2.00
4	Key of D, cocus with slide, G.S. mounts, Renab	$3.00
5	Key of D, cocus, G.S. mounts, American	$1.50
6	Key of C, cocus, G.S. mounts, American	$1.50
7	Key of F, cocus, G.S. mounts, American	$2.00
8	Key of F, cocus, slide, G.S. mounts, Renab	$3.00
9	Key of G, cocus, G.S. mounts, Renab	$1.86
10	Key of B flat, cocus, slide, G.S. mounts	$0.90

Flutes, 4 keys

11	Key of D, imitation ebony, G.S. mounts	$1.50
12	Key of D, boxwood, black with slide, G.S. mounts	$1.95
13	Key of D, grenadilla, slide, G.S. mounts	$2.25
14	Key of F, grenadilla, G.S. mounts	$1.92
15	Key of B flat, grenadilla, slide, cork joints, military [model?]	$1.80

Flutes, 6 keys

16	Key of D, boxwood, black, polished, tuning slide, G.S. mounts	$2.70
17	Key of D, grenadilla, polished, tuning slide, G.S. mounts	$2.85
18	Key of D, grenadilla, tuning slide, cork joints, G.S. mounts	$3.00
19	Key of B flat, grenadilla, tuning slide, cork joints, military	$2.00
20	Key of D, grenadilla, tuning slide, cork joints, American, Renab	$10.00
21	Key of F, grenadilla, tuning slide, cork joints, American, Renab	$10.00
22	Key of E flat, grenadilla, tuning slide, cork joints, American, Renab	$10.00
23	Key of B flat, grenadilla, tuning slide, cork joints, American, Renab	$9.00

Flutes, 8 keys

24	Key of D, grenadilla, G.S. mounts	$3.90
25	Key of D, grenadilla, G.S. caps, cork joints	$4.05
26	Key of D, grenadilla, G.S. embouchure, cork joints	$5.10
27	Key of D, grenadilla, ivory embouchure, cork joints	$10.50
28	Key of D, grenadilla, imitation Meyer, cork joints	$6.60
29	Key of D, grenadilla, imitation Meyer, ivory head, cork joints	$12.00
30	Key of D, grenadilla, cork joints, American, Renab	$18.75

Fifes

1	Key of B or C, maple, plain	$0.18
2	Key of B or C, imitation ebony, G.S. ferrules	$0.25
3	Key of B or C, rosewood, brass ferrules	$0.35

Musettes

1	Boxwood, stained	$2.50
2	Cast metal, nickel plated, reed protection	$1.05

Oboe, Buffet, Crampon & Co.

Ebony, 12 keys, 3 rings	$45.00

Saxophones, Buffet, Crampon & Co. (Evette & Schaeffer)

1	Key of B flat, soprano, brass, double B flat key	$64.20

2	Key of E flat, alto, brass, double B flat key	$72.00
3	Key of B flat, tenor, brass, double B flat key	$72.00
3	Key of E flat, baritone, brass, double B flat key	$79.20

Fifes

1	Key of B or C, maple, plain	$0.18
2	Key of B or C, imitation ebony, G.S. ferrules	$0.25
3	Key of B or C, rosewood, brass ferrules	$0.35
4	Key of B or C, cocus, brass ferrules	$0.45
5	Key of B or C, cocus, G.S. ferrules	$0.55
6	Key of B or C, ebony, G.S. ferrules	$0.65
7	Key of B or C, cocus, G.S. embouchure and ferrule	$0.85
8	Key of B or C, ebony, G.S. embouchure, and ferrules	$1.00
9	Key of B or C, cocus, long G.S. ferrules	$0.80
10	Key of B or C, ebony, long G.S. ferrules	$0.85
11	Key of B or C, nickel plated, raised holes, ebonite embouchure	$0.90
12	Key of B or C, nickel plated, ebonite embouchure, extra quality	$1.10
13	Key of B or C, cocus, Crosby model, long G.S. ferrules	$1.00
14	Key of B or C, ebony, Crosby model, long G.S. ferrules	$1.00
15	Key of B or C, grenadilla, Renab, artist model, long G.S. ferrules	$2.25
16	Key of B flat, grenadilla, jointed, 1 key, military model, American, Renab	$1.50
17	Key of B flat, grenadilla, jointed, 6 key, military model, American, Renab	$9.00

Flageolets

21	Key of C, cocus, 1 G.S. key and mounts	$1.50
22	Key of C, cocus, 4 G.S. keys and mounts	$1.95
23	Key of C, cocus, 6 G.S. keys and mounts	$2.40
24	Key of B, grenadilla, 1 key	$3.15
25	Key of B, grenadilla, 6 keys	$9.00
26	Key of C, grenadilla, 1 key	$3.15
27	Key of C, grenadilla, 6 keys	$9.00

Flageolet/Piccolo

28	Key of D, boxwood, 1 G.S. key and mounts	$1.50
29	Key of D, cocus, 1 G.S. key and mounts	$1.65
30	Key of D, cocus, 4 G.S. keys and mounts	$2.25
31	Key of D, cocus, 6 G.S. keys and mounts	$2.55

U.S. Eagle Flageolet

32	Key of B, C, D, E, F, and G, nickel plated	$0.20

French flageolets

33	Key of D, cast metal, nickel plated	$0.40
34	Key of D, cast metal, nickel plated	$0.50
35	Key of D, cast metal, nickel plated	$0.50

Clark's London flutes (tin whistles)

36	Tin	$0.10
37	Brass	$0.15
39	Nickel plated	$0.20

Tin flageolets

40	10 inch	$0.05
41	12 inch	$0.07
42	14 inch	$0.09
43	14 inch, better quality and finish	$0.12

Piccolos

1	Key of D or E flat, boxwood, 1 G.S. key and mounts	$2.45 *
2	Key of D or E flat, cocus, 1 G.S. key and mounts	$0.51 *
3	Key of D or E flat, cocus, 1 G.S key and mounts, and tuning slide	$0.66 *
4	Key of D or E flat, grenadilla, 4 G.S keys and mounts, and tuning slide	$1.11
5	Key of D or E flat, grenadilla, 4 G.S keys, caps, mounts, tuning slide, and cork joints	$1.26
6	Key of D or E flat, grenadilla, 6 G.S keys, caps, mounts, and tuning slide	$1.44
7	Key of D or E flat, grenadilla, 6 G.S keys, caps, mounts, and tuning slide	$1.50
8	Key of D or E flat, grenadilla, 6 G.S keys, caps, mounts, tuning slide, and ivory embouchure	$3.00
9	Key of D or E flat, grenadilla, 6 G.S keys, caps, mounts, tuning slide, ivory head joint	$3.36
10	Key of D or E flat, grenadilla, 6 G.S keys, caps, mounts, tuning slide, and embouchure	$2.04
11	Key of D or E flat, grenadilla, 6 G.S keys, caps, mounts, tuning slide, and head joint	$2.28

[The prices with an * are copied exactly from the catalog but are questionable.]

Piccolos

12	Key of D or E flat, grenadilla, imitation Meyer, 6 G.S keys, and cork joints	$2.70
13	Key of D or E flat, grenadilla, 6 keys, imitation Meyer, ivory head, cork joints	$4.50
14	Key of D or E flat, grenadilla, 6 keys, ivory head, cork joints	$7.12

Piccolos, George Cloos

15	Key of D or E flat, cocus, 1 G.S. key	$1.00
16	Key of D or E flat, grenadilla, 4 G.S. keys and tuning slide, cork joints	$7.50
17	Key of D or E flat, grenadilla, 6 G.S. keys and tuning slide, cork joints	$9.60
18	Key of D or E flat, grenadilla, 4 G.S. keys and tuning slide, cork joints, ivory head	$10.80
19	Key of D or E flat, grenadilla, 4 G.S. keys, head joint, tuning slide, cork joints	$9.00

Piccolo, Buffet

20	Key of D or E flat, grenadilla, 6 (G.S.?) keys	$10.80

Piccolos, stamped Renab

21	Key of D or E flat, grenadilla, G.S. ring keys	$45.00
22	Key of D or E flat, (unidentified) wood, silver covered keys	$82.25

Piccolos, Buffet, Crampon & Co.

23	Key of D or E flat (unidentified) wood, G.S. keys	$45.00

[This piccolo could be ordered in either high or low pitch.]

Theodor Berteling

According to a c.1915 musical instrument trade catalog in the Library of Congress, T. Berteling & Co. was founded by Theodor Berteling in New York City in 1848 to manufacture woodwind instruments. The company is known for making quality instruments, and Berteling received patents for the clarinet and flute. *NLI* (p. 28) states that the company was in Boston from 1848-1858, and then in New York City from 1859-c.1920. The following list was obtained from that catalog. All instruments in this list were made by this company. For additional instruments made by Berteling that appear in other companies' catalogs, see the Index.

Albert system clarinets

1	Grenadilla, 13 G.S. keys and mounts, 2 ring keys for F sharp right hand	$48.00
1½	Same as above, with 4 additional rollers for both little fingers	$53.25
2	Grenadilla, 15 G.S. keys and mounts, 2 ring keys, extra double C sharp key for trilling from B natural to C sharp and from C sharp to D sharp (middle register) also B flat or E flat trill key (side key)	$51.00
2½	Same as above, with 4 additional rollers for both little fingers	$56.25
3	Grenadilla, 15 G.S. keys and mounts, 4 ring keys same as 2 with extra double rings, on the upper joint for F sharp and C sharp without aid of F natural key	$54.00
3½	Same as above, with 4 additional rollers for both little fingers	$59.25
4	Grenadilla, 16 G.S. keys and mounts, 4 rings, same as number 3 with additional C sharp and G sharp trill lever for first finger of the right hand, also double E flat key for little finger of the left hand	$60.00
4½	Same as above, with 4 additional rollers for both little fingers	$65.25
5	Grenadilla, 16 G.S. keys and mounts, 4 rings, 4 rollers, same as number 4 ½ with an additional 4th ring on upper joint for perfect fork B flat in the staff	$66.00
6	Same as above, with an additional side key for G and A, or A and B flat trill	$69.00

Clarinets from Number 1 to 6 inclusive can be furnished with the articulated G sharp for additional $10.00.

Boehm system clarinets

7	Grenadilla, 17 G.S. keys and mounts, 6 rings	$85.50
8	Grenadilla, 17 G.S. keys and mounts, 7 rings, including the patent key for cross finger of B flat above the staff and E flat on the first line	$90.00
9	Same as number 7, with articulated G sharp and extra G sharp trill key for second finger of right hand, made in one piece	$97.50

Numbers 7 and 8 can be furnished with the articulated G sharp for an additional $13.50.

Simple system flutes

14	Grenadilla, 6 G.S. keys and mounts	$27.00
15	Grenadilla, 8 G.S. keys and mounts, C foot	$36.50
	Same as above, with ivory head	$46.50
16	Grenadilla, 10 G.S. keys and mounts, with C foot	$53.00
	Same as above, with ivory head	$63.00
17	Grenadilla, 11 G.S. keys and mounts, with B foot	$56.50
	Same as above, with ivory head	$66.50
18	Grenadilla, 13 G.S. keys and mounts, with B foot	$63.00
	Same as above, with ivory head	$73.00

Boehm system flutes

20	Grenadilla, cylinder bore, to C natural G.S. keys	$135.00
20½	Same as above, with nickel plated keys	$140.00
21	Grenadilla, cylinder bore, to C natural, real silver keys and mechanism	$175.00

The above instruments available with either open or closed G sharp keys, and pitched in either high or low pitch.

Simple system piccolos

24	Grenadilla, 6 G.S. keys and mounts	$18.00
24½	Same as above, with ivory head	$22.50

Boehm system piccolos

25	Grenadilla, G.S. keys, covered keys	$70.00
25½	Same as above, with ring keys	$60.00
26	Grenadilla, real silver, covered keys	$85.00
26½	Same as above, with ring keys	$75.00

The above instruments available with either open or closed G sharp keys, and either H.P. or L.P.

Bassoons

1	German model, maple wood, 19 G.S. keys and mounts, 2 crooks	$105.00
2	Improved model, maple wood, 22 G.S. keys and mounts, extending to B flat	$130.50

Berteling improved oboes

1	Grenadilla, 15 G.S. keys and mounts, 3 ring keys, extra C sharp key	$45.00
2	Grenadilla, 17 G.S. keys and mounts, self-changing octave key from G to A	$105.00

Albert system clarinets made by T. Berteling & Co.

No. 1 1/2   No. 2 1/2   No. 3 1/2   No. 4 1/4   No. 5   No. 6

Note the two roller keys for the little finger of the right hand. Boehm system clarinets are not known for this feature. This is the most obvious difference between the two clarinet key systems.

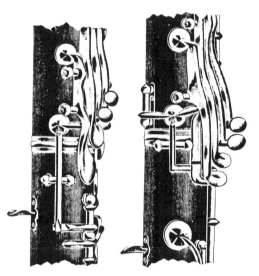

Boehm system
clarinets

No. 1   No. 2

Example 1 shows an articulated
G# key available on Nos.
1-6 for an addtiional $10.00

No. 7   No. 8   No. 9

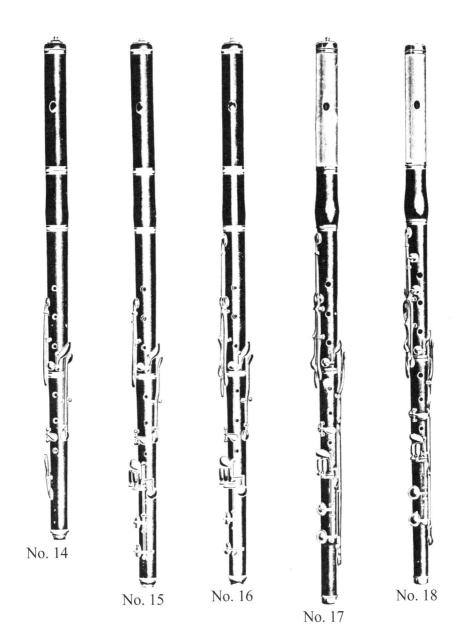

No. 14

No. 15

No. 16

No. 17

No. 18

Berteling improved
piccolo, simple
system

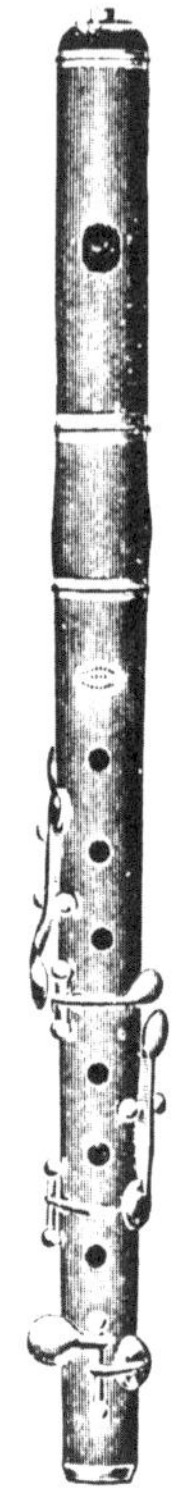

Boehm system
piccolo made
by Berteling

No. 24

No. 25 1/2
and 26 1/2

No. 25
and 26

Low clarinets and double reed
instruments made by T.
Berteling

Alto Clarinet
No. 1

Bass clarinet
No. 2

Oboe No. 2

Bassoon
No. 1 and 2

The easiest way to identify alto clarinets and bass clarinets of the 19th and 20th century is alto clarinets have only a slight upward bend in their necks, while bass clarinets have 2 bends.

Cundy-Bettoney

According to *NLI* (p. 77), Cundy-Bettoney was established in 1907 in Boston as an importer of musical instruments, and also music publisher. By 1912, the company began making woodwind instruments. By 1916, the company had evolved into one of the largest manufacturers of woodwind instruments in the U.S. While the company is best known for student-grade instruments today and also metal clarinets, the company also manufactured very high grade instruments, including a solid gold flute. The company, also known as Bettoney, was still in operation as of 1950. Instruments from this company are not presently well represented in museum collections. All information in this section is from the company's 1932 catalog. Note that this catalog did not include prices or complete information for all instruments listed here. Also, Bettonite is a form of ebonite.

Flutes

1 Alto or bass flute in low pitch G, closed G sharp, silver
2 Flute in low pitch C, closed G sharp, silver, in French style; high G to A and C sharp trills
3 Flute in low pitch C, closed G sharp, silver
4 Flute in low pitch C, closed G sharp, silver, with articulated F sharp and C sharp trill attachment; trill from high G to A, and C sharp trill
5 Flute in low pitch C, closed G sharp, silver plated with sterling keys
6 Flute in low pitch C, closed G sharp wood (discontinued)
7 Flute in low pitch C, open G sharp, Bettonite (discontinued)
8 Flute in low pitch D flat, closed D sharp, wood with metal head joint (discontinued)
9 Flute in high pitch C, closed G sharp, wood (discontinued)
10 Flute in high pitch C, closed G sharp, silver
11 Flute in low pitch D flat, open G sharp, silver
12 Flute in high pitch D flat, closed G sharp, silver
13 Flute in low pitch E flat, closed G sharp, silver
14 Flute in low pitch A flat, closed G sharp, wood (discontinued)
15 Piccolo in low pitch C, closed G sharp, silver conical bore
16 Piccolo in low pitch C, closed G sharp silver, cylindrical bore
17 Piccolo in low pitch C, open G sharp wood (discontinued)
18 Piccolo in low pitch, closed G sharp, Bettonite
19 Piccolo in low pitch D flat, closed G sharp, silver conical bore
20 Piccolo in low pitch D flat, open G sharp, wood (discontinued)
21 Piccolo in low pitch D flat, closed G sharp, silver, cylindrical bore
22 Piccolo in low pitch D flat, closed G sharp wood (discontinued)

Boehm system flute, open or closed G sharp keys, built in C for orchestra, or D flat for band

2000S	Silva-bet, sterling silver throughout, of seamless tubing, drop-forged keys, 14K gold springs, regulating screws, special pad seats, and bar supporting mechanism	$185.00
2000	Solid sterling silver body, keys and mechanism, regulating screws, 14 gold springs	$185.00
2000F	Same as 2000, in French model, open tone holes, 14 K gold springs	$200.00
2000X	Columbia Model, built like 2000, G.S. metal body, triple silver plated, mirror finish, sterling silver lip pate, non-rusting phosphor gold springs	$125.00
2000G	Same as 2000, same construction, 14 K gold throughout	$1000.00
2000GF	Same as 2000G, French model, open tone holes	$1100.00

Any of the above flutes can be equipped with thumb crutch at no extra charge.

Alto flutes (flute d'amour)

2000T	Boehm system, key of G, sold sterling silver body, keys and mechanism, regulating screws, 14 K gold springs, similar to 2000	$300.00

Piccolos

1004A	Key of A flat, Bettonite, conical bore, sterling silver keys, covered tone holes, 14 K gold springs, designed for Fife and drum corps	$90.00
1006X	Columbia model, G.S. body, triple silver plated, mirror finish, cylindrical bore, phosphor gold springs, sterling silver embouchure pate	$75.00
1005	Sterling silver throughout, conical bore	$100.00
1006	Same as 1005, cylindrical bore	$100.00

Clarinets, P.X. Laube, metal one-piece body, silver plated satin finish body, key work and inside of bell burnished

Boehm system

S318X	17 keys, 6 rings	$72.00
S318PO	Same as above, with covered finger holes	$90.00

Albert system

S398X	15 keys, rings, 4 rollers	$55.00

Screw sliding tuning barrel joints available for an additional 6.00

Clarinets, P.X. Laube, ebonite body

317K	Boehm system, 17 keys, 6 rings	$52.50
697K	Albert system, 15 keys, 4 rings, 4 rollers	$36.00

Boston wonder clarinets, G.S. one-piece body, available in B flat, A, and E flat, silver plated satin finish body, key work and inside of bell burnished

Boehm system

S218X	17 keys, 6 rings	$95.00
S218PO	Same as above, with covered holes, only available in B flat	$110.00
S238X	18 keys, 7 rings	$110.00

Albert system

S698X	15 keys, 4 rings, 4 rollers	$75.00

Screw sliding tuning barrel joints available for an additional | $6.00 |

Boston Wonder, Boehm system instruments (student-grade), cylindrical bore, G.S. body, triple silver plated, available in either closed G sharp key or open G sharp key on special order

1007	Piccolo, key of C for orchestra	$60.00
1007	Piccolo, key of D flat for band	$60.00
2007	Flute, key of C for orchestra	$95.00
2007	Piccolo, key of D flat for band	$95.00

Boehm system clarinets, Bettoney, available in B flat, A, C, and E flat, wood body

WS-21X	17 keys, 6 rings, patented forked B flat-E flat attachment, silver plated keys and mounts	$112.00
21X	Same as WS-21X, with G.S. keys and mounts	$100.00
WS-23X	17 keys, 7 rings, patented formed B flat-E flat attachment, silver plated keys and mounts	$122.00
23X	Same as WS-23X, with nickel plated keys and mounts	$110.00

Columbia Model clarinets, G.S. body and keys, one piece body, silver plated and burnished

S318½X	17 keys, 6 rings	$75.00

Clarinets, key of B flat are equipped with screw-sliding barrel joint
Clarinets, key of A are equipped with screw-sliding barrel joint
Clarinets, key of E flat are equipped with plain barrel joint

Madelon Boehm system flutes, cylindrical bore, available in either closed G sharp key or open G sharp key on special order, G.S. body, silver plated

2008	Flute, key of C for orchestra	$72.00

Madelon Boehm system clarinets

S418X	17 keys, 6 rings, one piece body, nickel plated	$55.00
S518X	17 keys, 6 rings, one piece body, silver plated throughout	$60.00
S518G	17 keys, 6 rings, one piece body, silver plated, inside of bell gold plated	$60.00
S518PO	17 keys, 6 rings, one piece body, silver plated throughout with covered tone holes	$75.00

Silva-Bet, Boehm system clarinets, all metal

The finishes for the Silva-Bet clarinets are as follows:

S950	Alto clarinet, key of E flat, 17 keys, 6 rings	
	Finish I	$225.00
	Finish II	$350.00
	Finish III	$400.00
S750	Bass clarinet, key of B flat, 17 keys, covered finger holes	
	Finish I	$275.00
	Finish II	$425.00
	Finish III	$500.00
S750E	Bass clarinet, key of B flat, 19 keys, range to low E flat, E flat-A flat lever, covered finger hole	
	Finish I	$300.00
	Finish II	$450.00
	Finish III	$535.00

Finish I: Silver plated body and keys, inside of bell gold plated, burnished throughout

Finish II: Gold plated, satin finish body, keys, and inside of bell burnished

Finish III: Gold plated and burnished throughout

[The catalog originally listed these finishes as Finish 4, Finish I, and Finish II.] Accessories for the above instruments could be ordered with gold plate upon request

B flat and A Silva-Bet clarinets are equipped with screw-sliding tuning barrel joints. E flat Silva-Bet clarinets are equipped with plain barrel joint.

Silva-Bet clarinets with O in the catalog number are one piece. Instruments with T in the catalog number are two piece.

Silva-Bet, Boehm system clarinet, metal body, 17 keys, 6 covered finger holes, Bettoney patented forked B flat-E flat attachment, silver plated and burnished

S21PO	One-piece body	$150.00
S21PT	Two-piece body	$150.00

Other models of Silva-Bet clarinets with covered keys may be ordered.

Silva-Bet Boehm system clarinets, metal body, open finger holes, Bettoney patented forked B flat-E flat attachment, silver plated and burnished

S21XT	17 keys, 6 rings	
	Stock finish	$135.00
	Finish I	$210.00
	Finish II	$230.00
	Finish III	$165.00
S21PT	Same as S21XT with covered keys	
	Stock finish	$150.00
	Finish I	$225.00
	Finish II	$245.00
	Finish III	$180.00
S23XT	17 keys, 7 rings, forked B flat-E flat made by an extra ring for 3rd finger left hand, and Bettoney patented B flat-E flat attachment	
	Stock finish	$150.00
	Finish I	$225.00
	Finish II	$245.00
	Finish III	$180.00
S28XT	Same as S21XT, with articulated F sharp-G sharp and B natural-C sharp attachment	
	Stock finish	$170.00
	Finish I	$225.00
	Finish II	$245.00
	Finish III	$180.00
S28XT	Same as S21XT, with articulated F sharp-g sharp and B natural-C sharp attachment	
	Stock finish	$170.00
	Finish I	$245.00
	Finish II	$266.00
	Finish III	$200.00
S30XT	Same as S28XT, low E flat key, and extra E flat-A flat lever kittle finger left hand	
	Stock finish	$180.00
	Finish I	$250.00
	Finish II	$276.00
	Finish III	$210.00

E flat-A flat lever little finger left hand applied on styles S28XT and S29XT clarinets for additional $10.00

S20XT	Same as S28XT, low E flat key, additional, extra E flat-A flat lever little finger left hand	
	Stock finish	$180.00
	Finish I	$250.00
	Finish II	$276.00
	Finish III	$210.00

S33XT 20 keys, 7 rings, low E flat key, forked B flat-E flat made by extra ring for 3rd finger left hand, articulated F sharp-G sharp attachment, extra E flat-A flat lever little finger left hand, full improved Boehm system

Stock finish	$190.00
Finish I	$265.00
Finish II	$287.00
Finish III	$220.00

Albert system clarinet, metal body
S69½XT 15 keys, 4 rings, 4 rollers

Stock finish	$110.00
Finish I	$175.00
Finish II	$192.00
Finish III	$135.00

Stock finish: Silver plated body, burnished finish, keys and inside of bell burnished

Finish I: Gold plated body, satin finish, keys and inside of bell burnished

Finish II: Gold plated body, burnished finish, keys and inside of bell burnished

Finish III: Silver plated body, burnished finish, keys and inside of bell gold plated and burnished

S21XO 17 keys, 6 rings, Bettoney patented forked B flat-E flat attachment

Finish III	$180.00

S23XO 17 keys, 7 rings, forked B flat-E flat made by extra ring for 3rd finger left hand, and by Bettoney patented B flat-E flat attachment

Stock finish	$150.00
Finish I	$225.00
Finish II	$245.00
Finish III	$180.00

Built only in B flat and A
S28XO Same as S21XO, with articulated F sharp-G sharp and B natural-C sharp attachments

Stock finish	$170.00
Finish I	$245.00
Finish II	$266.00
Finish III	$200.00

S29XO Same as S23XO, with articulated F sharp-G sharp and B natural-C sharp attachments

Stock finish	$175.00
Finish I	$250.00
Finish II	$271.00
Finish III	$205.00

E flat-A flat-lever, little finger left hand, applied on styles S28XO and S29XO for additional $10.00

S20XO Same as S28XO, with low E flat key additional, extra E flat-a flat lever little finger left hand

Stock finish	$180.00
Finish I	$250.00
Finish II	$276.00
Finish III	$210.00

S33XO $20 keys, 7 rings, low e flat key, forked B flat-E flat, extra ring for 3rd finger left hand, articulated F sharp-G sharp attachment, extra E flat-

A flat lever little finger left hand, full improved Boehm system

Stock finish	$190.00
Finish I	$265.00
Finish II	$287.00
Finish III	$220.00

Albert system clarinets
S69½XO 15 keys, 4 rings, 4 rollers

Stock finish	$110.00
Finish I	$175.00
Finish II	$192.00
Finish III	$135.00

Boston Wonder Oboes

650	$15 G.S. keys and mounts, 3 rings, register extending to B natural	$60.00
680	Conservatory model, regular double-effect octave key, a flat-b flat trill first finger right hand, register extending to low B flat, G.S. keys and mounts	$180.00
680½	Same as 680, with automatic single octave key	$200.00
686	Same as 680, with register extending to B natural	$165.00
686½	Same as 686, with automatic single octave key	$185.00

Oboes, Bettoney, black granadilla, G.S. keys, quadruple silver plated and burnished

655	Conservatory system, regular double-effect octave key; A flat-B flat trill, first ringer right hand, upper joint, additional lever placed beside the ring operated by the third finger right hand that allows the trill to C natural to C sharp to be made by the little finger right hand, register extension to low B flat	$200.00
655½	Same as 655, with automatic octave key	$220.00
660	Same as 655, with covered keys	$220.00
660½	Same as 655 ½, with covered keys	$240.00
661	Same as 660, automatic single octave key	$240.00

Boston Wonder oboe sax (simplified model), G.S. one piece body, silver plated, burnished finish body and keys

640	Two octave keys, without articulated F sharp, G sharp, plays to B natural	$120.00
641	Same as 640, with single automatic octave key	$140.00

Oboe sax, Bettoney
A new instrument that sounds the same as an oboe, having the same dimensions and placement of vent holes, but fingers like a saxophone. The instrument could be played either with a double reed or a specially designed mouthpiece with a single reed.

S656	Silver plated, burnished finish body and keys, 6 rings (like Boehm clarinet), single automatic octave key; articulated G sharp, range to low B flat, one piece body	$180.00
657	Grenadilla, silver plated and burnished keys, 6 rings (like Boehm clarinet), single automatic octave key, range to low B flat, three pieces body	$180.00

Bassoons, Bettoney

850	Paris Conservatory model, maple wood, hard rubber lined	$225.00
860	Bassoon, German style, 22 keys, stained and varnished maple wood, hard rubber lined, extra crook	$220.00

Flutes and piccolos made by Bettoney

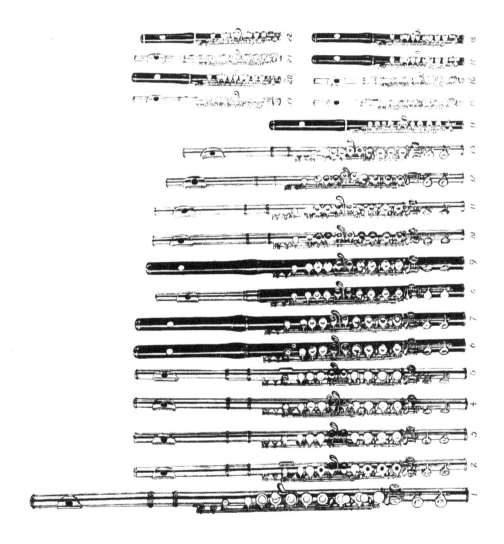

Clarinets made by Bettoney

No. S21XO   No. 269 1/2XO   No. S21PO   No. 21X

Styles of thumb keys and extra trill keys on Bettoney Boehm system flutes.

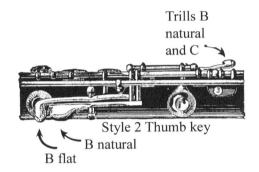

Trills B natural and C

Style 2 Thumb key

B natural

B flat

Style 10 trill key

High G to A trill key. C sharp to D trill

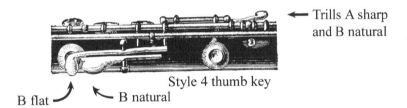

Trills A sharp and B natural

Style 4 thumb key

B flat   B natural

Trills B natural and C

Style 5 thumb key

B natural

B flat

Style 11 trill key

Trill G to A by first finger, right hand

Styles of *Silva-Bet* Clarinets

Skeletonized Boehm system clarinets

No. S23XO   No. S28XO   No. S29XO   No. S30XO   No. X33XO

Alto and bass clarinets made
by Bettoney

No. S950
Alto

No. S750E
Bass

Bassoons made by Bettoney

No. 860

No. 850
Front

No. 850
Back

Oboes made by Bettoney

No. 650   No. 657   No. 660   No. S656

No. S656 is one of the few metal oboes documented in this book. Note that it is a skeletonized form, slightly suggestive of a clarinet.

Boosey & Co.

Boosey & Co. began making flutes in 1851. The company has a complex history (see *NLI*, p. 40). The company is well known as a maker of Pratten system flutes. In an undated and incomplete catalog, descriptions of three different Pratten flutes are given. The main differences between the three Pratten flutes are the keys of their foot joints. The company also sold a Siccama model flute, and a Boehm system flute. The quality of instruments from this company varies, but for Pratten flutes, this is an important company as the company worked directly with Mr. R.S. Pratten. Pratten system flutes are easily identified as having two level keys for the little finger of the left hand, as does the Siccama flute the company made. By comparison, Boehm system flutes generally only have one key for the little finger of the left hand. All prices in the following list are in pounds, shillings, and pence. The first price is for instruments made of cocus. The second price is for ebonite. Also note that the descriptions in the catalog are very incomplete, and evidently relied upon illustrations that were partly missing from the catalog fragment.

Pratten system piccolos, key of D, E flat, or F

150	5 G.S. keys on G.S. knobs	1 0 0	1 2 6
151	5 G.S. keys and mounts on pillars, plain head	2 0 0	2 4 0
152	6 G.S. keys and mounts on pillars, tuning slide	3 3 0	3 10 0
153	6 silver keys and mounts on pillars, tuning slide	5 5 0	5 12 6

Fifes, key of B flat or C

154	4 G.S. keys and mounts on G.S. knobs	0 15 0	1 1 0
155	5 G.S. keys and mounts on G.S. knobs	0 18 0	1 4 0
156	4 G.S. keys and mounts on pillars	1 10 0	1 17 0
157	4 G.S. keys and mounts on pillars	2 0 0	2 7 6

Flutes, key of E flat or F

158	5 G.S. keys and mounts on G.S. knobs	1 10 0	2 5 0
159	5 G.S. keys and mounts on pillars, plain head	3 3 0	4 0 0
160	6 G.S. keys and mounts on pillars, plain head, tuning slide	5 5 0	6 6 0
161	8 G.S. keys and mounts on pillars, plain head, tuning slide	7 7 0	8 8 0
162	10 G.S. keys and mounts on pillars, plain head, tuning slide	8 18 6	9 19 6

This flute is equipped with cups covering the A and E holes, thereby obviating all unnatural extension of the fingers

163	12 G.S. keys and mounts on pillars, cylinder bore	10 10 0	11 11 0

Pratten concert flutes, (conical bore ?)

164	8 G.S. keys on knobs	4 4 0	5 15 6
165	8 G.S. keys on pillars	7 7 0	8 8 0
166	8 silver keys on pillars	10 10 0	11 11 0
167	10 G.S. keys on pillars	8 18 6	9 19 6
168	10 silver keys on pillars	12 12 0	13 13 0

Pratten concert flutes, cylinder bore

169	12 G.S. keys, 2 ring keys, pewter plugs on foot	8 8 0	10 0 0
170	12 silver keys, 2 ring keys, pewter plugs on foot	12 12 0	14 2 6

171	13 G.S. keys on pillars, superior foot joint (suggestive of Boehm system)	10 10 0	11 11 0
172	12 silver keys on pillars, superior foot joint (suggestive of Boehm system)	15 15 0	16 16 0

Extra keys for C natural

Thumb key so constructed as to enable the performer to play from B flat to C, and vice versa by the slightest movement of the thumb, thus rendering all the scales in flat keys extremely easy. In G.S. 1 1 0. In silver 1 1 6. This key can be added to any one of the above models (164 to 172).

Improved C key, giving the middle C natural with the second finger of the left hand with full tone and well in tune. In G.S. 1 11 6. In silver 2 2 0. This improvement is recommended to players who do not care for the thumb key (described above), and is applicable to the greater number of flutes with keys on pillars, including 173.

Pratten concert flute (large holes)

173	14 silver keys on pillars, cork and silver joints	23 2 0	24 3 0
174	17 silver keys on pillars, cork and silver joints, plateau keys	28 7 0	29 8 0

Metal body flutes

175	17 silver keys and mounts, silver body, cylinder body	30 9 0	
176	17 silver keys, gold mounts and embouchure, silver body, cylinder body	52 10 0	

Siccama flutes

177	11 G.S. keys on pillars	10 10 0	11 11 0
178	11 silver keys on pillars	15 15 0	16 16 0
179	13 silver keys on pillars (evidently with 2 ring keys), roller keys	23 2 0	24 3 0

This flute has large holes, same as 173 and 176.

Boehm system piccolo and flute

180	Piccolo, silver keys on pillars, tuning slide	16 16 0	16 16 0
181	Flute, G.S. keys on pillars, tuning slide	—	16 16 0

[Other flutes were offered. However, the catalog was incomplete.]

[The prices for the following instruments are in U.S. dollars. The catalog numbers are as they appear in the catalog.]

Piccolos

152	F, 6 keys, cocus	$22.00
151	E flat, 6 keys, cocus	$12.00
152	D, 6 keys, cocus (international pitch)	$22.00

Flutes

154	B flat, 5 keys, ebonite	$15.00
158	E flat, 5 keys, ebonite	$18.00
161	F, 8 keys cocus	$46.00
162	E flat, 8 keys, cocus, superior foot joint	$50.00

Concert flutes

167	8 keys, cocus, conical bore, superior foot joint	$58.00
171	12 keys, cylindrical bore, superior foot joint (suggestive of Boehm system)	$90.00
181	Boehm system, cylindrical bore, ebonite, Briccialdi action	$120.00
181	Boehm system, cylindrical bore, ebonite, international pitch	$120.00
183	Boehm system, cocus, cylindrical bore, silver keys, plateau keys	$210.00
181	Boehm system, ebonite, cylindrical bore, plateau keys	$225.00
181	Boehm system, ebonite, cylindrical bore, plateau keys, Briccialdi action, international pitch	$120.00
172	12 silver keys, cocus, cylindrical bore, superior foot joint (suggestive of Boehm system)	$120.00
164	8 keys, cocus, conical bore	$86.00
169	12 keys, cocus, cylindrical bore, 2 ring keys, pewter plugs on foot	$76.00
—	F, Boehm system, cocus, conical bore	$120.00
159	F, 6 keys, ebonite	$15.00
155	B flat, 6 keys, cocus	$14.00

Piccolos

152	D, 6 keys, cocus	$22.00
152	E flat, 6 keys, ebonite	$23.00
150	F, 5 keys, cocus	$11.00

Clarinets

107	B flat, African black wood, extra C sharp key	$74.00

108	B flat, ebonite, extra C sharp and B flat trill keys	$81.00
107	B flat, cocus, international pitch	$74.00
107	A, African black wood	$74.00
108	A, ebonite, extra C sharp and B flat trill keys	$81.00

Boehm system piccolo

180	Ebonite, cylindrical body, international pitch	$130.00

Saxophones, military model

1	B flat, soprano	$100.00
2	E flat, alto	$116.00
3	B flat, tenor	$120.00
4	B flat, baritone	$126.00

Oboes

125	Cocus, descending to B flat, international pitch	$125.00
124	Ebonite, descending to B natural	$120.00
123r	Cocus, descending to B natural	$76.00
126	Ebonite, descending to B flat	$136.00

Bassoons

128	Ebonite	$160.00
127	Rosewood	$150.00

Clarinets

116	Alto, ebonite	$136.00
118	Bass, ebonite	$170.00
115	Alto, cocus	$130.00
107	A, cocus, patent B flat key, international pitch	$64.00
107	B flat, African black wood	$64.00
107	C, African black wood	$64.00
108	E flat, ebonite	$77.00
106	E flat, cocus, extra C sharp key	$69.00
108	C, ebonite, extra C sharp key, and B flat trill key	$77.00
107	B flat, cocus, 4 rollers, international pitch	$86.00
114	B flat, ebonite, Spencer model, international pitch	$130.00

41

Piccolos and flutes sold by Boosey & Co.

E flat piccolo. A152 & 153

Concert piccolo, Boehm system. A180

Concert flute, Pratten system, conical. A167 & 168

Concert flute, Pratten system, cylinder. A169 & 170

Concert flute, Pratten system, cylinder. A171 & 172

Concert flute, Pratten system, cylinder. A174

Concert flute, Improved Siccama system. A179

Concert flute, Boehm system, cylinder. A181

Concert flute, Boehm system, cylinder. A183

Buegeleisen & Jacobson

Buegeleisen & Jacobson began in about 1890 in New York City primarily as an importer of instruments. The company is not listed in *NLI*, and appears to have been a retailer. The information found here was obtained from the company's 1930-31 catalog. Possibly because of the difficult economic times, instruments that had become all but obsolete were still offered by this company. By comparison, the company sold Meyer system flutes for $27 and $36.

The company sold instruments made by Coudet & Cie, Evette and Schaeffer, V. Kohlert and Sons, and Martin frères. The company sold instruments with the following trade marks: Boston Wonder, Abbott (evidently Martin frères), and Salvadore de Durro (mainly string instruments and accessories). The company also sold a large number of plucked string instruments.

Abbott Premier metal clarinets, all clarinets were made with two-piece G.S. bodies

A4497	Albert system, low B flat, 15 G.S. keys, 4 rings, 4 rollers	$40.00
A4498	Boehm system, low B flat, 17 G.S. keys, 6 rings	$66.00
A4495	Boehm system, low B flat, 17 G.S. keys, 6 rings, triple plated, satin finish, burnished keys and bell, tuning barrel	$75.00
A4499	Boehm system, low B flat, 17 keys, 6 rings, triple silver-plated, gold plated keys and gold burnished bell, tuning barrel	$90.00

Metal clarinets, Coudet & Cie

A4492	Albert system, low B flat, 15 keys, 4 rings, 4 rollers, nickel-plated one-piece body	$34.00
A4493	Boehm system, low B flat, 17 keys, 6 rings	$50.00

Abbott ebonite clarinets

A3497	Albert system, low B flat, 15 G.S. keys, 4 rings, 4 rollers	$29.00
A3496	Same as No. A3497, low A	$29.00
A3495	Same as No. A3497, low E flat	$29.00
A3498	Boehm system, low B flat, 17 G.S. keys, 6 rings	$56.00
A3490	Same as No. 3498, low A	$56.00
A3491	Same as No. 3498, low E flat	$56.00

Abbott wood clarinets

A2497	Albert system, low B flat, grenadilla, 15 G.S. keys, 4 rings, 4 rollers	$29.00
A2496	Same as 2497, low A, grenadilla, 15 G.S. keys, 4 rings, 4 rollers	$29.00
A2495	Same as 2497, low E flat, grenadilla, 15 G.S. keys, 4 rings, 4 rollers	$29.00
A2498	Boehm system, low B flat, grenadilla, 17 G.S. keys, 6 rings	$56.00
A2490	Same as A2498, low A, grenadilla, 17 G.S. keys, 6 rings	$56.00
A2491	Same as A2498, low E flat, grenadilla, 17 G.S. keys, 6 rings	$56.00

Buffet clarinets

A451	Boehm system, low B flat only, grenadilla, 17 G.S. keys, 6 rings	$120.00

Boston Wonder metal clarinets, presumably G.S. body

A4501	Boehm system, low B flat, 17 keys, 6 rings, silver-plated	$114.00

A4503	Boehm system, low B flat, 17 keys, 7 rings, silver-plated, satin finish	$132.00

Clarinets in low A and E flat were available upon special order

Boston Wonder metal flutes, nickel silver

A4504	Boehm system, pitched in C for orchestra, heavily silver-plated	$114.00
A4504½	Boehm system, pitched in D flat for band, heavily silver plated	$114.00

Boston Wonder metal piccolo, nickel silver

A4505	Boehm system, pitched in C for orchestra, heavily silver-plated	$72.00
A4505½	Boehm system, pitched in D flat for band, heavily silver plated	$72.00

Abbott Premier professional saxophones, brass finish

A10	B flat soprano, pearl finger tips, curved shape	$100.00
A20	B flat soprano, pearl finger tips, straight shape	$100.00
A30	C soprano, pearl finger tips, straight shape	$104.00
A40	E flat alto, pearl finger tips, curved shape	$104.00
A50	C melody, pearl finger tips, curved shape	$114.00
A60	B flat tenor, pearl finger tips, curved shape	$116.00
A70	B flat baritone, pearl finger tips, curved shape	$174.00

Abbott Premier professional saxophones, silver-plated satin finish, with gold bell

AS10	B flat soprano, curved shape	$116.00
AS20	B flat soprano, straight shape	$116.00
AS30	C soprano, curved shape	$116.00
AS40	E flat alto, curved shape	$120.00
AS50	C melody, curved shape	$136.00
AS60	B flat tenor, curved shape	$138.00
AS70	E flat baritone, curved shape	$200.00

Meyer system flutes

A2463	Low C for orchestra, grenadilla wood, hard rubber head and first joint, 8 G.S. keys, G.S. tuning slide and mounts, cork joints	$27.00
A2464	Low D flat for band, otherwise same as above	$27.00

A2469 Low C for orchestra, grenadilla, 13 G.S. keys, G.S. tuning slide and mounts, imitation ivory head joint, hard rubber first joint, cork joints $36.00

A2470 Low D flat for band, otherwise same as above $36.00

Meyer system piccolos

A464 Low C for orchestra, grenadilla, hard rubber head joint, 6 G.S. keys, G.S. tuning slide, cork joints $6.00

A4654 Low D flat for band, otherwise same as above $6.00

A466 Low C for orchestra, grenadilla, 6 G.S keys, G.S. tuning slide, imitation ivory head joint $12.00

A467 Low D flat for band, otherwise same as above $12.00

Oboes, V. Kohlert and Sons

A5000 Conservatory model, grenadilla, nickel silver keys, automatic octave key, automatic half-hole key, descending to low B flat $222.00

A5001 Military model, grenadilla, 15 G.S. keys, 3 rings $60.00

Bassoons, V. Kohlert and Sons

A5002 Heckel system, curly maple body stained brown, 22 G.S. keys, lined with rubber, piano-mechanism, automatic octave key, ivory rim on bell $220.00

A5003 Same as above, but with extra G-sharp key $235.00

Charles Gerhard Conn

Charles Gerhard Conn (C.G. Conn) began his company making mouthpieces for cornets shortly after the end of the Civil War. Upon buying the Boston Musical Instrument Manufactory in 1887, Conn began making brass wind instruments. He eventually built a second factory in Elkhart, Indiana. Between 1875 and 1879, the company was called Conn-Dupont. In 1898, he closed the Boston factory. At an undetermined time (pre 1900), C.G. Conn began making woodwind instruments. Ferdinand August Buescher, then working for Conn, made the first saxophone in the U.S., in 1888. Instruments from this company range from highly prized professional quality to low-quality student instruments of very modest value. The founder was perhaps the most colorful figure in the U.S. musical instrument making industry. In 1892-94, Conn was a U.S. Congressmen, but offered no significant legislation. Conn engaged in a vicious legal battle with J.W. Pepper. Theories vary, but evidently Conn objected to Pepper importing student-grade instruments from Europe. Conn used his *The Musical Truth,* a quasi-catalog and magazine, to lambaste Pepper. He even had Pepper imprisoned for slander. Pepper retaliated, and in 1922, Conn was compelled to publish a retraction that appeared in *The Musical Courier,* an important trade publication of the day. The implication of the letter was that Conn was addicted to cocaine, a commonly available substance at the time. Conn eventually retired from the company and retired to southern California. The following list is obtained from various Conn catalogs, and includes catalog numbers only in the 1927 catalog. As Conn was such an ardent opponent of imported musical instruments, it is rather likely that all instruments listed below were made by C.G. Conn. See also *NLI* (p. 69-70), and the bibliography.

CONN 1893

Albert system, all metal double wall clarinets, 15 keys, extra C sharp key, 2 ring keys, 3 part body in either E flat, C, B flat, or A

Finish I: silver plated, gold plated keys	$40.00
Finish II: heavily nickel plated	$30.00

All instruments stamped with company name on the bell
Solid silver clarinets with solid silver keys available on special order.

CONN 1907

Boehm system flutes

All metal flutes

Finish I: engraved, heavily gold-plated, burnished or sand blast velvet finish, mother of pearl inlay finger pieces	$100.00
Finish II: silver-plated body with gold-plated keys and trimmings, burnished or sand blast velvet finish	$60.00
Finish III: nickel-plated and highly polished throughout	$50.00

All examples made of metal with conical head joint and cylindrical body, and ebonite lip plate.

Metal flute with ebonite head joint

Finish I: engraved, heavily gold-plated, sand-blast velvet finish, keys and finger-hole caps burnished and inlaid with mother of pearl	$100.00
Finish II: heavily silver-plated, sand-blast velvet finish, keys and finger hole caps gold plated and burnished	$70.00
Finish III: durably nickel-plated, highly polished	$60.00

All examples made of metal with conical head joint and cylindrical body

Wood flutes

Finish I: gold-plated keys, and trimming	$115.00
Finish II: silver-plated keys, and trimmings	$100.00

All examples made of metal with conical head joint and cylindrical body

Ebonite metal-lined flutes

Finish I: gold-plated keys, and trimmings	$100.00
Finish II: silver-plated keys, and trimmings	$85.00

All examples made of metal with conical head joint and cylindrical body

Piccolos with ebonite head joint and metal body

Finish I: silver-plated metal body, gold plated keys and metal trimmings, ebonite head joint with gold-plated end caps and tuning slide ferrule	$50.00
Finish II: nickel-plated metal body, keys and metal trimmings, ebonite head joint with nickel-plated end caps and tuning slide ferrule	$40.00

All flutes and piccolos are Boehm system, and available with either open or closed G sharp keys, and in either high or low pitch. For piccolos, an extra head joint could be bought for $9.00 that would change the pitch to international pitch (A=440).

Clarinets

Albert system, with Pupeschi G sharp key, patented in 1894

Wood or ebonite, white metal nickel-plated keys and trimmings	$55.00

Available "in any desired pitch or key" evidently all at the same price. The instrument retains the Albert system keys for the lower right hand fingers, and 5 ring keys

Albert system clarinet (Wonder clarinet)

Wood or ebonite, 15 keys, 2 ring keys, metal ferrules	$34.00

Available in A, B flat, or C

Albert system clarinet (Wonder clarinet) improved model

Wood or ebonite, 17 keys, 5 ring keys, metal ferrules	$44.00

Available in A, B flat, or C

Boehm system clarinet (Wonder clarinet)

Wood or ebonite	$65.00

Available in A, B flat, or C

Saxophones

[All examples available as described below but for about $10.00 less. One significant feature, however, is that the artistic finish offered in the circa 1910 catalog was only available in the 1907 catalog as a custom order extra.]

CONN, 1910 CATALOG

Boehm system metal flutes

Artist finish: engraved, heavily gold plated, the body sand blast velvet finish, keys and trimmings burnished, pearl inlaid finger pieces, and gold springs

Finish I: heavily silver plated, body and sand blast velvet finish, the keys heavily gold plated, burnished finish, and gold springs

Finish II: heavily silver plated all over, body sand blast velvet finish, the keys furnished finish, and gold springs

Finish III: heavily nickel plated all over

Ebonite embouchure, 2 piece body, plateau keys

Artist finish	$130.00
Finish I	$90.00
Finish II	$75.00
Finish III	$65.00

Wood or ebonite head joint, 2 piece body, plateau keys

Artist finish	$140.00
Finish I	$95.00
Finish II	$80.00
Finish III	$70.00

Full ebonite body, metal lined, 2 piece body, plateau keys

Artist finish	$140.00
Finish I	$130.00
Finish II	$110.00

All wood flute, 2 piece body, plateau keys

Artist finish	$160.00
Finish I	$150.00
Finish II	$130.00

All the above flutes could be had in either C for orchestra, or E flat (terz) or D flat for band

Piccolos

Ebonite head joint, 2 piece metal body, plateau keys

Artist finish	$90.00
Finish I	$70.00
Finish II	$60.00
Finish III	$50.00

All ebonite or wood, 2 piece body, plateau keys

Finish I	$100.00
Finish II	$75.00
Finish III	$60.00

All the above piccolos could be had in either C for orchestra, or D flat for band

Albert system clarinets

Ebony, grenadilla, or ebonite, 15 keys (G.S.?) and 2 ring keys	$37.50
Ebony, grenadilla, or ebonite, 15 keys (G.S.?) and 4 ring keys	$45.00
Ebony, grenadilla, or ebonite, 15 keys (G.S.?) and 5 ring keys	$52.00

Boehm system clarinets

Ebony, grenadilla, or ebonite, 17 (G.S.?) keys and 6 ring keys	$75.00
Ebony, grenadilla, or ebonite, 17 (G.S.?) keys and 6 ring keys, low B flat added	$85.00

Saxophones

Artist finish: heavily gold plated, burnished keys, inlaid with pearl, pearl rollers, artistically engraved

Finish I: engraved, quadruple silver plated, sand blast velvet finish, keys and finger hole caps, inside of bell and engraving gold plated, burnished

Finish II: heavily silver plated, sand blast velvet finish, inside of bell gold plated

Finish III: heavily nickel plated throughout and highly polished

Finish IV: heavily polished brass throughout

B flat soprano

Artist finish	$140.00
Finish I	$100.00
Finish II	$90.00
Finish III	$75.00
Finish IV	$60.00

E flat alto

Artist finish	$150.00
Finish I	$105.00
Finish II	$95.00
Finish III	$80.00
Finish IV	$65.00

C melody

Artist finish	$160.00
Finish I	$110.00
Finish II	$100.00
Finish III	$85.00
Finish IV	$70.00

B flat tenor

Artist finish	$170.00
Finish I	$115.00
Finish II	$105.00
Finish III	$90.00
Finish IV	$75.00

E flat baritone

Artist finish	$200.00
Finish I	$145.00
Finish II	$135.00
Finish III	$110.00
Finish IV	$95.00

Monster contra bass

Artist finish	$270.00
Finish I	$200.00
Finish II	$190.00
Finish III	$145.00
Finish IV	$125.00

Special prices upon application for duplicate keys, screws, springs extra finish, and engraving.

Oboe, Boehm system, cocus or grenadilla, white metal keys and mounts	$50.00

Bassoon, cocus or grenadilla, white metal keys and mounts $115.00

B flat fife, cocus or grenadilla, inverse conical wind way, adjustable cord head joint, tuning slide, 2 white metal keys and mounts $7.50

This instrument was designed to play the B flat cornet part in marching bands and is made in high and low pitch.

CIRCA 1927 CATALOG

Finish 00: Quadruple gold plate, completely hand burnished, bell richly engraved, finger tips pearl inlaid, and on saxophones, pearl rollers

Finish 0: Quadruple gold plate over all, sand blast finish, interior of bell, valve caps, keys, water keys, ferrules, etc. as well as engraving background are hand burnished, finger tips pearl inlaid, and on saxophones, pear rollers

Finish 1: Quadruple silver plating over all, sand blast finish, gold plated and hand burnished interior of bell, ferrules, engraving, water keys, knobs, etc. finger tips pearl inlaid, and on saxophones, pear rollers. On wood instruments this finish simply represents heavily gold plated keys posts and rods.

Finish 2: Quadruple silver plated, sand blast finish, points burnished, with inside of bell gold plated and burnished, finger tips pear inlaid, and on saxophones, pearl rollers.

Finish 4: Highly polished brass, with neat engraving design.

Finish 6: Body heavily nickel-plated and highly polished, pearl finger tips, and on saxophones pearl rollers. On wood instruments this finish simple represents nickel-plated keys, posts and rods.

Metal Boehm system flutes, two-piece body, New Wonder

Finish	0	1	3	6
10-O C, closed G#, low pitch	$150.00	$100.00	$80.00	
11-O C, closed G#, high pitch	$150.00	$100.00	$80.00	
12-O C, open G#, low pitch	$150.00	$100.00	$80.00	
13-O C, open G#, high pitch	$150.00	$100.00	$80.00	
14-O D flat, closed G#, low pitch	$150.00	$100.00	$80.00	
15-O D flat, closed G#, high pitch	$150.00	$100.00	$80.00	
16-O D flat, open G#, low pitch	$150.00	$100.00	$80.00	
17-O D flat, open G#, high pitch	$150.00	$100.00	$80.00	

Sterling silver Boehm system flute, low pitch, New Symphony model, three-piece body

60-O C, closed G#	$150.00
62-O C, open G#	$150.00
64-O D flat, closed G#	$150.00
66-O D flat, open G#	$150.00
100-O C, closed G#, B natural foot	$200.00
110-O C, closed G#, C foot	$225.00

[No indication given of finishes available.]

Metal Boehm system piccolos, low pitch, New Wonder

Finish	0	1	3	6
40-P C, closed G#	$90.00	$75.00	$60.00	$50.00
42-P C, open G#	$90.00	$75.00	$60.00	$50.00
44-P D flat, closed G#	$90.00	$75.00	$60.00	$50.00
46-P D flat, open G#	$90.00	$75.00	$60.00	$50.00

Sterling silver Boehm system piccolos, low pitch

30-P C, closed G#	$85.00
32-P C, open G#	$85.00
34-P D flat, closed G#	$85.00
36-P D flat, open G#	$85.00

Albert system clarinets

48N E flat, low pitch, 15 keys, 4 rings	$55.00
49N E flat, high pitch, 15 keys, 4 rings	$55.00
46N C, low pitch, 15 keys, 4 rings	$55.00
47N C, high pitch, 15 keys, 4 rings	$55.00
44N B flat, low pitch, 15 keys, 4 rings	$55.00
45N B flat, high pitch, 15 keys, 4 rings	$55.00
42N A, low pitch, 15 keys, 4 rings	$55.00
43N A, high pitch, 15 keys, 4 rings	$55.00
8N E flat, low pitch, 15 keys, 5 rings	$70.00
9N E flat, high pitch, 15 keys, 5 rings	$70.00
6N C, low pitch, 15 keys, 5 rings	$70.00
7N C, high pitch, 15 keys, 5 rings	$70.00
4N B flat, low pitch, 15 keys, 5 rings	$70.00
5N B flat, high pitch, 15 keys, 5 rings	$70.00
2N A, low pitch, 15 keys, 5 rings	$70.00
3N A, low pitch, 15 keys, 5 rings	$70.00
18N E flat, low pitch, 17 keys, 5 rings	$75.00
19N E flat, high pitch, 17 keys, 5 rings	$75.00
16N C, low pitch, 17 keys, 5 rings	$75.00
17N C, high pitch, 17 keys, 5 rings	$75.00
14N B flat, low pitch, 17 keys, 5 rings	$75.00
15N B flat, high pitch, 17 keys, 5 rings	$75.00
12N A, low pitch, 17 keys, 5 rings	$75.00
13N A, high pitch, 17 keys, 5 rings	$75.00

Large Albert system clarinets, no cases

60N Alto, E flat, low pitch	$125.00
70N Bass, B flat, low pitch	$165.00

[Neither instrument offered in high pitch.]

Metal Boehm system clarinets, 4-part body

524N B flat, 17 keys, 6 rings	$125.00
624N B flat, 17 keys, 6 rings, Deluxe	$175.00

[Prices on gold metal clarinets could be had as a special order. No prices given.]

Wood Boehm system clarinets

28N E flat, low pitch, 17 keys, 6 rings	$100.00
29N E flat, high pitch, 17 keys, 6 rings	$100.00
26N C, low pitch, 17 keys, 6 rings	$100.00
27N C, high pitch, 17 keys, 6 rings	$100.00
24N B flat, low pitch, 17 keys, 6 rings	$100.00
25N B flat, high pitch, 17 keys, 6 rings	$100.00
22N A, low pitch, 17 keys, 6 rings	$100.00
23N A, high pitch, 17 keys, 6 rings	$100.00
34N B flat, low pitch, 18 keys, 7 rings	$105.00
35N B flat, high pitch, 18 keys, 7 rings	$105.00
32N A, low pitch, 18 keys, 7 rings	$105.00
33N A, high pitch, 18 keys, 7 rings	$105.00
20N B flat, low pitch, 20 keys, 7 rings, E flat attachment	$110.00
21N B flat, high pitch, 20 keys, 7 rings, E flat attachment	$110.00

Larger Boehm system clarinets

40N E flat, low pitch $150.00
50N Bass, B flat $190.00

Oboe

2Q C, low pitch, French system, 12 keys, 5 rings $70.00
4Q C, low pitch, Conservatory system, 20 keys, 6 rings $200.00
6Q C low pitch, Artists Symphony model, full conservatory with plateau keys
$250.00
8Q C low pitch, New Improved Conservatory system $150.00

Heckle system bassoons

2R C, low pitch, Professional model $175.00
4R C, low pitch, Symphony model $275.00

English horns

14Q Military model $165.00
16Q Conservatory model $250.00

Saxophones

Finish	00	0	1	2	4	6
20M E flat, Soprano, low pitch						
	$200.00	$175.00	$145.00	$120.00	$100.00	$110.00
2M C Soprano, low pitch						
	$200.00	$175.00	$140.00	$120.00	$95.00	$105.00
18M B flat Soprano, low pitch, straight body						
	$200.00	$170.00	$135.00	$115.00	$95.00	$100.00
19M B flat Soprano, high pitch, curved body						
	$210.00	$180.00	$140.00	$120.00	$100.00	$110.00
22M F, low pitch, Conn-O-sax						
	$260.00	$220.00	$185.00	$145.00	$110.00	$120.00
24M F, mezzo soprano, low pitch						
	$250.00	$210.00	$175.00	$135.00	$100.00	$110.00
6M E flat, Alto, low pitch						
	$250.00	$210.00	$175.00	$135.00	$100.00	$110.00
7M E flat, Alto high pitch						
	$250.00	$210.00	$175.00	$135.00	$100.00	$110.00
8M C, Melody, low pitch						
	$255.00	$215.00	$180.00	$140.00	$105.00	$115.00
9M C, Melody, high pitch						
	$255.00	$215.00	$180.00	$140.00	$105.00	$115.00
10M B flat, Tenor, low pitch						
	$275.00	$235.00	$195.00	$155.00	$115.00	$125.00
11M B flat, Tenor, high pitch						
	$275.00	$235.00	$195.00	$155.00	$115.00	$125.00
12M E flat, Baritone, low pitch						
	$380.00	$325.00	$260.00	$190.00	$150.00	$160.00
13M E flat, Baritone, high pitch						
	$380.00	$325.00	$260.00	$190.00	$150.00	$160.00
14M B flat, Bass, low pitch						
	$510.00	$430.00	$335.00	$260.00	$220.00	$240.00

Sarrusophone (unidentified metal)

16V E flat contrabass						
	$440.00	$400.00	$350.00	$325.00	$275.00	$295.00

Regular System Clarinet   Regular System Clarinet   Regular System Clarinet   Boehm System Clarinet   Boehm System Clarinet

C.G. Conn's 1892 double wall metal clarinets

Eb CLARINET.

C CLARINET.

Bb CLARINET.

A CLARINET.

Oboe and bassoon
made by C.G. Conn

Couesnon

Couesnon, later Couesnon & Cie, is a very respected maker based in Paris. *NLI* (p. 72-73) states that the company began in 1882 and continued until at least 1950. The following information is from a catalog printed in 1900. The illustrations of instruments were too poor in quality to reproduce here. Instruments range from professional to student instruments. Many instruments from this company are found in public and private collections. The following information is a free translation from the French.

Instrument	Models						
Saxophones	scolaire	Universel	National	Armee	Armee	Opera	Monopole
Soprano	174	180	190	200	220	240	250
Tenor	208	220	230	240	280	300	325
Baritone	230	240	250	260	290	340	400
Bass	400	410	420	430	440	450	460
Ebony piccolos	130	140	160	170	180	190	200
Metal piccolos	180	190	200	210	220	230	240
Metal flute	220	275	330	340	350	360	370
Clarinets	170	200	210	220	230	240	250
Bassoons	290	340	350	390	430	460	500

Instrument	brass	nickel
Saxophones		
Sopranino	250	270
Soprano (straight body)	250	270
Soprano (bent body)	300	328
Alto	300	328
Tenor	325	355
Tenor in C	325	355
Tenor in C, Dupaquier system	400	430
Baritone	400	440
Bass	460	530
Sarrusophones		
Bass	360	400
Contrabass in E flat	440	500
Contrabass in C	500	560
Contrabass in B flat	500	560

Boehm system piccolos in either C or E flat, cylindrical-conical body

G.S. keys and mounts	240
Silver keys and mounts	340

Boehm system flutes, cylindrical

G.S. keys and mounts	370
Silver keys and mounts	580

Boehm system clarinet (G.S. keys and mounts?)

A flat, E flat, C or B flat, ebony	250
Alto, ebony	400
Bass, ebony	520

Triébert model oboe (conservatoire model)

Ebony, double C sharp, adopted for the army	450

Bassoon

Triébert model (conservatoire model)	500

[All the above models not otherwise indicated were evidently Monopole model.]

Czechoslovak Music

The following information is from Czechoslovak Music's catalog of 1931. Images were not suitable for use here. This company is not listed in *NLI*, and only is a retailer.

Clarinets made of ebonite unless otherwise indicated, all keys, rings and mounts were probably made of G.S., instruments evidently marked Bourdain (Paris). [This name is not listed in *NLI*.]

230	Key of B flat, Albert system, 14 keys, 2 rings	$20.00
235	Key of A, Albert system, 15 keys, 4 rings, and 4 rollers	$22.00
236	Key of B flat, Albert system, 15 keys, 4 rings, and 4 rollers	$22.00
237	Key of C, Albert system, 15 keys, 4 rings, and 4 rollers	$22.00
238	Key of E flat, Albert system, 15 keys, 4 rings, and 4 rollers	$22.00
240	Key of A, Boehm system	$40.00
241	Key of B flat, Boehm system	$40.00
242	Key of C, Boehm system	$40.00
243	Key of E flat, Boehm system	$40.00

Clarinets, grenadilla, all keys, rings and mounts were probably made of G.S., evidently marked Greville (Paris). [Listed in *NLI* as a trade name, no maker identified.]

245	Key of A, Albert system, 15 keys, 4 rings, and 4 rollers	$32.00
246	Key of B flat, Albert system, 15 keys, 4 rings, and 4 rollers	$32.00
247	Key of C, Albert system, 15 keys, 4 rings, and 4 rollers	$32.00
248	Key of E flat, Albert system, 15 keys, 4 rings, and 4 rollers	$32.00
250	Key of A, Boehm system	$64.00
251	Key of B flat, Boehm system	$64.00
252	Key of C, Boehm system	$64.00
253	Key of E flat, Boehm system	$64.00
255	Key of A, Boehm system, 17 keys, 7 rings, articulated G sharp key	$64.00
256	Key of B flat, Boehm system, 17 keys, 7 rings, articulated G sharp key	$64.00
257	Key of C, Boehm system, 17 keys, 7 rings, articulated G sharp key	$64.00
258	Key of E flat, Boehm system, 17 keys, 7 rings, articulated G sharp key	$64.00
262	Key of A, full Boehm system, 20 keys, 7 rings	$110.00
263	Key of B flat, full Boehm system, 20 keys, 7 rings	$110.00

Metal clarinets, evidently marked Greville

275	Key of B flat, Albert system, 15 keys, 4 rings, 4 rollers, one piece construction	$27.00
276	Key of A, Boehm system, nickel plated, 1 piece construction	$40.00
277	Key of B flat, Boehm system, nickel plated, 1 piece construction	$40.00
278	Key of C, Boehm system, nickel plated, 1 piece construction	$40.00
279	Key of E flat, Boehm system, nickel plated, 1 piece construction	$40.00
286	Key of A, Boehm system, silver plated, 1 piece construction	$45.00
287	Key of B flat, Boehm system, silver plated, 1 piece construction	$45.00
288	Key of C, Boehm system, silver plated, 1 piece construction	$45.00
289	Key of E flat, Boehm system, silver plated, 1 piece construction	$45.00

Clarinets made of metal, evidently marked Beaumont. [*NLI* states that this trade name was used by C. Meisel.]

299	Key of B flat, Albert system, 15 keys, 4 rings, 4 rollers, tuning barrel, 2 piece, silver plated	$38.00
290	Key of A, Boehm system, 17 keys, 6 rings, tuning barrel, 2 piece construction, silver plated	$62.00
291	Key of B flat, Boehm system, 17 keys, 6 rings, tuning barrel, 2 piece construction, silver plated	$62.00
292	Key of C, Boehm system, 17 keys, 6 rings, tuning barrel, 2 piece construction, silver plated	$62.00
293	Key of E flat, Boehm system, 17 keys, 6 rings, tuning barrel, 2 piece construction, silver plated	$62.00
295	Key of A, Boehm system, 17 keys, 7 rings, articulated G sharp key, tuning barrel, 2 piece construction, silver plated	$62.00
296	Key of B flat, Boehm system, 17 keys, 7 rings, articulated G sharp key, tuning barrel, 2 piece construction, silver plated	$62.00
297	Key of C, Boehm system, 17 keys, 7 rings, articulated G sharp key, tuning barrel, 2 piece construction, silver plated	$62.00
298	Key of E flat, Boehm system, 17 keys, 7 rings, articulated G sharp key, tuning barrel, 2 piece construction, silver plated	$62.00

J. Howard Foote

John Howard Foote began this company in 1852 as an importer, and eventually became a maker of brass wind instruments. The company evidently made no woodwind instruments. The company was based in New York City, and ended operation in 1896, according to *NLI* (p. 120). The following information is from an 1893 catalog.

Boehm system flutes, key of C

350	Martin frères, grenadilla wood, G.S. keys and mounts	$125.00
353	Charles Bertin, ebony, cylinder bore, G.S. keys and mounts	$200.00
354	Buffet, ebony, cylinder bore, G.S. keys and mounts	$210.00
355	Charles Bertin, G.S. body and keys, cylinder bore, superior to number 354	$275.00
356	Key of C. Buffet. G.S. body and keys, cylinder bore	$250.00

[All instruments are described as best quality, and all but the first instrument are described as American models, without further explanation.]

Boehm system piccolos

370	Buffet, key of E flat, grenadilla, G.S. keys and mounts	$82.50
371	Buffet, key of D, grenadilla, G.S. keys and mounts	$82.50
372	Charles Bertin, key of E flat, ebony, G.S. keys and mounts	$85.00
373	Charles Bertin, key of D, ebony, G.S. keys and mounts	$85.00
374	Godfroy, key of E flat, grenadilla, solid silver keys and mounts	$175.00
375	Godfroy, key of D, grenadilla, solid silver keys and mounts	$175.00

Saxophones, Buffet

330	Key of B flat, soprano, brass, improved scale	$115.00
331	Key of E flat, alto, brass, improved scale	$130.00
332	Key of B flat, tenor, brass, improved scale	$130.00
333	Key of E flat, baritone, brass, improved scale	$145.00

Cuckoos

334	Boxwood, ivory tipped, improved model	$6.50

[The instrument is described as best Paris make, and could be ordered in any desired key, or combination of three different keys at prices between $10 and $25.00. The instrument is a novelty member of the fipple family.]

Clarinets, "genuine Albert patent clarionets," all made with patent tuning slide, body of metal and ebonite

310	Key of E flat, G.S. keys, 2 rings, and patent C sharp key and B flat trill key	$145.00
311	Key of C, G.S. keys, 2 rings, G.S. keys, 2 rings, and patent C sharp key and B flat trill key	$145.00
312	Key of B flat, G.S. keys, 2 rings, and patent C sharp key and B flat trill key	$145.00
313	Key of A, G.S. keys, 2 rings, and patent C sharp key and B flat trill key	$145.00

[The telescopic tuning slide is threaded so that turning it can raise or lower the instrument's pitch.]

Clarinets, "genuine Eugene Albert clarionets," best model

318	Key of E flat, ebony, 15 G.S. keys, and patent C sharp key	$84.00
319	Key of C, ebony, 15 G.S. keys, and patent C sharp key	$84.00
320	Key of B flat, ebony, 15 G.S. keys, and patent C sharp key	$84.00
321	Key of A, ebony, 15 G.S. keys, and patent C sharp key	$84.00

Musette

335	Boxwood, plain, improved model, best quality, Paris make	$4.00

Oboes

337	Martin frères, key of C, ebony, 12 G.S keys and G.S. mounts, 2 rings	$60.00
338	Buffet, key of C, ebony, 15 G.S. keys and mounts, 2 rings for right hand (F#), on ring (C#), for left hand	$80.00

Bassoon

339	Key of B flat, maple (stained), 15 G.S. keys, G.S. mounts, improved model, Paris make	$138.00

Sarrussophones

340	Key of B flat, soprano, brass, best quality	$138.00
341	Key of E flat, alto, brass, best quality	$146.00
342	Key of B flat, tenor, brass, best quality	$155.00
343	Key of E flat, baritone, brass, best quality	$164.00
344	Key of B flat, bass, brass, best quality	$181.00

The following information appears at this point in the catalog: "Alto and Bass clarionets, Saxophones, and Sarrussophones should be introduced into American Bands whenever possible."

Eugene and Jacques Albert's new patent clarinets

Mr. Albert, and his son Jacques Albert, have recently perfected and patented a new system of Clarionets, which surpass all hitherto made. The body of the new instrument is metal of the most exact proportions to produce correct tune and sympathetic tone, and is covered with an indestructible preparation of ebonite, which forms the most durable and beautiful instrument that can be made.

F flutes

5306	Maple body, 1 brass key	$0.75
5307	Boxwood stained black, 1 G.S. key, bone tipped	$1.65
5309	Grenadilla, 1 G.S. key, G.S. mounts	$2.40
5312	Grenadilla, 6 G.S. keys, G.S. mounts	$5.25

D flutes

5318	Maple, 1 brass key	$0.85
5324	Grenadilla, 1 G.S. key, G.S. mounts	$2.80
5335	Grenadilla, 4 G.S. key, G.S. mounts, sliding joints	$5.00
5344	Grenadilla, 6 G.S. keys, G.S. mounts, sliding joints	$7.00

5353   Grenadilla, 8 G.S. keys, G. S. mounts, extra fine quality, sliding joints
                                                                                        $18.00

Flute, Charles Bertin

5356   Key of D, Portugal ebony, 8 G.S. keys, G.S. mounts, sliding joints
                                                                                        $40.00

Flutes, Meyer system

5360   Key of D, grenadilla, 11 G.S. keys, G.S. mounts $30.00
5361   Key of D, grenadilla, 11 G.S. keys, G.S. mounts $42.00
5362   Key of D, grenadilla, 11 G.S. keys, G.S. mounts, ivory head joint
                                                                                        $63.00

Flutes, H.F. Meyer

5363   Key of D, grenadilla, 11 G.S. keys, G.S. mounts, made especially for
         solo artists $137.50
5364   Key of D, grenadilla, 11 G.S. keys, G.S. mounts, extra fine quality, ivory
         embouchure joint, made especially for solo artists $150.00

[All genuine Meyer flutes and piccolos are stamped on each joint "H.F. Meyer, Hanover" and also stamped with a crown.]

Piccolos

5383   Key of E flat, grenadilla, 1 G.S. key, G.S. mounts, best quality, sliding
         joint $1.30
5384   Key of D, grenadilla, 1 G.S. key, G.S. mounts, best quality, sliding
         joint $1.30
5386   Key of B flat, grenadilla, 1 G.S. key, G.S. mounts, best quality, sliding
         joint $1.80
5387   Key of B flat, grenadilla, 6 G.S. key, G.S. mounts, best quality, sliding
         joint $3.75
5392   Key of E flat, grenadilla, 4 G.S. keys, G.S. extra fine quality, mounts,
         sliding joint $3.50
5393   Key of D, grenadilla, 4 G.S. keys, G.S. mounts, extra fine quality,
         sliding joint $3.50
5400   Key of E flat, grenadilla, 6 G.S. keys, G.S. mounts, fine quality,
         sliding joint $4.00
5401   Key of D, grenadilla, 6 G.S. keys, G.S. mounts, fine quality, sliding
         joint $4.00

Piccolos, Chas. Bertin

5404   Key of E flat, cocus, 6 G.S. keys, G.S. mounts, extra fine $15.00
5405   Key of D, cocus, 6 G.S. keys, G.S. mounts, extra fine $15.00

[Both 5404 and 5405 were designed for professional use.]

Piccolos, H.F. Meyer

5408   Key of E flat, grenadilla, 6 G.S. keys, G.S. mounts, ivory embou-
         chure joint, especially made for solo artists $50.00
5409   Key of D, grenadilla, 6 G.S. keys, G.S. mounts, ivory embouchure
         joint, made especially for solo artists $50.00

Clarinets, Martin frères, no system given

5262   Key of E flat, boxwood, 6 brass keys, brass mounts $8.00
5263   Key of C, boxwood, 6 brass keys, brass mounts $8.00
5264   Key of B flat, boxwood, 6 brass keys, brass mounts $8.00
5265   Key of A, boxwood, 6 brass keys, brass mounts $8.00

Albert system clarinets, Martin frères

5285   Key of E flat, grenadilla, 13 G.S. keys, G.S. mounts, 2 rings finest
         quality, tuning slide $42.50
5286   Key of D, grenadilla, 13 G.S. keys, G.S. mounts, 2 rings finest
         quality, tuning slide $42.50

5287   Key of C, grenadilla, 13 G.S. keys, G.S. mounts, 2 rings finest
         quality, tuning slide $42.50
5288   Key of B flat, grenadilla, 13 G.S. keys, G.S. mounts, 2 rings finest
         quality, tuning slide $42.50
5289   Key of A, grenadilla, 13 G.S. keys, G.S. mounts, 2 rings finest
         quality, tuning slide $42.50

Albert system clarinets, genuine Challenge clarinets (brand name)

5273½   Key of E flat, Portugal ebony, 13 G.S. keys, G.S. mounts, 2 rings
                                                                                        $26.00
5275½   Key of C, Portugal ebony, 13 G.S. keys, G.S. mounts, 2 rings $26.00
5276½   Key of B flat, Portugal ebony, 13 G.S. keys, G.S. mounts, 2 rings
                                                                                        $26.00
5277½   Key of A, Portugal ebony, 13 G.S. keys, G.S. mounts, 2 rings $26.00

Albert system clarinets, Chas. Bertin

5279   Key of E flat, Portugal ebony, 13 G.S. keys, G.S. mounts, 2 rings
                                                                                        $26.00
5281   Key of C, Portugal ebony, 13 G.S. keys, G.S. mounts, 2 rings $26.00
5282   Key of B flat, Portugal ebony, 13 G.S. keys, G.S. mounts, 2 rings
                                                                                        $26.00
5283   Key of A, Portugal ebony, 13 G.S. keys, G.S. mounts, 2 rings $26.00

Clarinets, Chas. Bertin, Albert system

5291   Key of E flat, Portugal ebony, 15 G.S. keys, G.S. mounts, 2 rings,
         patent C# and side B flat trill key $44.00
5293   Key of C, Portugal ebony, 15 G.S. keys, G.S. mounts, 2 rings, patent
         C# and side B flat trill key $44.00
5294   Key of B flat, Portugal ebony, 15 G.S. keys, G.S. mounts, 2 rings,
         patent C# and side B flat trill key $44.00
5295   Key of A, Portugal ebony, 15 G.S. keys, G.S. mounts, 2 rings, patent
         C# and side B flat trill key $44.00

Clarinets, Barret system

5298   Key of E flat, Portugal ebony, 15 G.S. keys, G.S. mounts, 4 rings
                                                                                        $60.00
5299   Key of C, Portugal ebony, 15 G.S. keys, G.S. mounts, 4 rings
                                                                                        $60.00
5300   Key of B flat, Portugal ebony, 15 G.S. keys, G.S. mounts, 4 rings
                                                                                        $60.00
5301   Key of A, Portugal ebony, 15 G.S. keys, G.S. mounts, 4 rings
                                                                                        $60.00

Flageolets

5423   Key of D, maple stained, 1 G.S. key, English model, good quality
                                                                                        $1.40
——   Key of D, grenadilla, 1 G.S. key, G.S. mounts, English model, best
         quality $1.40
5438   Key of A, boxwood, 4 G.S. keys, G.S. mounts French model, best
         quality $10.25
5440   Key of A, ebony, 4 G.S. keys, G.S. mounts, French model, best
         quality $14.50

Flageolet and piccolo

5442   Key of D, grenadilla, 6 G.S. keys, G.S. mounts, best quality $5.00

Ocarinas, J.H.F.

7200   Key of C, soprano, clay body $0.30
7201   Key of D, alto, clay body $0.45
7202   Key of C, alto, clay body $0.50
7203   Key of C, bass, clay body $2.25

Clair Godfroy aîné

The following list is from a possibly incomplete two-page trade catalog of circa 1878 in the Dayton C. Miller Flute Collection. Miller wrote that he obtained this catalog in November 1922. According to *NLI* (p. 139), this important maker of wood-wind instruments operated from 1814 to 1888, and was based in Paris. All prices are in French francs. The catalog included no illustrations, and descriptions are incomplete.

Wood Boehm system cylindrical flutes

1	Ebony or grenadilla, silver keys and mounts, B foot	525
2	Ebony or grenadilla, silver keys and mounts, C foot	475
3	Ebony or grenadilla, G.S. keys and mounts, B foot	425
4	Ebony or grenadilla, G.S. keys and mounts, C foot	375

Metal non-Boehm system cylindrical flutes

5	Silver body and keys, B foot	575
6	Silver body and keys, C foot	526
7	G.S. body and keys, B foot	475
8	G.S. body and keys, C foot	425
9	G.S. body and keys, B foot	425
10	G.S. body and keys, C foot	375

Boehm system conical flutes

11	Ebony or grenadilla, silver keys and mounts, B foot	475
12	Ebony or grenadilla, silver keys and mounts, C foot	425
13	Ebony or grenadilla, G.S. keys and mounts	260
14	Ebony or grenadilla, G.S. keys and mounts, without C foot	210

Boehm system piccolos

15	Ebony or grenadilla, silver keys and mounts	210
16	Ebony or grenadilla, G.S. keys and mounts	160
17	G.S. throughout	150

Simple system flutes, ebony or grenadilla, silver keys, embouchure, and mounts

18	4 keys	185
19	5 keys	200
20	6 keys	215
21	8 keys, C foot	300
22	8 keys, B foot	350
23	10 keys, trill key for Re/Me	380
24	11 keys, trill keys for Re/Me and Si/La	400
25	12 keys	420

Simple system flutes, ebony or grenadilla, G.S. keys, embouchure, and mounts

26	4 keys	80
27	5 keys	90
28	6 keys	100
29	8 keys, C foot	140
30	9 keys, B foot	170
31	10 keys	190
32	11 keys	200
33	12 keys	210

Simple system flutes, ebony or grenadilla, silver plated keys, embouchure, and mounts

34	4 keys	100
35	5 keys	110
36	6 keys	120
37	8 keys, C foot	170
38	9 keys, B foot	185
39	10 keys, trill key for Re/Mi	200
40	11 keys, trill key for Re/Me and a key for Fa	220
41	12 keys	230
42	Same as above, ivory head	260

Simple system wood piccolos, silver keys, embouchure, and mounts

43	4 keys	70
44	5 keys	80
45	4 keys, ivory ferrules	60
46	5 keys, ivory ferrules	65
47	4 keys, G.S. keys	50
48	5 keys, G.S. keys	60

New system clarinets in A, B flat, C, E flat [Boehm system?]

49	Ebony, silver keys and mounts	430
50	Ebony, G.S. keys and mounts	280
51	Boxwood, brass keys and mounts	200
52	Boxwood, incomplete	180
53	Alto in F, G.S. keys and mounts	320
54	Alto in F, brass keys and mounts	250

Ordinary clarinets, ebony or grenadilla, silver keys [Albert system?]

55	15 keys	300
56	14 keys	280
57	13 keys	270
58	13 G.S. keys	170
59	13 G.S. keys, ivory ferrules	150
60	13 brass keys	130

New system oboes [conservatoire?]

61	Palissader or ebony, silver keys and ferrules	400

62	Palissader or ebony, 4 keys	360
63	Boxwood, G.S. keys and ferrules	260
64	Boxwood, 4 keys	235
65	Boxwood, brass keys	180

Ordinary oboe

66	Ebony or palissader, 8 silver keys and mounts	180
67	Ebony or palissader, 10 silver keys and mounts	200
68	Ebony or palissader, 12 silver keys and mounts	240
69	Ebony or palissader, 8 G.S. keys and mounts	110
70	Ebony or palissader, 10 G.S. keys and mounts	120
71	Ebony or palissader, 12 G.S. keys and mounts	150
72	Ebony or palissader, 8 brass keys and mounts	85
73	Ebony or palissader, 10 brass keys and mounts	95
74	Ebony or palissader, 12 brass keys and mounts	125

Perfected bassoons [evidently made of wood]

| 75 | 8 G.S. keys and mounts | 250 |
| 76 | 8 brass keys and mounts | 210 |

Ordinary bassoons [evidently made of wood]

77	8 G.S. keys and mounts	135
78	10 G.S. keys and mounts	170
79	12 G.S. keys and mounts	185
80	15 G.S. keys and mounts	210
81	8 brass keys and mounts	105
82	10 brass keys and mounts	140
83	12 brass keys and mounts	155
84	15 brass keys and mounts	180

John C. Haynes & Co.

This company operated in Boston between 1861 and 1900, and had a relationship with Oliver Ditson Co. Haynes began as an importer, but by 1894 began making flutes, having acquired the tools from William Sherman Haynes. The company used the Bay State trade name. *NLI* (p. 165-166) is indispensable for sorting out the various family members either making or selling instruments during this time. Unless otherwise stated, no maker is mentioned for these instruments. The following information is from an 1889 catalog. This catalog does not always indicate when an instrument has G.S. mounts. However, from the associated illustrations, and surviving instruments, all clarinets, flutes, oboes, and bassoons surely had G.S. mounts, unless otherwise indicated below. This company is not to be confused with William S. Haynes. William S. Haynes is still business making very high-quality professional flutes.

Albert system clarinets, "Best French"

20	Key of B flat, boxwood, 6 brass keys, horn mounts	$6.00
20 C	Same as above in key of C	$6.00
20 E	Same as above in key of E flat	$6.00
20 A	Same as above in key of A	$6.00
21	Key of B flat, boxwood, 8 brass keys, horn mounts	$9.00
21 C	Same as above in key of C	$9.00
21 E	Same as above in key of E flat	$9.00
21 A	Same as above in key of A	$9.00

Albert system clarinets

1½	Key of B flat, ebony, 13 G.S. keys and mounts	$23.00
1½ C	Same as above in key of C	$23.00
1½ E	Same as above in key of E flat	$23.00
1½ A	Same as above in key of A	$23.00
90	Key of B flat, ebony, 13 G.S. keys	$26.00
90 C	Same as above, in key of C	$26.00
90 E	Same as above, in key of E flat	$26.00
90 A	Same as above, in key of A	$26.00
91	Key of B flat, ebony	$33.00
91 C	Key of C, ebony	$33.00
91 E	Key of E flat, ebony	$33.00
91 A	Key of A, ebony	$33.00

Albert system clarinets, Henry Gunkel, Paris, 13 G.S. keys, 2 rings

2½	Key of B flat, ebony	$30.00
2½ C	Key of C, ebony	$30.00
2½ E	Key of E flat, ebony	$30.00
2½ A	Key of A, ebony	$30.00

Albert system clarinets, Henry Gunkel, Paris, 15 G.S. keys, 2 rings, 2 mouthpieces, extra B flat and C sharp

2¾	Key of B flat, ebony	$47.50
2¾ C	Key of C, ebony	$47.50
2¾ E	Key of E flat, ebony	$47.50
2¾ A	Key of A, ebony	$47.50

Albert system clarinets, George Cloos, American, 13 G.S. keys, 2 rings

30	Key of B flat, grenadilla	$54.00
30 C	Key of C, grenadilla	$54.00
30 E	Key of E flat, grenadilla	$54.00
30 A	Key of A, grenadilla	$54.00

Albert system clarinets, George Cloos, American, 15 G.S. keys, 2 rings, extra B flat and C sharp keys

35	Key of B flat, grenadilla	$80.00
35 C	Key of C, grenadilla	$80.00
35 E	Key of E flat, grenadilla	$80.00
35 A	Key of A, grenadilla	$80.00

Albert system clarinets, Buffet, Crampon & Co., Paris, 15 G.S. keys, 4 rings, extra B flat, C sharp, and E flat keys

19	Key of B flat, ebony	$80.00
19 C	Key of C, ebony	$80.00
19 E	Key of E flat, ebony	$80.00
19 A	Key of A, ebony	$80.00

Albert system clarinets, A. Hilleron, Paris, 15 G.S. keys, 2 rings, extra B flat and C sharp keys

95	Key of B flat, ebonite	$46.00
95 C	Key of C, ebonite	$46.00
95 E	Key of E flat, ebonite	$46.00
95 A	Key of A, ebonite	$46.00

Saxophones, Buffet, Crampon & Co. (Evette & Schaeffer)

55	Key of B flat soprano, brass, straight body, double B flat key	$105.00
55¾	Key of B flat soprano, silver plated, double B flat key	$155.00
56	Key of E flat alto, brass double B flat key	$120.00
56¾	Key of E flat alto, silver plated, double B flat key	$170.00
57	Key of B flat tenor, brass, double B flat key	$120.00
57¾	Key of B flat tenor, silver plated, double B flat key	$182.00
58	Key of E flat baritone, brass, double B flat key	$130.00
58¾	Key of E flat baritone, silver plated, double B flat key	$192.50

Bassoons

1	Buffet, Crampon & Co. (Evette & Schaeffer), rosewood	$172.00
2	Rudall, Carte & Co.	$410.00

Musette

15	Boxwood, dark stained, no keys	$3.50

Fifes

20	Key of B, maple, plain	$2.75
20c	Key of C, maple, plain	$2.75
24	Key of B, imitation ebony, G.S. ferrules	$4.50
24c	Key of C, imitation ebony, G.S. ferrules	$4.50
26	Key of B, rosewood, brass ferrules	$6.38
26c	Key of C, rosewood, brass ferrules	$6.38
28	Key of B, cocus, brass ferrules	$9.18
28c	Key of C, cocus, brass ferrules	$9.18
30	Key of B, cocus, brass ferrules	$10.00
30c	Key of C, cocus, brass ferrules	$10.00
32	Key of B, cocus, G.S. embouchure and ferrules	$16.85
32c	Key of C, cocus, G.S. embouchure and ferrules	$16.85
34	Key of B, ebony, G.S. ferrules	$12.50
34c	Key of C, ebony, G.S. ferrules	$12.50
36	Key of B, ebony, G.S. embouchure and ferrules	$20.00
36c	Key of C, ebony, G.S. embouchure and ferrules	$20.00
37	Key of B, cocus, long G.S ferrules	$13.38
37c	Key of C, cocus, long G.S ferrules	$13.38
39	Key of B, ebony, long G.S ferrules	$15.00
39c	Key of C, ebony, long G.S ferrules	$15.00
81	Key of B, nickel plated, raised holes, ebonite embouchure	$15.88
81c	Key of C, nickel plated, raised holes, ebonite embouchure	$15.88
38	Key of B, cocus, Crosby model, long G.S. ferrules	$1.88
38c	Key of C, cocus, Crosby model, long G.S. ferrules	$1.88
40	Key of B, ebony, Crosby model, long G.S. ferrules	$2.00
40c	Key of C, ebony, Crosby model, long G.S. ferrules	$2.00
41	Key of B, dark grenadilla, for artists, long G.S. ferrules	$5.63
41c	Key of C, dark grenadilla, for artists, long G.S. ferrules	$5.63

American flageolets

121	Key of B, grenadilla, 1 key	$5.25
122	Key of B, grenadilla, 6 keys	$15.00
123	Key of C, grenadilla, 1 key	$5.25
124	Key of C, grenadilla, 6 keys	$15.00

Flageolet and piccolo combination

20	Key of D, boxwood, 1 G.S. key and mounts	$3.20
24	Key of D, cocoa, 1 G.S. key and mounts	$3.75
26	Key of D, cocoa, 4 G.S. keys and mounts	$4.50
70	Key of D, cocoa, 6 G.S. keys and mounts	$5.00

Tin whistles, U.S. Eagle (described as a flageolet in the catalog), marked with an eagle above "U.S." and pitch in circle

In the keys of B, C, D, and E, nickel plated. Per dozen	$3.13

Clark's London flutes (tin whistles)

Tin	$1.50
Brass	$2.20
Nickel plated	$2.50

Tin whistles (described as flageolets in catalog) narrows toward the instrument's end

3	10 inch	$0.45
4	12 inch	$0.65
5	14 inch	$0.85
9	14 inch, better quality and finish	$1.25

Flutes, 1 key (evidently French made)

1	Key of D, maple, bone ferrules	$1.10
2	Key of D, boxwood stained black, bone ferrules	$2.10
3	Key of D, boxwood stained black, G.S. mounts	$2.50
4	Key of D, cocus, George Cloos, G.S. mounts	$3.33
5	Key of D, cocus, George Cloos, tuning slide, G.S. mounts	$5.00
11	Key of B, cocus, George Cloos, G.S. mounts	$2.50
11½	Key of C, cocus, George Cloos, G.S. mounts	$2.50
7	Key of F, cocus, George Cloos, G.S. mounts	$3.25
8	Key of F, cocus, George Cloos, tuning slide, G.S. mounts	$5.00
10	Key of G, cocus, George Cloos, G.S. mounts	$3.10

Flutes, 4 keys (probably G.S., evidently French made)

12	Key of D, imitation ebony, G.S. mounts	$2.50
13	Key of D, boxwood stained black, tuning slide, G.S. mounts	$4.00
14	Key of D, grenadilla, tuning slide, G.S. mounts	$4.50
15	Key of F, grenadilla, G.S. mounts	$4.00

Flutes, 6 keys (probably G.S., evidently French made)

16	Key of D, boxwood stained black, tuning slide, G.S. mounts	$5.00
17	Key of D, grenadilla, tuning slide, G.S. mounts	$5.50
19	Key of D, grenadilla, tuning slide, G.S. mounts, cork joints	$6.00
121	Key of D grenadilla, George Cloos, tuning slide, G.S. mounts, cork joints	$16.65
21	Key of F, grenadilla, George Cloos, tuning slide, G.S. mounts, cork joints	$16.65

Piccolos

18	Key of E flat, grenadilla, George Cloos, tuning slide, G.S. mounts, cork joints	$16.65
122	Key of B flat, grenadilla, George Cloos, tuning slide, G.S. mounts, cork joints	$15.00

Flutes, 8 keys (probably G.S., evidently French made)

23	Key of D, grenadilla, G.S. mounts	$8.68
24	Key of D, grenadilla, G.S. mounts, cork joints	$9.00
25	Key of D, grenadilla, G.S. embouchure, cork joints	$11.00
26	Key of D, grenadilla, G.S. tuning slide, G.S. head joint, G.S. mounts, cork joints	$16.00
27	Key of D, grenadilla, ivory head joint, cork joints	$16.50
28	Key of D, grenadilla, imitation Meyer system, cork joints	$14.00
29	Key of D, grenadilla, imitation Meyer system, ivory head joint, cork joints	$26.50
30	Key of D, grenadilla, George Cloos, cork joints	$33.00
31	Key of D, grenadilla, George Cloos, ivory head joint, cork joints	$48.00

Flutes, 11 keys (probably G.S., evidently French made)

128	Key of D, imitation Meyer system	$22.00
128½	Key of D, imitation Meyer system, ivory head joint	$35.50
59	Key of D, grenadilla, George Cloos	$54.00
61	Key of D, grenadilla, George Cloos, ivory head joint	$60.00

61½   Key of D, grenadilla, George Cloos, ivory head joint and mounts
$68.00

Flutes, 13 keys (probably G.S., evidently French made)

40	Key of D, imitation Meyer system	$26.00
44	Key of D, imitation Meyer system, ivory head	$38.50

Boehm system flute, Buffet, Crampon & Co.

215	Unidentified wood, G.S. keys	$175.00

Boehm system flutes, Rudall, Carte & Co.

220	Cocus wood, G.S. keys	$287.50
225	Cocus wood, solid silver keys	$425.00
130	Ebonite, G.S. keys	$287.00
135	Ebonite, solid silver keys	$425.00

All Rudall, Carte & Co.'s flutes are cylindrical in bore, with a tapering or "parabola" head-joint; sakes [trill keys] for B natural, C natural, and C sharp; extra regulating set screws, thumb rest for the left had. Each instrument is also provided with extra fittings, including flattening rings (for lowering the pitch), etc.

Piccolos, no makers given, G.S. mounts

22	Key of D, boxwood, 1 key	$0.93
22e	Key of E flat, boxwood, 1 key	$0.93
25	Key of D, cocus, 1 key	$1.00
25e	Key of E flat, cocus, 1 key	$1.00

Piccolos, G.S. mounts, tuning slide

26	Key of D, grenadilla, 4 keys	$2.50
26e	Key of E flat, grenadilla, 4 key	$2.50
26½	Key of D, grenadilla, 4 keys, cork joints, G.S. caps	$2.75
26½e	Key of E flat, grenadilla, cork joints, G.S. caps	$2.75
27	Key of D, grenadilla, 6 keys	$3.00
27e	Key of E flat, grenadilla, 6 keys	$3.00
27 ½	Key of D, grenadilla, 6 keys, cork joints, G.S. caps	$3.30
27½e	Key of E flat, grenadilla, 6 keys, cork joints, G.S. caps	$3.30
86	Key of D grenadilla, 6 keys, ivory embouchure, cork joints, G.S. caps	$5.75
86e	Key of E flat, grenadilla, 6 keys, ivory embouchure, cork joints, G.S. caps	$5.75

29	Key of D grenadilla, 6 keys, ivory head, cork joints	$8.75
29e	Key of E flat, grenadilla, ivory head, cork joints	$8.75
40	Key of D, grenadilla, 6 keys, G.S. embouchure and caps, cork joints	$4.50
40e	Key of E flat, grenadilla, G.S. embouchure and caps, cork joints	$4.50
41	Key of D, grenadilla, 6 keys, G.S. head and caps, cork joints	$5.00
41e	Key of E flat, cork joints, G.S. head and caps, cork joints	$5.00
102	Key of D, grenadilla, 6 keys, imitation Meyer, cork joints	$5.50
102e	Key of E flat, grenadilla, 6 keys, imitation Meyer, cork joints	$5.50
108	Key of D, grenadilla, 6 keys, ivory head, imitation Meyer, cork joints	$10.50
108e	Key of E flat, grenadilla, ivory head, imitation Meyer, cork joints	$10.50
600	Key of D, grenadilla, 6 keys, ivory head, cork joints	$13.13
900e	Key of E flat, grenadilla, 6 keys, ivory head, cork joints	$13.13

Piccolos, George Cloos

4	Key of D, cocus, 1 key	$1.68
4e	Key of E flat, cocus, 1 key	$1.68

Piccolos, George Cloos, tuning slide, cork joints

5	Key of D grenadilla, 4 keys	$10.83
5e	Key of E flat, grenadilla, 4 keys	$10.83
10	Key of D, grenadilla, 6 keys	$16.50
10e	Key of E flat, grenadilla, 6 keys	$16.50
11	Key of D, grenadilla, ivory head, 6 keys	$20.00
11e	Key of E flat, grenadilla, ivory head, 6 keys	$20.00
12	Key of D, grenadilla, 6 keys, G.S. embouchure	$15.00
12e	Key of E flat, grenadilla, 6 keys, G.S. embouchure	$15.00

Boehm piccolos

1	Key of D, Buffet, unidentified wood, G.S. keys	$75.00
1e	E flat, Buffet, unidentified wood, G.S. keys	$75.00
2	Key of D, Rudall, Carte & Co., ebonite, pure silver keys	$225.00
2e	Key of E flat, Rudall, Carte & Co., ebonite, pure silver keys	$225.00

Wilhelm Heckel

This company operated a factory in Biebrich, Germany, making woodwind instruments from 1831 and is still in business as of 2004. The Heckel family consisted of a large number of makers (see *NLI*, p. 167-68) constructing instruments always of the highest quality, much favored even today by professional musicians, and museums. From an undated catalog (circa 1902) in the Dayton C. Miller Flute Collection, Wilhelm Heckel stated that all instruments made in his factory were made with G.S. keys, nickel plated G.S. keys, or upon special order sterling silver plated G.S. keys. The catalog included illustrations (provided here) that included catalog numbers for each instrument. Because of the cramped design of the illustrations, these numbers were removed for this book. This company is especially known for making professional-quality bassoons, and for having invented the Heckelphone, a relatively rare family of double reed instruments with a large bulbous bell suggestive of an oboe d'amore bell. The Heckelphone, however, is considerably larger and includes two large resonance holes. The company also invented less well known instruments such as the German schalmai (a double reed instrument similar to the Renaissance shawm, also called Deutsche schalmai) and the Heckel-clarina (a single reed instrument).

In the following list, prices in column one are for instruments with just G.S. keys. Column two is for nickel plated G.S. keys. Column three is for silver plated G.S. keys. All prices are in German Marks. Heckel continued to offer obsolete and outdated instruments into the 20th century, such as the clarinet d'amore in G or A flat; bass clarinets in A and C; and a contrabass clarinet in F. The following information is a free translation from the German by the author of this book.

Clarinets [probably made of African blackwood]

1f	In high G or A flat with F sharp ring key, B natural-C sharp, C sharp-D sharp trill keys	110	150	210
1g	In high F with F sharp ring key, B natural-C sharp, C sharp-D sharp trill keys	110	150	210

Clarinets in either A, B flat, C, D, or E flat

2	13 keys, F sharp ring key, B natural-C sharp, C sharp-D sharp trill keys	115	155	215
2b	14 keys, F sharp ring key	110	150	210
2c	15 keys, F sharp ring keys on the upper and lower joints	120	165	225
3	16 keys, F sharp ring keys on the upper and lower joints, forked B flat ring key	125	170	235
3	16 keys, enclosing F sharp ring on the upper and lower joint and forked B flat ring	125	170	235
4	14 keys, enclosing F sharp ring, B natural-C sharp, C sharp-D sharp trill key	125	170	235
4a	Like Nr. 4, 15 keys enclosing F sharp ring on the upper and lower joint	125	185	245
5	16 keys enclosing F sharp ring on the upper and lower joint and forked B flat ring, B natural-C sharp, C sharp-D sharp trill key	140	190	255
7	19 keys enclosing F sharp ring on the upper and lower joint and forked B flat ring, C-D trill key, curved F key and forked F mechanism on the upper joint, B natural-C sharp, C sharp-D sharp trill key, forked F-B flat mechanism and E flat lever on the lower joint	190	250	330
8	Bärmann system, 20 keys, enclosing F sharp ring on the upper and lower joints, C-D trill key. 2 F keys on the upper joint, C sharp lever, E flat and F lever on the lower joint	160	215	285
9	14 keys enclosing B flat-E flat and C-F trill key on the upper joint, B natural-C sharp, C sharp-D sharp trill key	155	210	270
10	15 keys enclosing B flat-E flat and C-F trill key and long B flat trill key on the upper joint, B natural-C sharp, C sharp-D sharp trill key and forked F-B flat mechanism on the lower joint	185	245	325
11	15 keys, enclosing B flat-E flat and C-F trill key on the upper joint, F sharp-G sharp, B natural- C sharp trill key for the right index finger, forked F-B mechanism on the lower joint	190	250	335
14	Half-Boehm, 20 keys enclosing F sharp ring on the upper and lower joint and forked B flat ring, curved F key and forked F mechanism on the upper joint, F sharp-G sharp, B natural-C sharp trill key for the right index finger	185	245	335
14a	Like Nr. 14, 19 keys, without ring and without forked F mechanism on the upper joint also without F sharp-G sharp, B natural-C sharp trill key for the right index finger	140	190	255
16	Boehm system 6 ring, 17 keys, with F sharp-G sharp, B natural-C sharp trill key	225	295	375
16a	Like Nr. 16, but without F sharp-G sharp, B natural-C sharp trill key	200	265	340
17	Boehm system, 7 ring, 18 keys enclosing E flat-A flat lever, F sharp-G sharp, B natural-C sharp trill key for the right index finger, forked B flat-E flat ring	270	340	420

The instruments listed above are not equipped with roller keys. For roller keys, add 2.50

An F sharp-G sharp, B natural-C sharp trill key for the right index finger	25	30	50
The above clarinets can be ordered descending to low E flat	30	35	50

Larger clarinets

18	Basset horn in F, with F sharp ring on the upper and lower joint, automatic B flat mechanism, B natural-C sharp, C sharp-D sharp trill key, descending to C	250	330	480
18c	Alto clarinet in F, like Nr. 18, descending to E	205	285	435
18f	Clarinet d'amore in G or A flat, with F sharp ring on the upper and			

lower joint, B natural-C sharp, C sharp-D sharp trill key

		195	275	360

19	Bass clarinet in A, B flat, or C, upright form with all the ring and coupling, B natural-C sharp, C sharp-D sharp trill key, automatic B flat mechanism descending to low E flat	320	450	600
19a	Like Nr. 19, descending to low D	360	490	660
19B	Like 19, descending to low E	300	430	570
19g	Like Nr. 19, with upward curving support	350	480	655
20	Contrabass in F, outfit and price upon agreement			
20a	Contrabass in B flat, outfit and price upon agreement			
20b	Pedal clarinet in B flat, outfit and price upon agreement			

Flutes with other key positions and metal bodies are available upon agreement.

The following flutes have a conical bore, short middle joint, long lower joint, metal-India rubber head joint and tuning slide, B natural foot.

21	11 keys enclosing D-E trill key	115	160	215
21a	12 keys enclosing F sharp mechanism with E-F sharp and high A-B flat trill key	135	185	240
21d	14 Keys enclosing F sharp-G sharp trill key, C key for the left middle finger, C sharp ring	155	205	270
22	11 keys, rollers on the C and C sharp keys, obliquely positioned B natural lever, B flat key in front, F key behind	120	165	220
22b	17 keys enclosing F sharp mechanism in back, E-F sharp and high A-B trill keys, rollers on the C and C sharp keys, obliquely positioned B natural, B flat in front, F key hinter, E flat key with the left thumb, C key for the left middle finger, F sharp-G sharp, C-D, high G-A, G sharp-A trill, thumb G sharp key	200	260	345

The following flutes have conical bore, short foot joint, metal-India rubber head joint, and tuning slide, C sharp key with rollers, B natural foot.

23	11 keys enclosing A flat-B, D-E, E-F, C-D, C sharp-D, high G-A, G sharp-A trill key	135	185	250
23a	12 keys enclosing F sharp mechanism with E-F sharp and high A-B trill key, A flat-B, D-E, E-F, C-D, C sharp-D, high G-A, G sharp-A trill key	155	210	270
23b	14 keys enclosing F sharp-G sharp trill key and C sharp ring	190	250	335
24	10 keys enclosing D-E trill key, B flat and C ring and lever mechanism	150	200	265
24b	13 keys enclosing F sharp key with C-D, C sharp-D, high G-A, G sharp-A, D-E trill key, 2 C keys	140	190	245

The addition of F sharp-G sharp trill keys cost an additional

		10	14	20

The following Boehm system flutes have a conical bore, metal head joint and tuning slide, roller on the C sharp key; key position for the left thumb with desire.

27	Flutes with ring keys, closed G sharp key, B natural-C trill key lever, C foot	185	205	265
27a	Like Nr. 27, with B natural foot	225	250	270

The following Boehm system flutes have cylindrical bore, India rubber or wood head joint and tuning slide, roller on the C sharp key; key position for the left thumb if desired.

28	Open G sharp key, B natural-C and A flat-B flat trill key lever, B flat lever to the overlap with the left index finger, F sharp lever for the right hand middle finger, B natural foot	250	270	370
28f	Open G sharp key, B natural-C and A flat-B natural trill key lever, B flat lever to the overlap with the left index finger, F sharp lever for the right			

	middle finger, B natural foot	300	325	420
29	Closed G sharp key with automatic E mechanism produces a faultless high E with the same excellent and clear intonation as the Boehm system flutes, with open G sharp key, B natural-C and A flat-B natural trill key lever, C foot	265	285	385
29f	Closed G sharp key with E mechanism like Nr. 29, in the rest like Nr. 28f, B natural foot	315	340	435

The above Boehm system flutes are made with trill key levers for the right index finger. Without this arrangement the instruments are less expensive. [No price given in the catalog.]

30	Cylindrical bore, India rubber head joint with tuning slide, roller on the C sharp key, similar hand position to the above simple conical flutes, 14 keys enclosing 6 covered keys, C foot	190	215	300
31	Terz flute in E flat, conical bore, 9 keys, metal-India rubber head joint, tuning slide, C foot	100	135	180
31a	Like Nr. 31, 10 keys close fitting close fitting F sharp mechanism with E-F sharp trill key	120	155	215

The following piccolos have conical bore, metal-India rubber head joint and tuning slide.

32	6 keys	40	55	80
32b	6 keys and F sharp mechanism	60	80	120
33	System Boehm, open G sharp key	120	135	180
33b	System Boehm, closed G sharp key	130	145	195
33x	Flute d'amore in A, conical bore, metal head joint with tuning slide, 16 keys close fitting 6 covered keys, F sharp mechanism, C sharp key with roller, C foot	350	440	550
33z	Alto flute, outfit and price provided if requested			

Conical flutes with ivory heads cost an additional	20
Boehm system flutes with ivory heads cost an additional	75
Piccolos with ivory heads cost an additional	15

With regards to durability and agility, India rubber is comparable with ivory; but for ivory I can provide no guarantee against splitting.

Raised mouthpiece can be provided if desired.

All key mechanisms and key position can be moved to a special hand position for the little finger, upon special agreement.

If not desired, the key position are manufactured like those pictured.
All oboes can be manufactured descending to low B if so ordered.

The fingering of the following listed oboes is just like by the best German oboes. The instruments have automatic closing mechanism, thumb B flat lever, B natural-C sharp trill key on the upper joint and F sharp ring provided; descending to low B natural.

The following oboes have simple octave keys

35a	Oboe with one octave key	130	165	225
35ab	Oboe with two octave keys for the thumb	135	170	230
35ac	Oboe with just one octave key for the thumb and index finger	135	170	230
35ad	Oboe with two octave keys, modified so that the thumb key can be pressed down and remain down when the index finger key is opened	140	180	240

The following oboes have 2 separate keys that are adjustable according to the need of the note.

35b	Oboe with F sharp ring key	150	195	270
35c	Oboe with F sharp-G sharp trill key and F sharp ring	160	205	280
35d	Oboe with forked F mechanism	160	205	280

| 35q | Oboe like Nr. 35c, descending to low B flat | 195 | 245 | 330 |

The following oboes have 3 separate keys that are adjustable according to the need of the note.

35o	Oboe with F sharp key	175	225	300
35p	Oboe with F sharp-G sharp trill key and F sharp ring	185	235	310
	A higher-priced oboe with a B-flat key on the back opposite a B-flat key	35	40	50

Where not mentioned above, the following rings and keys will cost:

One C sharp ring on the upper joint	10	14	20
One half hole key	5	7	10
A half hole ring in connection with the brill key for the left ring finger, which closes itself as needed	20	28	40
One G sharp key for the left thumb	10	14	20
One forked F mechanism	10	14	20
A B natural-C sharp trill key on the lower joint	10	14	20
An F sharp-G sharp trill key	10	14	20

The design and the touch of the following oboes are like the French oboes. The instruments are equipped with self closing mechanism for the D trill key on the upper joint and F sharp ring, descending to low B natural.

The following oboes have 3 individual octave keys that can be adjusted according to the need of the tone.

35r	Oboe with half hole key	185	235	310
35f	Oboe with F sharp-G sharp trill key, B flat-C trill key ring with thumb plate, self closing half hole ring in connection with the ring for the left index finger, low C-E flat connection	285	335	435
35y	Oboe with F sharp-G sharp trill key, double G sharp lever, A sharp-B flat trill key self closing half hole key, B flat-C trill key ring in connection with the ring on the lower joint, with a special fingering for the index finger, C sharp and D trill key, the last one with a second fingering on the lower joint, low C-E flat connection, C lever for the right ring finger, descending to low B flat	370	420	525

The following oboes have 3 individual octave keys that can be adjusted according to the need of the tone.

35v	Oboe, with mechanism just like Nr. 35y, however without the third octave and low B flat key	310	360	465
35u	Oboe with F sharp-G sharp, A flat-B flat trill key, automatic hole ring connection with the ring for right index finger, low C-E flat connection	235	280	365
35x	Oboe with half hole and C sharp ring	205	350	335
35w	Oboe, with a 1 octave key for the thumb and half hole key for the index finger	145	185	265

Any additional key placements are possible if so desired. When ordering an oboe, I ask to be sent an oboe that has previously been used by the player in an orchestra and found to be satisfactory. This is necessary so that I can build the instrument based on the size of the tube. Because of the variation in tube construction and length, this is absolutely necessary.

The following oboes d'amore have half hole key, F sharp ring, thumb B flat lever, B natural-C sharp trill key on the upper joint; descending to low B natural; German fingering.

| 37e | Oboe d'amore, with 3 individual octave keys that can be adjusted according to the need of the tone | 255 | 305 | 405 |

The following models are especially qualified for use in the Symphonia Domestica of Dr. Richard Strauss.

37g	Oboe d'amore, like Nr. 37e with 2 self closing octave keys	230	275	380
37f	Oboe d'amore, with just 1 octave key for the thumb and the index finger	175	215	320
37y	The design and fingering are like the French instruments, D trill key on the upper joint, simple B flat and C trill ring key, low C-E flat connection, simple half hole ring and 3 individual octave keys that can be adjusted according to the need of the tone	295	345	445

Alternate keys mechanism and hand position are available upon agreement.

The following English horns have half hole key, F sharp ring, thumb B flat lever, B natural-C sharp trill key on the upper joint; descending to low B natural; German fingering.

39f	English horn with 3 individual octave keys that can be adjusted according to the need of the tone	280	365	470
39a	Like Nr. 39f, with 2 self closing octave keys	250	335	440
39d	Like Nr. 39a, with forked F mechanism	270	360	464
39h	With 1 octave key for the thumb and the index finger	205	270	355
39i	With 2 individual octave keys that can be adjusted according to the need of the tone, forked F mechanism, descending to low B flat	320	420	535

The design and the fingering of the following listed English horns are like the French type of English horns. The instruments are provided with D trill key on the upper joint and F sharp ring, descending to low B natural.

39w	English horn, with half hole key, simple B flat-C trill ring key, low C-E flat connection and 2 octave keys, modified so that the thumb key can be pressed down and remain down when the index finger key is opened	250	335	440
39x	Like Nr. 39w with 2 octave keys that can be adjusted according to the need of the tone	285	370	475
39y	Like Nr. 39w, with 3 individual octave keys that can be adjusted according to the need of the tone	315	415	530

All English horns can be ordered descending to low B flat.

| Higher prices for E flat English horns with B flat in back, an E flat like the B natural | 50 | 60 | 75 |

Alternate keys mechanism and fingering are available upon agreement.

39n	Baritone oboe (also wrongly called Bass oboe) with 2 octave keys, half hole key, C-E flat connection, descends to B natural	350	470	655
37o	Tristan schalmei in F with half hole key, specially made for use in "Die Lustige Weise," similar in tone color to the English horn, however darker in tone	45	55	75
37p	Musette with one octave key and half hole key	75	90	135
40	Fagottino [small bassoon] in F with E-F sharp trill key and D sharp key on wing joint, yet with self closing G ring; fingering like on the Heckel-bassoons	350	470	655

The following Heckelphones have B natural-C sharp trill key on the upper joint, thumb B flat lever, F sharp ring and half hole key. The hand position is just like on the Heckel-oboe (German design).

36	Heckelphone, descending to low B natural	350	470	655
36a	Heckelphone, descending to low B flat	385	505	690
36b	Heckelphone, descending to low A natural	425	545	730

The following Heckelphones have a B-C trill brill key on the wing joint. The half hole brill key also closes itself through the Brill ring for the left finger. The key position for both of the small fingers is placed according to French oboe fingering practice.

36g	Heckelphone, descending to low B natural	370	490	675
36h	Heckelphone, descending to low B flat	405	525	710
36i	Heckelphone, descending to low A natural	445	565	750

Alternate key position and hand position are available upon agreement.

The piccolo Heckelphone in the highest tone produces a healthy, strong, but high class oboe tone. Such a safe and clear height of an oboe instrument has never before been achievable. The instruments are in high F and have a chromatic range like the oboe from B flat to E. The tube is similar to the oboe tube.

36m	Piccolo-Heckelphone in F with 2 individual octave keys that can be adjusted according to the need of the tone, half hole key, thumb B flat lever F sharp ring. The hand position is just like the Heckel-oboe (German design)	150	180	235
36o	Like Nr. 36m; the key position for the right small finger is like French work	155	185	240

Heckel bassoons

40a	Bassoon descending to low A, with all the needed keys and modern establishments, key position and hand position like 41a	490	700	1250
40b	Like Nr. 40a, but descending to low B flat	400	600	1125

The following bassoons descend to low B flat

41a	Bassoon, with C sharp-D sharp and F sharp-G sharp trill key	310	410	775
41b	Bassoon with 19 keys	276	370	690
41c	Bassoon with F sharp-G sharp trill key	286	380	715
41e	Bassoon with C sharp-D sharp and F sharp-G sharp trill key, self closing G ring	335	435	810
41f	Bassoon with 19 keys and self closing G ring	310	410	775
41g	Bassoon with F sharp-G sharp trill key and self closing G ring	320	420	785
41h	Bassoon with C sharp-D sharp, F sharp-G sharp, E-F sharp and high C trill key, thumb D sharp lever on the butt joint, self closing G ring	370	480	890
41i	Bassoon with C sharp-D sharp and F sharp-G sharp trill key, automatic G ring, with automatic mechanism for the hole in the bocal from the low E-covered out of operating and other lever for the left thumb operating and other lever for the left thumb	365	475	880
41d	Bassoon with F sharp-G sharp trill key and self closing G ring, descending to low A	425	575	1015

The following new bassoons are made like the famous Heckel-bassoon. The outer shape of the instruments, the key placement and grip plate are like the French bassoon, so that switching from those instruments to a real Heckel bassoon should be very easy. The fingering of these instruments is the same as the French bassoons, with the exception of a few tones in the highest ranges.

42a	Bassoon with automatic mechanism for the left little finger, E-F sharp trill key, D sharp key and 2 C sharp keys on wing joint, E key, B flat lever for the right thumb, descending to low B flat	330	430	805
42c	Bassoon with whisper key closing mechanism for the left thumb as well as the small finger, E-F sharp, D sharp key, G trill key, and 2 C sharp keys, E key, B and C sharp thumb lever, independent G-brill key down to B natural	390	500	920

The following items will be mounted on the listed bassoons according to the customer's wants, unless these particular ones have not already been mentioned with particular models.

E-F sharp trill key on wing joint	10	14	20
Simple D sharp keys on wing joint	10	14	20
Self closing E ring on wing joint	25	30	45
C trill key on wing joint, B natural-C and C-C sharp trill keys	10	14	20
D sharp lever on the butt joint for the thumb	5	7	10
Independent closing mechanism for the hole in the bocal, functioning from the lower E key and special lever for the left thumb	25	30	45
G-B and A sharp-B natural ligature and trill key on the foot	20	25	35

On the image in front of you is a butt joint and a headpiece with dampening mechanism for lower tones. If you order these parts instead of the usual parts, no additional cost will be incurred. If another is used, which is recommended, with exception of the usual parts like head, butt joint with dampening mechanism, the price of a bassoon without the self actuating closing mechanism for the hole in the bocal will be higher.

Every bassoon that descends to B will also be made to descend to low A, at an additional cost of:	85	105	180
Every other key position can be made, upon agreement	90	120	185

Alternate key position etc. are available, upon agreement.

Contrabassoons

The instruments are made of three pieces of wood and are fingered like the Heckel-bassoons, so that bassoonists can immediately learn to play without special study.

43	Contrabassoon with straight wood head, down to C	395	530	910
43b	Contrabassoon with the metal head joint bend downward, therefore reaching only chest high, are constructed like the one prior. On the wing an E-F sharp trill is attached, in addition to a C sharp key for the left small finger. Especially suited for march music	470	700	1600
43a	Robust contrabassoon, organ-like tone, long, straight metal head joint, descending to low B flat	590	890	1850
43d	Robust contrabassoon, organ-like tone, with bent wood head joint, therefore reaching only chest high, descending to low A	620	895	1675
43e	Contrabassoon, organ-like tone, descending to low A	745	1050	1975

The following contrabassoons are in design etc. just like the preceding. On the wing joint, an E-F sharp trill is attached, in addition to a C sharp key for the left small finger. The key position for the left thumb etc. is like the French bassoons, so that the bassoonist who knows the French bassoon can play these contrabassoons immediately without special study.

43h	Contrabass bassoon, like Nor. 43	420	555	945
43i	Contrabass bassoon, like Nr. 43b	495	725	1635
43k	Contrabass bassoon, like Nr. 43a	615	915	1885
43l	Contrabass bassoon, like Nr. 43d	635	920	1710
43m	Contrabass bassoon, like Nr. 43e	770	1075	2010

If the head piece of the contrabass bassoon is built to come apart for early transportation, an additional charge of 30 is due.

The klarina resembles in its tone and in the fingering that of the saxophone. The tone, though, due to the particular construction of the instrument is much larger and finer. The klarina forms a transition from sheet-metal to wood sheet-metal instruments. With this instrument a new and important factor of the orchestra is gained.

100   Heckel-clarina are entirely made of metal, with a mouth piece similar to a clarinet mouth piece (made of wood), with two individual octave keys that can be adjusted according to the need of the tone. The fingering in general is like the oboe, and the conical flutes, so that musicians can play the Heckel-clarina without special study.   250   380

100a   Heckel-clarina like Nr. 100, sopranino in E flat   240   360

The following saxophones have a compact design and simple keys. Other keys can be added with specification and agreement.

96	Soprano in B flat	200	220	340
97	Alto in E flat	240	265	420
98	Tenor in B flat	250	280	505
99	Baritone in E flat	290	320	610

[The upper prices are as follows: column 1 totally made of brass; column 2 nickel plate, column 3 G.S. plate.]

Ophiclides, Sarrusophones and other instruments are available upon special order.

Heckel clarinets

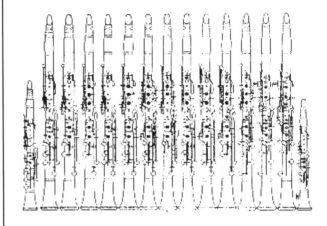

Heckel alto and bass clarinets

Heckel flutes

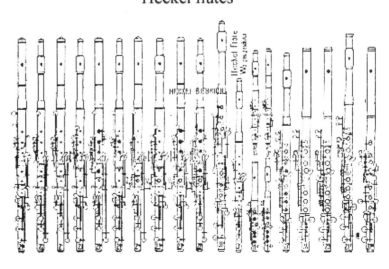

Heckel bassoons

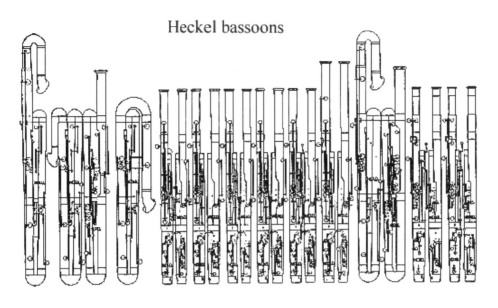

Heckel double reeds

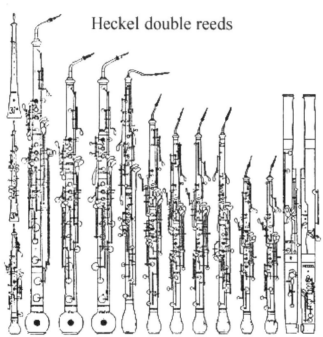

Heckel oboes

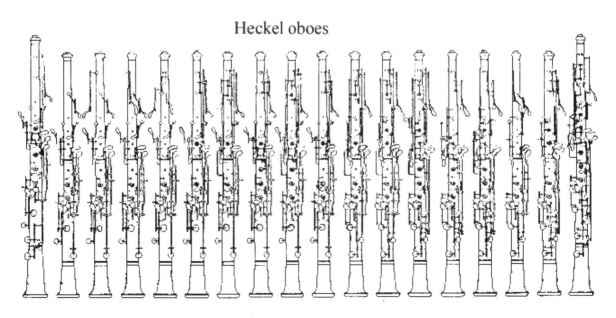

J.R. Holcomb & Co.

This company was based in Cleveland, Ohio, according to a catalog dated 1901. The company is not listed in *NLI*, and the company appears to have been just an importer of inexpensive European-made instruments. Though the catalog does not list any makers of the following instruments, one illustration of a clarinet is clearly marked "Henry Gunkel/Paris."

Albert system clarinets in the key of A, B flat, C, D, or E flat

10	Boxwood, 6 keys (no material identified), horn mounts	$5.30
12	Boxwood, 10 keys (no material identified), horn mounts	$8.00
14	Grenadilla, 10 G.S. keys and mounts	$11.00
16	Grenadilla, 13 G.S. keys and mounts, 2 rings	$16.00
18	Grenadilla, 15 G.S. keys and mounts, 2 rings, C and B flat trill keys $20.00	

Fifes

1	Maple stained black, G.S. ferrules	$0.30
2	Cocus, G.S. ferrules	$0.60
3	Ebony, G.S. ferrules	$0.75
4	Ebony, G.S. blow hole, G.S. ferrules	$1.10

Fifes, raised finger holes

20	Brass	$0.20
21	Nickel plated	$0.25

[These instruments were identified in the catalog as flageolet-fifes.]

Flageolets

3	Key of B, C, or D, cocus, 1 G.S. key and mounts	$2.00
4	Cocus, 4 G.S. keys and mounts, C or D	$2.75
5	Cocus, 6 G.S. keys and mounts, C only	$3.00

Piccolo flageolets

13	Grenadilla, 4 G.S. keys and mounts, alternate piccolo or flageolet heads $3.50	
14	Grenadilla, 6 G.S. keys and mounts, alternate piccolo or flageolet heads $4.00	

Simple system wood flutes [key of F?]

73	Cocus, 1 G.S. key and mounts	$2.00
74	Cocus, 4 G.S. keys and mounts, tuning slide	$3.75
75	Key of F, cocus, 6 G.S. keys and mounts, tuning slide, cork joints $5.00	

[Only the pitch for number 75 was given in the catalog.]

Simple system wood flutes, key of D

78	Grenadilla, 4 G.S. keys and mounts, tuning slide	$3.60
79	Same as 78, close fitting cork joints	$4.50
80	Grenadilla, 6 G.S. keys and mounts, tuning slide, caps, cork joints	$5.00
81	Grenadilla, 8 G.S. keys and mounts, tuning slide, caps, cork joints	$7.50
82	Grenadilla, Meyer system, ivory head, 8 G.S. keys and mounts, caps, cork joints	$16.00

[Number 83 was described as "Finest for Professional Use".]

Simple system wood piccolos, [metal not identified], key of D or E flat, grenadilla

3	1 key, side	$1.50
4	4 keys, tuning slide	$2.00
5	4 keys, tuning slide, cork joints	$2.25
6	6 keys, tuning slide, cork joints	$2.50
7	G.S. mouth-piece, 6 keys, tuning slide, cork joints	$3.50
8	G.S. head joint, 6 keys, tuning slide, cork joints	$4.00
9	Meyer system, ivory head joint, 6 keys, tuning slide, cork joints	$7.50

G. & A. Klemm

NLI (p. 206) states that George and August Klemm operated in Neukirchen, Germany between about 1851 and 1930. Little information exists about this company. From a trade catalog of circa 1890, the company exported instruments to English and Spanish-speaking countries. The catalog does not clearly state that this company actually made instruments. The company could have simply been an exporter, but more research is clearly needed, as many of the unsigned instruments found on online auctions are very similar to instruments in this catalog. No relationship has yet been discovered with Klemm Brothers of Philadelphia. Prices in this catalog are in Saxon Marks. Not all instruments are fully described. Keys and mounts are probably made of G.S. unless otherwise indicated. The following information is a free translation from the German by the author of this book.

Simple system piccolo in D or E flat, pitch of A=435 or A=888 (Vienna) [Prices for instruments in this first group are per dozen.]

2840	Pear wood, Black, bone rings, 1 G.S. key	14.40
2842	Boxwood, black or yellow, brass ferrules, 1 key	24.00
2843	Grenadilla or cocus, 1 G.S. key and mounts	38.00
2844	Grenadilla or cocus, 1 G.S. key, G.S. mounts	44.00
2845	Grenadilla or cocus, 4 G.S. keys	64.00
2846	Grenadilla or cocus, 4 G.S. key, cork joints	72.00
2847	Grenadilla or cocus, 4 G.S. key, cork joints better quality	132.00
2848	Grenadilla or cocus, 6 G.S. key	84.00
2849	Grenadilla or cocus, 6 G.S. key, cork joints,	
2849½	Grenadilla or cocus, 6 G.S. key, cork joints, better quality	150.00
2850	Grenadilla or cocus, 6 G.S. keys, G.S. finger holes	108.00
2851	Grenadilla or cocus, 6 G.S. keys, G.S. G.S. embouchure band, G.S. lined finger holes	120.00
2852	Grenadilla or cocus, 6 G.S. keys, G.S. head joint	120.00
2854	Grenadilla or cocus, 6 G.S. keys, Ivory lined finger holes	126.00
2855	Grenadilla or cocus, 6 G.S. keys, and G.S. lined finger holes	150.00

Simple system piccolos with metal head joints [Prices for the following instruments are per piece, not per dozen as above.]

2856	Grenadilla or cocus, 6 G.S. keys and mounts	16.50
2857	Meyer system, grenadilla or cocus, 6 G.S. keys and mounts	8.00
2857½	Meyer system, grenadilla or cocus, 6 G.S. keys, better quality	13.00
2858	Meyer system, grenadilla or cocus, 6 G.S. keys	18.00
2858½	Meyer system, grenadilla or cocus, 6 G.S. keys	25.00

Meyer system flutes, C foot

2905	Grenadilla, 8 G.S. keys and mounts	21.00
2906	Grenadilla, 8 G.S. keys and mounts, better quality	28.00
2908	Grenadilla, 8 G.S. keys and mounts, G.S. finger holes	22.00
2909	Grenadilla, 8 G.S. keys and mounts, G.S. finger holes, better quality	32.00
2910	Grenadilla, 8 G.S. keys and mounts, lip plate	23.00
2911	Grenadilla, 8 G.S. keys and mounts, lip plate and set out hole	26.00
2912	Grenadilla, 8 G.S. keys and mounts, ivory-lined finger holes	30.00
2914	Grenadilla, 8 G.S. keys and mounts, ivory-lined finger holes and set out hole	35.00
2915	Grenadilla, 8 G.S. keys and mounts, ivory head joint	46.00
2918	Grenadilla, 8 G.S. keys and mounts, ivory head joint, better quality	60.00

Meyer system flutes, B flat foot

2920	Grenadilla, 9 G.S. keys and mounts	36.00
2921	Grenadilla, 9 G.S. keys and mounts, ivory head joint	60.00
2922	Grenadilla, 10 G.S. keys and mounts	38.00
2924	Grenadilla, 10 G.S. keys and mounts ivory head joint	62.00
2925	Grenadilla, 11 G.S. keys and mounts	40.00
2926	Grenadilla, 11 G.S. keys and mounts ivory head joint	64.00
2928	Grenadilla, 12 G.S. keys and mounts	42.00
2930	Grenadilla, 12 G.S. keys and mounts ivory head joint	66.00
2932	Grenadilla, 13 G.S. keys and mounts	44.00
2934	Grenadilla, 13 G.S. keys and mounts ivory head joint	68.00

Meyer system concert flutes with B flat foot

2935	Grenadilla, 9 G.S. keys	60.00
2936	Grenadilla, 9 G.S. keys, ivory head joint	84.00
2938	Grenadilla, 10 G.S. keys	63.00
2939	Grenadilla, 10 G.S. keys, ivory head joint	87.00
2940	Grenadilla, 11 G.S. keys	66.00
2941	Grenadilla, 11 G.S. keys, ivory head joint	90.00
2942	Grenadilla, 12 G.S. keys	69.00
2944	Grenadilla, 12 G.S. keys ivory head joint	93.00
2945	Grenadilla, 13 G.S. keys	72.00
2946	Grenadilla, 13 G.S. keys ivory head joint	96.00
2947	Grenadilla, 14 G.S. keys	75.00
2947½	Grenadilla, 14 G.S. keys, ivory head joint	99.00
2948	Grenadilla, 15 G.S. keys	78.00
2948½	Grenadilla, 15 G.S. keys, ivory head joint	102.00

Pratten [?] system flutes

2949	Grenadilla, cylindrical bore, covered finger holes, no ferrule	135
2949/S	Grenadilla, cylindrical bore, covered finger holes, ferrule	150

Flutes, simple system, Grenadilla or Kings grenadilla

2952½	13 [metal?] keys, ivory head joint, C and C# rollers, B foot	150
2950E	8 [metal?] keys, Ebony head joint, C foot	116
02951	11 [metal?] keys, ivory head joint, B flat foot	105

02952	11 G.S. keys, C and C# rollers, ebony head joint, B flat foot	140
2952½	13 G.S. keys, C and C# rollers, ebony head joint, B flat foot	150

Flute, Schwedler Kruspe system

2953	G.S. keys, ivory head joint, B foot	160
2953E	G.S. keys, ebony head joint, B foot	210
2953M	G.S. keys, G.S. head joint, B flat foot	200

Flute, Ziegler system, G.S. keys

2954Z	13 keys, 3 rollers, wood head joint, B flat foot	108
02954Z	15 keys, 3 rollers, wood head joint, B flat foot	120
2954M	11 keys, metal head joint, hard rubber mouthpiece, B flat foot	135
2954½M	13 keys, metal head joint, hard rubber mouthpiece, B flat foot	142

Flutes 2954Z and 02954Z can be had in ebony for 54 marks more.

Flute, Boehm system, Grenadilla or cocobolo, closed or open G# key

2955½	B flat-C trill, C foot	300
	B flat foot	325
2956	G-A and B flat-C trills, C foot	400
	B flat foot	430
2957½	Metal head joint, G-A and B flat-C trills, C foot	445
	B flat foot	470
2959½	G.S. body, G-A and B flat-C trills, C foot	420
	B flat foot	435
5961½	Silver body, G-A and B flat-C trills, hard rubber mouthpiece, C foot	620
	B flat foot	645

Clarinets in E flat, D, C, B flat, and A, A=435 or A=444

3031	Key of E flat, unstained maple, 5 brass keys	10.50
3031	Key of D, unstained maple, 5 brass keys	10.50
3031	Key of C, unstained maple, 5 brass keys	11.40
3031	Key of B flat, unstained maple, 5 brass keys	11.40
3031	Key of A, unstained maple, 5 brass keys	11.40
3033	Key of E flat, maple stained black, 5 nickel-plated brass keys	10.50
3033	Key of D, maple stained black, 5 nickel-plated brass keys	10.50
3033	Key of C, maple stained black, 5 nickel-plated brass keys	13.20
3033	Key of B flat, maple stained black, 5 nickel-plated brass keys	13.20
3033	Key of A, maple stained black, 5 nickel-plated brass keys	13.20
3036	Boxwood, 5 brass keys, without sheet screws	18.00
3038	Boxwood, 8 brass keys, without sheet screws	22.50
3040	Boxwood, 5 brass keys, without sheet screws	19.00
3041	Boxwood, 8 brass keys, without sheet screws	23.50
3042	Boxwood, 10 brass keys, without sheet screws	26.50
3044	Boxwood, 13 brass keys, without sheet screws	31.20
3046	Boxwood, 5 G.S., with Sheet screws and cup-shaped ring	23.40
3048	Boxwood, 8 G.S., with Sheet screws and cup-shaped ring	29.00
3049	Boxwood, 10 G.S., with Sheet screws and cup-shaped ring	34.00
3050	Boxwood, 13 G.S., with Sheet screws and cup-shaped ring	40.50
3052	Boxwood, 13 G.S., with Sheet screws and cup-shaped ring	46.00

Albert system clarinets, grenadilla, current quality

3053	8 G.S. keys	36.00
3054	10 G.S. keys	42.00
3054½	12 G.S. keys	48.00
3055	13 G.S. keys	51.00
3056	13 G.S. keys, 1 ring key	60.00

3057	13 G.S. keys, 1 ring key, India rubber rollers	69.00

With steel springs und Steel screw for an additional 8 Marks

Clarinets, grenadilla, good quality, German model, tapered keys, steel springs and screws

3058	10 G.S. keys	48.00
3059	12 G.S. keys	54.00
3060	13 G.S. keys	57.00
3061	13 G.S. keys, 1 ring key	66.00
3062	13 G.S. keys, 1 ring key and rollers	75.00
3063	13 G.S. keys, 2 ring keys	78.00
3064	13 G.S. keys, 2 ring keys and rollers	87.00
3065	14 G.S. keys, 1 ring key	69.00
3066	14 G.S. keys, 1 ring key and rollers	90.00
3067	14 G.S. keys, 2 ring keys	81.00
3068	14 G.S. keys, 2 ring keys and rollers	99.00
3069	15 G.S. keys, 1 ring key	72.00
3070	15 G.S. keys, 1 ring key and rollers	93.00
3071	15 G.S. keys, 2 ring keys	84.00
3072	15 G.S. keys, 2 ring keys and rollers	108.00

With hard rubber mouthpiece for an additional 12 Marks

Clarinets, Buffet-Crampon model, grenadilla, steel springs and screws

F/150	13 G.S. keys	54
F/151	13 G.S. keys, 1 ring key	63.00
F/152	14 G.S. keys, 1 ring key	66.00
F/153	14 G.S. keys, 2 ring keys	75.00
F/154	14 G.S. keys, 1 ring key, H-C sharp trill	72.00
F/155	15 G.S. keys, 2 ring keys, H-C sharp trill	81.00
F/156	13 G.S. keys, 1 ring key, 4 rollers	72.00
F/157	13 G.S. keys, 2 ring keys, 4 rollers	81.00
F/158	14 G.S. keys, 1 ring key, 4 rollers	75.00
F/159	14 G.S. keys, 2 ring keys, 4 rollers	84.00
F/150	15 G.S. keys, 1 ring key, 4 rollers, H-C sharp trill	78.00
F/151	15 G.S. keys, 2 ring keys, 4 rollers, H-C sharp trill	87.00

Albert system clarinets, grenadilla, steel springs and screws

A/170	13 G.S. keys, 1 ring key	63.00
A/171	14 G.S. keys, 1 ring key	66.00
A/172	15 G.S. keys, 1 ring key, B natural-C sharp trill	72.00
A/173	13 G.S. keys, 2 ring keys	72.00
A/174	14 G.S. keys, 2 ring keys	75.00
A/175	15 G.S. keys, 2 ring keys, B natural-C sharp trill	81.00

Concert clarinets, grenadilla, G.S. keys, with steel springs, and roller screws, cup-shaped ring, sheet screws, metal housing in the G-hole

K/260	13 G.S. keys, 1 ring key, G sharp lever	69.00
K/262	14 G.S. keys, 1 ring key, G sharp lever	72.00
K/264	14 G.S. keys, 1 ring key, 4 rollers, G sharp lever	82.50
K/266	15 G.S. keys, 1 ring key, 4 rollers, G sharp and Es-lever	87.00
K/267	16 G.S. keys, 1 ring key, 4 rollers, G sharp and Es- lever, H-C sharp-trill	95.00
K/268	14 G.S. keys, 2 ring keys, 4 rollers, G sharp lever	93.00
K/270	15 G.S. keys, 2 ring keys, 4 rollers, G sharp and E flat levers	96.00
K274	14 G.S. keys, 2 ring keys, 4 rollers, G sharp lever and B natural-C sharp trill key	106
K/278	15 G.S. keys, 2 ring keys, 4 rollers, G sharp and E flat levers, B natural-C sharp trill key	108

Fine solo clarinet, grenadilla, supple keys, ebonite head joint, with string or sheet screws.

S/300	14 keys, 1 ring key, 4 rollers, G sharp lever	122.00
S/304	14 keys, 2 ring keys, 4 rollers, G sharp lever	135.00
S/305	15 keys, 1 ring key, 4 rollers, G sharp and E flat levers	176.00
S/306	15 keys, 2 ring keys, 4 rollers, G sharp and E flat levers	190.00
S/308	16 keys, 2 ring keys, 4 rollers, G sharp and E flat levers, B natural-C sharp trill key	202.00
S/310	16 keys, 5 ring keys, 4 rollers, B natural-C sharp trill keys, forked B mechanism, E flat and G sharp levers	216.00
S/315	15 keys, 5 rings, 4 rollers, forked B mechanism, E flat and G sharp levers	216.00

Clarinets made of ebonite available for an additional 40 marks.

Boehm system clarinet, grenadilla or ebony

S/320½	Boehm, 18 keys, 2 rings	195.00
S/324	18 keys, 6 rings	250.00
B/326	19 keys, 7 rings, F sharp-G sharp trill, forked B mechanism, 2 rollers	338.00
B/330	20 keys, 7 rings, F sharp-G sharp trill, forked B mechanism, 2 rollers, E flat lever, double G sharp keys	380.00

Alto clarinet in E flat or F, wood lined with trimmings

3073½	Long form, extending to E, nickel plated keys	430.00
3074½	Long form, extending to E flat, nickel plated keys	460.00
3075½	Long form, extending to C, nickel plated keys	540.00
3076½	Long form, extending to E, Boehm system	460.00

Bass clarinets in A, B or C

3077½	Long form, extending to E, nickel plated keys	485.00
3078½	Long form, extending to E flat, nickel plated keys	510.00
3079½	Long form, extending to C, nickel plated keys	610.00
3080½	Long form, extending to E flat, Boehm system	540.00

Bassoons, flamed maple, stained brown, 2 crooks, 2 cane reeds

3108	16 G.S. keys and mounts	340.00
3109	18 G.S. keys and mounts	360.00
3111	20 G.S. keys and mounts, with G ring key	400.00
3111½	20 G.S. keys and mounts, with G ring key, F sharp-G sharp and C sharp-D sharp trill keys, ebonite lined wind way	500.00
3112	22 G.S. keys, with G ring key, F sharp-G sharp and C sharp-D sharp trill keys, ebonite lined wind way	670.00
3112K	Contrabass bassoon, extending to C	800.00
3113K	Contrabass bassoon, extending to B	1000.00

Oboes, grenadilla or Kings grenadilla

3118	13 keys, no ring keys	108.00
3120	13 keys, F sharp ring key, closed C key	116.00
3121	14 keys, F sharp ring key, closed C key	120.00
2122½	14 keys, F sharp ring key, 2 octave keys, voice key	148.00
3123	15 keys, F sharp ring key, 2 octave keys, forked F mechanism	200.00
3124	16 keys, F sharp ring key, 2 octave keys, forked F mechanism, F sharp-G sharp trill key, half block key, voice key	240.00
3125	Boehm system	250.00

Flutes sold by G.& A. Klemm

2949/S

2952 1/2

2953/E

2953/M

2954 1/2/M

2956

[no catalog number]

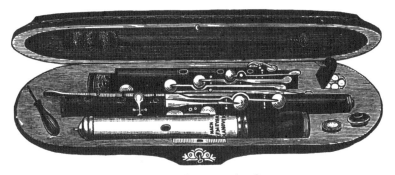

[no catalog number]

71

Simple system piccolos

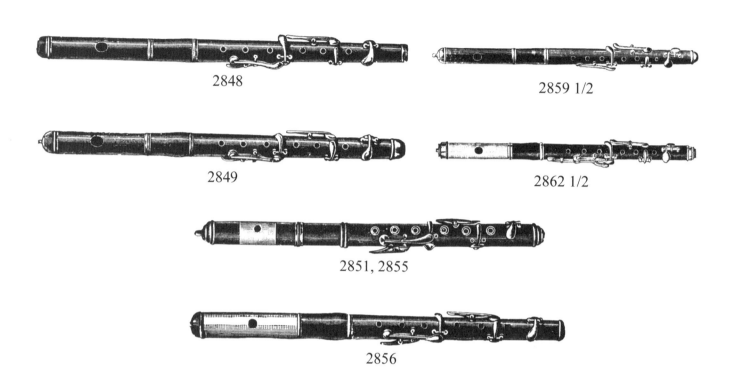

2848

2859 1/2

2849

2862 1/2

2851, 2855

2856

2865 3/4

Though this piccolo has rods and posts, and plateau keys suggestive of a Boehm system piccolo, this instrument also has lever keys, and rods on both sides of the body, which are characteristic of efforts to create a hybrid of the Boehm and simple system. Examples of this effort are not common.

Boehm system piccolo

B/2865

Military flute, or Band flute

2990, 2992, 2993

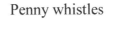

2994

Band flutes are more common in England than in the U.S. Band flutes are easily confused with piccolos. Band flutes tend to have wider bores than piccolos to produce a louder sound than piccolos.

Penny whistles

2998, 2999

3002, 3004

Note that penny whistles have a fipple head, and are not tuneable. Instruments are almost always made of sheet metal.

2997 Pan pipe

Pan pipes are also called Andean pipes, and can be found in many non-western cultures.

73

Albert system concert clarinet

K/278

Albert system solo clarinet

S/306

S/310

Note the roller keys for the little finger of the right hand; characteristic of Albert system clarinets but not Boehm system clarinets.

Boehm system clarinets

B/324

B/330

Note the multiple keys for the little finger of the right hand; characteristic of Boehm system clarinets, but not found on Albert system clarinets.

Albert system clarinets

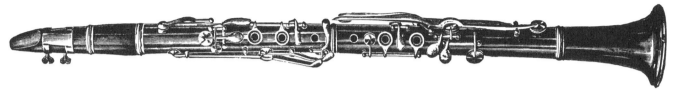

F/150, F/151, F/152, F/153, F/154, F/155, F/156, F/157, F/158, F/159

A/170, A171, A172, A173, A174, A175

K/260, K/262, K/264, K/266, K/267

Flageolets in C

3006, 3012, 3014, 3015

Piccolo-Flageolet

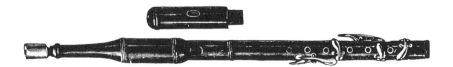

3016, 3017, 3018

Saxophones

10S 10A 10T 10B

20S 20A 20T 20B

G. Leblanc

George Leblanc founded the company G. Leblanc in Paris, but had a New York office (*NLI*, p. 227). His son Leon opened a factory in Kenosha, Wisconsin. Instruments made for the U.S. market as of circa 1925 were pitched in A=440. All instruments were equipped with G.S. keys and mounts. The company made professional quality instruments for the most part, especially the bass and contrabass clarinets, which were made by almost no other maker. This list is from a circa 1930 catalog.

Boehm system clarinets, key of B flat

136	Grenadilla, 17 keys, 6 rings	$150.00
156	Grenadilla, 18 keys, 6 rings, same as 136, with articulated G sharp	$174.00
177	Grenadilla, 17 keys, 7 rings, with new clear B flat improvement	$162.00
187	Grenadilla, 18 keys, 7 rings, same as 177, with B flat fork	$186.00
197	Grenadilla, 19 keys, 7 rings, with B flat fork and G sharp articulated, new B flat improvement	$198.00
217	Grenadilla, 21 keys, 7 rings, same as the above with double E flat key, and low E flat, and double C sharp	$216.00

Boehm system alto clarinet

30	Grenadilla, covered keys, new patented model, low E flat key, improved B flat key	$240.00

Boehm system bass clarinet

35	Grenadilla, covered keys, low E flat key	$336.00

Boehm system bass clarinet

62	G.S. throughout, covered keys one piece body, bent body, with bell positioned above the instrument, suggestive of a bassoon, range of 5 octaves beginning at low C	$390.00

Boehm system bass clarinet

52	Similar to 62	$450.00

Lyon & Healy

Lyon & Healy, based in Chicago, Illinois, was the largest retailer of musical instruments in the Midwest during the late 19th century. The company also was a major music publisher. Around 1890, the company began making plucked string instruments. According to *NLI* (p. 245), the company eventually made wind instruments between 1923 and 1930. However, because the factory burned several times, determining when the company began making woodwind instruments will require more research, possibly in Chicago newspapers. The company is still in business making professional-quality concert harps. The following information is from an 1896 catalog owned by the Library of Congress.

Saxophones, Buffet, Crampon & Co.

Soprano, key of B flat

25	Brass	$67.00
25½	Brass, silver plated, satin finish	$80.00
26	Brass, nickel plated	$76.00
26½	Brass, silver plated, finely burnished	$84.00

Alto, key of E flat

27	Brass	$76.00
27½	Brass, silver plated, satin finish	$94.00
28	Brass, nickel plated	$88.00
28½	Brass, silver plated finely burnished	$99.00

Tenor, key of B flat

29	Brass	$73.00
29½	Brass, silver plated, satin finish	$99.60
30	Brass, nickel plated	$93.00
30½	Brass, silver plated, finely burnished	$104.60

Baritone, key of E flat

31	Brass	$83.75
31½	Brass, silver plated, satin finish	$111.75
32	Brass, nickel plated	$100.00
32½	Brass, silver plated, finely burnished	$115.75

Alto and bass clarinets

52	Key of E flat, grenadilla wood, 13 G.S. keys, 2 rings for F sharp and extra B flat trill key	$106.66
54	Key of E flat, Boehm system alto, grenadilla wood	$130.00
56	Key of B flat, bass, grenadilla wood, 13, G.S. keys, 2 rings for F sharp and extra B flat trill key	$133.33
58	Key of B flat, Boehm system bass, grenadilla wood	$109.00

Plated saxophones were only available on special order. Numbers 25 to 32½ were made by Evette & Schaeffer's (successors to Buffet, Crampon & Co.) latest system of fingering, which consists of additional F sharp trill key, new system G sharp trill key, and extra key for low B flat.

Piccolos

27	Key of E flat, cocus, tuning slide, 1 key, G.S. mounts	$1.25
29	Key of E flat, grenadilla, tuning slide, 4 keys, G.S. mounts	$1.75
31	Key of E flat, grenadilla, tuning slide, 4 keys, G.S. mounts, cork joints	$2.30
33	Key of E flat, grenadilla, tuning slide, 6 keys, G.S. mounts	$2.15
35	Key of E flat, grenadilla, tuning slide, 6 keys, G.S. mounts, cork joints	$3.10
35 ¾	Key of E flat, grenadilla, G.S. head, 6 keys, G.S. mounts, tuning slide, and cork joints	$3.45
37	Key of E flat, grenadilla, ivory head, 6 keys, G.S. mounts, tuning slide, and cork joints	$6.35

Piccolos, Meyer system

53	Key of E flat, grenadilla, ivory head, 6 keys, G.S. mounts, tuning slide, cork joints	$7.60

Piccolos, George Cloos

42	Key of E flat, grenadilla, 6 keys, G.S. mounts	$12.00
43	Key of E flat, grenadilla, 6 keys, ivory head, G.S. mounts	$16.00

Piccolos genuine H.F. Meyer, Hanover

54	Key of D, grenadilla, ivory head, 6 keys, G.S. mounts, tuning slide, cork joints	$31.70
55	Key of E flat, grenadilla, ivory head, 6 keys, G.S. mounts, tuning slide, cork joints	$31.70

Piccolos, Buffet, Crampon & Co. Boehm system

60	Key of E flat, cocus, G.S. keys and mounts	$46.50

Available in either low or new standard (high) pitch. Any of the above piccolos could be furnished in the key of D at the same price

Fifes

3	Key of B flat, maple, natural color, brass ferrules	$0.33
4	Key of C, maple, natural color, brass ferrules	$0.33
5	Key of B flat, imitation ebony, G.S. ferrules	$0.40
6	Key of C, imitation ebony, G.S. ferrules	$0.40
5½	Key of B flat, rosewood, brass ferrules	$0.53
6½	Key of C, rosewood, brass ferrules	$0.53
7	Key of B flat, cocus, brass ferrules	$0.66
8	Key of C, cocus, brass ferrules	$0.66
9	Key of B flat, cocus, brass ferrules, nickel plated	$0.80
10	Key of C, cocus, brass ferrules, nickel plated	$0.80
11	Key of C, ebony, brass ferrules, nickel plated	$1.00
12	Key of C, ebony, brass ferrules, nickel plated	$1.00
13	Key of B flat, brass, nickel plated, raised finger holes	$1.33
14	Key of C, brass, nickel plated, raised finger holes	$1.33

15	Key of B flat, G.S., raised finger holes, and embouchure	$1.50
16	Key of C, G.S., raised finger holes, and embouchure	$1.50
21	Key of B flat, nickel plated, raised finger holes, gutta-percha embouchure	$1.65
22	Key of C, nickel plated, raised finger holes, gutta-percha embouchure	$1.65
23	Key of B flat, nickel plated, professional model, full bore, raised embouchure plate, extra fine	$1.40
24	Key of C, nickel plated, professional model, full bore, raised embouchure plate, extra fine	$1.40

U.S. Army fife, for professional players, Crosby

17	Key of B flat, cocus, long tapering G.S. ferrules, large caliber	$1.33
18	Key of C, cocus, long tapering G.S. ferrules, large caliber	$1.33
19	Key of B flat, ebony, long tapering G.S. ferrules, large caliber	$1.33
20	Key of C, ebony, long tapering G.S. ferrules, large caliber	$1.33

Military flutes

181	F, cocus, 1 key, G.S. mounts	$1.90
182	F, cocus, 4 keys, tuning slide, G.S. mounts	$3.35
185	F, grenadilla, 6 keys, tuning slide, G.S. mounts, cork joints	$4.60
38	Key of B flat, cocus, 1 key, tuning slide	$1.65
184	Key of B flat, cocus, 4 keys, tuning slide, G.S. mounts	$3.35
139	Key of B flat, grenadilla, 6 keys, tuning slide, G.S. mounts, cork joints	$4.65

Boehm system flutes

1020	F. Delaure & Co., Paris, cocus, G.S. keys, closed G sharp key, in new standard (high) pitch	$87.75
1022	F. Delaure & Co., Paris, silver plated over G.S., G.S. keys, closed G sharp key, in new standard (high) pitch	$100.55
1016	George Cloos, grenadilla, G.S. keys, set screws, C sharp and B keys, roller keys	$186.65
1018	George Cloos, grenadilla, pure silver keys, set screws, C, C sharp, and B keys, roller keys in new standard (high) pitch	$220.00
1014	Buffett, Crampon & Co., Paris, pure silver body and keys, B key, in new standard (high) pitch	$219.35

Flute, half Boehm system, cylinder bore

| 1010 | Granadilla, G.S. keys, C key | $32.60 |

[This flute is fingered like an ordinary 8 key flute, but has covered keys, suggestive of Boehm system flutes.]

Flute, simple system (nach Meyer)

1205	Grenadilla, 8 keys, tuning slide, cork joints, Morocco velvet lined case	$12.55
1206	Grenadilla, ivory keys, 8 keys, tuning slide, cork joints, Morocco velvet lined case	$20.00
1209	Grenadilla, 10 keys, tuning slide, cork joints, Morocco velvet lined case	$18.80
1210	Grenadilla, ivory keys, 10 keys, tuning slide, cork joints, Morocco velvet lined case	$28.00
1211	Grenadilla, 11 keys, tuning slide, cork joints, Morocco velvet lined case	$29.50
1212	Grenadilla, ivory heads, 13 keys, tuning slide, cork joints, Morocco velvet lined case	$22.50
1213	Grenadilla, 13 keys, ivory heads, tuning slides, cork joints, Morocco velvet lined case	$31.50

Flute, H. F. Meyer, Hanover

| 1218 | Grenadilla, ivory head, 11 G.S. keys, tuning slide, cork joints, finest Morocco case, etc. | $95.00 |

Double reed instruments, F. Delaure & Co.

2	Musette, ebony, 5 keys, ivory mounts	$8.00
12	Oboe, 15 keys, 2 rings	$39.00
15	English horn, grenadilla, 15 keys, 2 rings	$56.40

Double reed instruments, Buffet, Crampon & Co.

4	Musette, grenadilla, 4 keys	$10.35
14	Oboe, grenadilla, 17 keys, 2 rings	$84.60
31B	English horn, grenadilla, 15 keys, 2 keys	$94.00
2	Jancourt's system bassoon, rosewood, first quality, 15 keys with third finger of the right hand for A natural and ring for second finger in B natural	$122.20

Numbers 14, 31B, and 2 available in either high or low pitch

Clarinets

[The 1896 catalog included the following: "For some time the boxwood clarionets have been falling into disrepute, and within recent years the yellow instrument has been regarded as a 'Hoo Doo.' We have omitted them from our catalogues, and instead present grenadilla wood clarionets at about the same price. …"]

Clarinets, F. Delaure & Co., Paris

6½	Key of B flat, grenadilla, 6 brass keys, and mounts	$7.00
9½	Key of E flat, grenadilla, 6, brass keys, and mounts	$7.00
21½	Key of B flat, grenadilla, 10 G.S. keys, and mounts	$10.00
34½	Key of E flat, grenadilla, 10 G.S. keys, and mounts	$10.00

Albert system clarinets, F. Delaure & Co., Paris, ne plus ultra instruments, Imperial model

| 146 | Key of B flat, grenadilla, 13 G.S. keys, 2 rings, cork joints | $23.70 |
| 149 | Key of E flat grenadilla, 13 G.S. keys, 2 rings, cork joints | $23.70 |

Clarinets, F. Delaure & Co., Paris, ne plus ultra instruments

| 171 | Key of B flat, grenadilla, 15 G.S. keys, 2 rings, cork joints half-Boehm system (extra B flat and C sharp keys) | $28.75 |
| 174 | Key of E flat, grenadilla, 15 G.S. keys, 2 rings, cork joints, Half-Boehm system (extra B flat and C sharp keys) | $28.75 |

Any of the above description of clarionets furnished in the additional letters of A, C, or D at the same price.

Albert system clarinets, F. Delaure & Co., Paris, professional model

| 76 | Key of B flat, grenadilla, 15 G.S. keys, 2 rings, metal lined finger holes, roller keys | $30.00 |
| 79 | Key of E flat, grenadilla, 15 G.S. keys, 2 rings, metal lined finger holes, roller keys | $30.00 |

Clarinets, Buffet, Crampon & Co., Evette & Schaeffer, successors

81	Key of B flat, grenadilla, 15 G.S. keys, 2 rings, cork joints, double C and B keys	$37.55
84	Key of E flat, grenadilla, 15 G.S. keys, 2 rings, cork joints, double C and B keys	$37.55
81½	Key of B flat, grenadilla, 15 G.S. keys, 2 rings, cork joints, double C and B keys, new standard or low pitch	$37.55
84½	Key of E flat, grenadilla, 15 G.S. keys, 2 rings, cork joints, double C and B keys, new standard or low pitch	$37.55

Clarinets, Buffet, Crampon & Co., Evette & Schaeffer, successors, full Boehm system

| 91 | Key of B flat, grenadilla, 17 G.S. keys, 6 rings | $76.60 |
| 94 | Key of E flat, grenadilla, 17 G.S. keys, 6 rings | $76.60 |

We furnish the above clarinets in A, C or D at same prices

Ocarinas, Ch. Mathieu, Paris, metal body

1001½	Key of C, nickel plated	$0.15
1002½	A, nickel plated	$0.20
1003½	F, nickel plated	$0.30
1004½	Key of D, nickel plated	$0.35
1005½	Key of C, nickel plated	$0.40
1006½	Key of C, nickel plated, tuning slide	$0.50
1007 ½	A, nickel plated, tuning slide	$0.50

Ocarinas, Fiehn, Vienna, clay body

1101	Key of C, soprano	$0.20
1102	Key of B flat, soprano	$0.20
1103	G, soprano	$0.25
1104	F, soprano	$0.25
1104½	E, soprano	$0.25
1104¾	Key of E flat, alto	$0.25
1105	Key of D, alto	$0.30
1105½	Key of D, alto	$0.30
1107	Key of B flat, alto	$0.30
1107½	A, alto	$0.40
1108½	Key of A flat, alto	$0.45
1109	G, alto	$0.55
1110	F, alto	$0.60
1111	E, alto	$0.80
1111½	Key of E flat, alto	$0.80
1112	Key of D, bass	$0.85
1113	Key of C, bass	$1.15
1114	Key of B flat, bass	$1.45

1115	A, bass	$1.60
1117	G, bass	$2.10
1118	F, contra bass	$2.25
1119	Key of E flat, contra bass	$2.50
1120	Key of D, great bass	$3.00
1121	Key of C, contra bass	$3.25
1030	Quartettes, 1st and 2nd tenor, 1st and 2nd bass	$3.25
1035	Sextettes, soprano, 1st and 2nd tenor, 1st and 2nd bass, and contra bass	$8.50

Pan pipes, metal, no maker given

113	13 notes	$0.65
120	20 notes	$1.15
124	24 notes	$2.00

Zobophones (kazoos shaped like brass wind instruments)

5	Polished wood, metal mounts	$0.12
7	Key of Cornet, polished brass	$1.00
8	Alto cornet, polished brass	$1.25
9	Saxophone, polished brass	$2.00
10	Bass horn, polished brass	$4.00

Midway Musette

Nickel plated, with reed	$1.00

Described as having made a great sensation at the Columbian Exposition, and "The introduction of this instrument into any band or orchestra cannot fail to make it popular." However, many subsequent articles decry the poor intonation, tone quality, playability, etc. of this novelty instrument.

William Meinl, Son & Co.

Wenzel Meinl began the company in 1899 in New York. Mr. Meinl studied instrument making in Germany where he was born, according to *NLI* (p. 259). The company ended operation around 1921. The company made high-grade clarinets, flutes, oboes, and bassoons, but is best known for its clarinets. Meinl (pronounced Mine-L) is not to be confused with William F. Meinell (pronounced my-Nell) who was also making instruments in New York around the same time. Mr. William F. Meinell is best known for making quality flutes, having worked for A.G. Badger.

The following information comes from a circa 1901 trade catalog. Slight changes have been made to the text either because of written-in price changes or to modernize grammar. One vexing feature of this catalog is that few makers are identified. It is very likely that larger instruments were made by Meinl. However, not all instruments listed here were made by this firm.

All clarinets are available in B flat, A, C, and E flat, high or low pitch (A=455, or A=435).

Albert system clarinets

No. 356	Grenadilla, 15 G.S. keys, 2 rings, with C sharp key for trill	$32.48
No. 357	Grenadilla, 15 G.S. keys, 4 rings, with C sharp key for trill	$36.50
No. 358	Grenadilla, 16 G.S. keys, 4 rings, with C sharp key for trill	$45.00

Boehm system clarinet

No. 359	Grenadilla, 17 G.S. keys, 6 rings	$84.60

Perfected new bore Albert system clarinets, no rollers

No. 356½ Grenadilla, 15 hammered G.S. keys, extra C sharp B flat or E flat key for trilling $41.00

No. 357½ Grenadilla, 15 hammered G.S. keys, 4 rings, extra C sharp, B flat, or E flat key for trilling, F sharp and C sharp without the aid of the F sharp key $46.90

Perfected new bore Albert system clarinets, with rollers

No. 358½ Grenadilla, 16 hammered G.S. keys, 4 rings, extra C sharp, B flat, or E flat key for trilling, F sharp and C sharp without the aid of the F sharp key, also C sharp and G sharp trilling key with the first finger of the right hand, 4 rubber rollers on keys for little finger of both hands $51.90

No. 360 Grenadilla, 17 hammered G.S. keys, with extra E flat key for the little finger of the left hand $53.98

No. 361 Grenadilla, 18 hammered G.S. keys, same as No. 360, with the addition of the third ring on the upper joint to make the B flat D flat correct in tune with the fork fingering. The upper C sharp is simplified by using the thumb hole and Octave key. The F sharp is perfect with the thumb hole alone. Extra key for the little finger of the left hand, 4 rubber rollers on keys, for little finger of both hands $79.70

No. 362 Grenadilla, 19 hammered G.S. keys, 5 rings, same as 361, with the addition of the B trill key for the right hand, first finger for trilling B and C, 5 rubber rollers on the keys for the little fingers of right and left hand $84.95

Boehm system clarinets

No. 359½ Grenadilla, 18 hammered G.S keys, 6 rings, with extra key for trill

from B flat to C sharp, and from C sharp to G sharp $96.70

No. 364 Grenadilla, 18 hammered G.S keys, 7 rings, including patent key for cross fingering of B flat above the line and E flat on the first line, also an extra B flat key for the little finger of the left hand $119.98

No. 365 Grenadilla, 20 hammered G.S. keys, 7 rings, with additional key to trill from B natural to C sharp and from F sharp to G sharp, also a second G sharp key for the first finger of the right hand and double E flat for the little finger of the left hand with low E flat key, the key joint in one piece $150.00

No. 356½ Same as No. 365, but with covered fingerholes $175.00

Clarinets made of ebonite are available as special order [no price given].

The company's patent was designed to make Albert system clarinets more in line with Boehm system clarinets by adding additional keys. Rather than giving up the Albert system fingering, this patent improved playing passages difficult on the Albert system clarinet.

No. 363 Patent clarinet, grenadilla wood, 20 hammered G.S. keys, 6 rings $94.95

[no number] Patent clarinet, same as above with covered finger holes, special order only $114.95

Albert system bass clarinets in B flat

No. 366 Grenadilla, 14 G.S. keys, 2 rings for F sharp or B natural, side B flat key $195.00

No. 366½ Grenadilla, 14 G.S. keys, 2 rings for F sharp or B natural, side B flat key, with rubber rollers for the little finger of the right hand $199.98

Full Boehm system bass clarinets

No. 367	Key of B flat, grenadilla	$237.50
No. 367½	Key of E flat, grenadilla, covered fingerholes	$324.00

The following clarinets were available upon special order: alto clarinets in E flat or F, Bass clarinets in C or A, and Contrabass clarinets

Boehm system flutes

No. 369 Grenadilla, G.S., open or closed G sharp key $106.00

No. 370 Artist grade, grenadilla, G.S. keys, with latest improvements set screws for regulating the pads, thumb rest, open or closed G sharp key, high or low pitch $145.40

No. 383	Same as above, with solid silver keys and trimmings, gold springs	$224.98
No. 384	Metal body, G.S. throughout	$172.50
No. 385	Same as above, heavy silver plate	$197.25
No. 386	Metal body, solid silver throughout, gold springs	$291.75

Boehm system piccolos

No. 387	Professional grade, grenadilla, G.S keys and trimmings	$67.45
No. 388	Artist grade, grenadilla, best G.S. keys, latest improvements, set screws	$74.98
No. 389	Same as above, with solid silver keys, gold springs	$99.90

Simple system flutes, G.S. keys and mounts

No. 374	Grenadilla, 1 key, with mounts	$2.98
No. 375	Grenadilla, 1 key, with mounts and tuning slide	$3.95
No. 376	Grenadilla, 4 key, with mounts and tuning slide	$5.00
No. 377	Grenadilla, 6 G.S. keys and caps, cork joints, extra fine workmanship	$6.75
No. 378	Grenadilla, 8 G.S. keys and caps, cork joints, tuning slide, fine quality	$10.30
No. 379	Grenadilla, 8 G.S. keys and caps, cork joints, ivory head joint, tuning slide, fine quality	$23.75
No. 380	Grenadilla, 10 G.S. keys and caps, cork joints, finest Meyer imitation	$14.00
No. 381	Grenadilla, 10 G.S. keys and caps, cork joints, ivory head, finest Meyer imitation	$38.00
No. 381 ½	Pratton system (?), grenadilla, 11 G.S. keys and mounts, finest workmanship, covered fingerholes, cylinder bore, cork joints, tuning slide	$89.95

Grand concert flutes, in C, with B foot, Meyer model, G.S. keys and mounts, cork joints, tuning slide

No. 382	Grenadilla, 11 keys	$25.75
No. 383½	Grenadilla, 13 keys	$28.50
No. 384½	Grenadilla, 11 keys, ivory head joint	$41.50
No. 385½	Grenadilla, 13 keys, ivory head joint	$44.75
No. 386	Grenadilla, 11 keys, Artist grade, Meyer model, ivory head	$59.50

Military band flutes, in D flat (E flat) to substitute for D flat (E flat) piccolos

No. 386	Grenadilla, 6 G.S. keys, tuning slide	$7.48
No. 387	Grenadilla, 8 G.S. keys, tuning slide, fine workmanship	$10.95
No. 388	Grenadilla, 8 G.S. keys, tuning slide, ivory head joint	$34.25
No. 389	Grenadilla, 10 G.S. keys, tuning slide, fine workmanship	$33.95
No. 390	Grenadilla, 10 G.S. keys, tuning slide, ivory head joint	$37.75

D flat flutes with 11 or 13 keys made to order [no price given]

Simple system piccolos in C (D) for orchestra, D flat (E flat) for military band, grenadilla

No. 395	1 G.S. key and mounts	$1.10
No. 376	1 G.S. key and mounts, tuning slide	$1.30
No. 397	4 G.S. keys and mounts, tuning slide, fine quality	$2.70
No. 398	6 G.S. keys and mounts, tuning slide, fine quality	$3.00
No. 399	6 G.S. keys and mounts, tuning slide, fine quality	$4.25

Professional quality piccolos, simple system, high or low pitch, grenadilla

No. 400	6 G.S. keys and mounts, tuning slide, fine quality	$4.85
No. 401	6 G.S. keys and mounts, tuning slide, ivory head	$9.50
No. 402	6 G.S. keys and mounts, extra fine, G.S. inlaid fingerholes	$17.50
No. 402½	6 G.S. keys, Meyer model, ivory head joint	$18.50

| No. 403 | Pratton system (?), 6 G.S. keys, covered fingerholes | $38.50 |

Flageolets, in C

No. 404	Grenadilla, 1 G.S. key	$2.50
No. 405	Grenadilla, 4 G.S. keys	$3.95
No. 406	In high or low pitch [no other data]	$485

Flageolets made to order in any system

Piccolo flageolets, in C

No. 407	Grenadilla, 1 G.S. key and mounts	$3.75
No. 408	Grenadilla, 4 G.S keys and mounts	$5.50
No. 409	Grenadilla, 6 G.S. keys and mounts	$6.25

Metal fifes, flutes and flageolets [no other data provided]

No. 410	Key of C, cast metal, nickel plated	per dozen $7.00
No. 411	Key of C, cast metal nickel plated	per dozen $9.00
No. 412	Key of C, cast metal nickel plated	per dozen $4.75

Clark (London make) flageolets, in C, 11 inches long

No. 413	Tin, 11	per dozen $1.35
No. 414	Brass	per dozen $2.00
No. 415	Nickel	per dozen $2.45

U.S. nickel flageolets

| No. 416 | Key of B, C, D, E, F, or G, nickel plated | per dozen $2.85 |

Tin fifes

No. 417	13 inches, with wood plug mouthpiece	per dozen $0.75
No. 418	14 inches, with wood plug mouthpiece	per dozen $0.90
No. 419	14 inches, with metal mouthpiece	per dozen $1.25

Drum fifes in C or B

No. 420	Rosewood, brass ferrules	$0.55
No. 421	Rosewood, G.S. ferrules	$0.60
No. 422	Cocus, brass ferrules	$0.80
No. 423	Cocus, G. S. ferrules	$0.90
No. 424	Ebony, G.S. ferrules, extra quality	$1.35
No. 425	Ebony, "Crosby model," extra quality	$1.75
No. 426	Cocus, "Crosby model," extra quality	$1.75

B flat band fife

No. 412	Grenadilla, 1 G.S. key and mounts	$3.00
No. 413	Grenadilla, 4 G.S. keys and mounts	$4.00
No. 414	Grenadilla, 6 G.S. keys and mounts	$4.75

Fifes [no additional data]

| No. 415 | Grenadilla, 4 G.S. keys, tuning slide | $2.45 |
| No. 416 | Grenadilla, 6 G.S. keys, tuning slide | $4.00 |

Oboes made by William Meinl

No. 456	Grenadilla, [?] G.S. drop forged keys, 3 rings, extra C sharp key	$65.00
No. 457	Grenadilla, 17 G.S. G.S. keys, 4 rings, extra thumb mechanism for B flat and C natural, with E flat key for facilitating the passing from low C to E flat with the little finger of the right hand	$80.00
No. 458	William Meinl's Special Model, favorite of the N.Y. Professional, same as No. 457, grenadilla, 17 G.S. keys, with self-changing octave key from upper G to A	$95.00
No. 459	Grenadilla, full Boehm system, with connecting rings, latest improvement	$118.00

No. 460 Grenadilla, Conservatory system, 19 G.S. keys, 4 rings, with a ring for the first finger of the right hand for the middle B flat and C natural, also plate for the upper D, and an E flat key for facilitating the passing from C to E flat by using the little finger of the right hand only, simplifying the two trills C sharp and D, also a double G sharp key, and an F sharp and G sharp trill key, also extra plate for the thumb for the B flat and C natural key for the first finger of the right hand $149.00

No. 461 Grenadilla, Conservatory system, same as No. 460, with self-changing key and covered fingerholes $199.40

English horns manufactured on the same system as oboes, in high or low pitch, surely made by William Meinl

No. 456½ Grenadilla, 16 G.S. keys, 3 rings, with self-changing double octave key $112.45

No. 459½ Conservatory system, with self-changing double octave key $212.45

Bassoons with patent key for the low D sharp, surely made by William Meinl

No. 494 Maple, 19 G.S. keys, 2 crooks $138.00

No. 494½ Maple, 22 G.S. keys, extending to B flat with C sharp, D sharp, F sharp and G sharp trill keys $183.00

New patent key for the low E flat. This new patent key is placed upon the lower joint of the bassoon, close to the new D sharp key, and enables the performer to produce the low E flat with the thumb of the right hand.

The wing joint of bassoons No. 495, 496, and 497 are lined with rubber to limit cracking.

No. 495 Rosewood, 17 G.S. keys, long key for the little finger of the left hand to close the vent hole for the lower notes with addition of a key for the thumb to shake from E natural to F sharp $223.80

No. 496 Rosewood, 18 G.S. keys. In addition to the mechanism of No. 495, the 18th key is added to the lower joint for the second finger of the right hand, and is used to trill from C natural to D flat; also D natural and E flat, between and above the lines, the upper G natural with the A natural, and A natural with the B flat. Fitted with moveable cork $238.00

Same as above, maple $138.00

Patented latest improved and perfected bassoons, in high or low pitch, surely made by William Meinl

No. 497 Rosewood, 22 G.S. keys, with a long key for the little finger of the left hand to close the vent hole for the lower notes, and additional key for the thumb of the left hand, which also closes the vent hole. The 18th key is on the lower joint and is used for the following trills, C natural, D flat, also D natural and E flat between and above the staff, the upper G natural with the A natural, and A natural with the A flat. The 19th key is a plate for A natural for the third finger of the right hand. The 20th key is for the top F natural; also two rings, one for the second finger of the right hand for B natural and one for the second finger of the left hand for E natural, moveable cork $315.00

No. 498 Same as above, maple $260.00

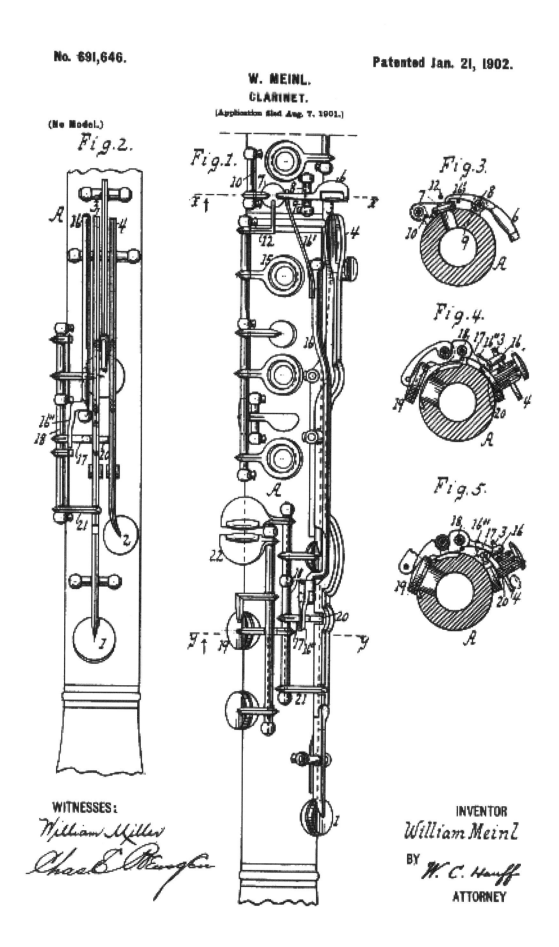

No. 691,646.

W. MEINL.
CLARINET.
(Application filed Aug. 7, 1901.)

Patented Jan. 21, 1902.

(No Model.)

Fig.2.

Fig.1.

Fig.3.

Fig.4.

Fig.5.

WITNESSES:
William M. Miller
Chas. E. Ringler

INVENTOR
William Meinl
BY
W. C. Hauff
ATTORNEY

Meinl's improvement to the Albert system clarinet

Clarinets made by William Meinl

No. 356 1/2 No. 357 1/2 No. 358 1/2 [image of bell reconstructed] No. 360 No. 356 No. 357 No. 359

Note that only numbers 356 and 359 are Boehm system clarinets. All others are Albert system clarients.

Examples of clarinets made by
William Meinl and Sons

No. 359 1/2   No. 362   No. 364   No. 365   No. 365 1/2   No. 358   No. 363   No. 363 1/2

Note that Numbers 359 1/2, 362, 364, 365, and 365 1/2 are all Boehm system clarinets. Numbers 358, 363, and 363 1/2 are all Albert system clarinets. The most obvious differences are the keys for the little fingers of both hands.

Bassoons offered by
William Meinl & Sons

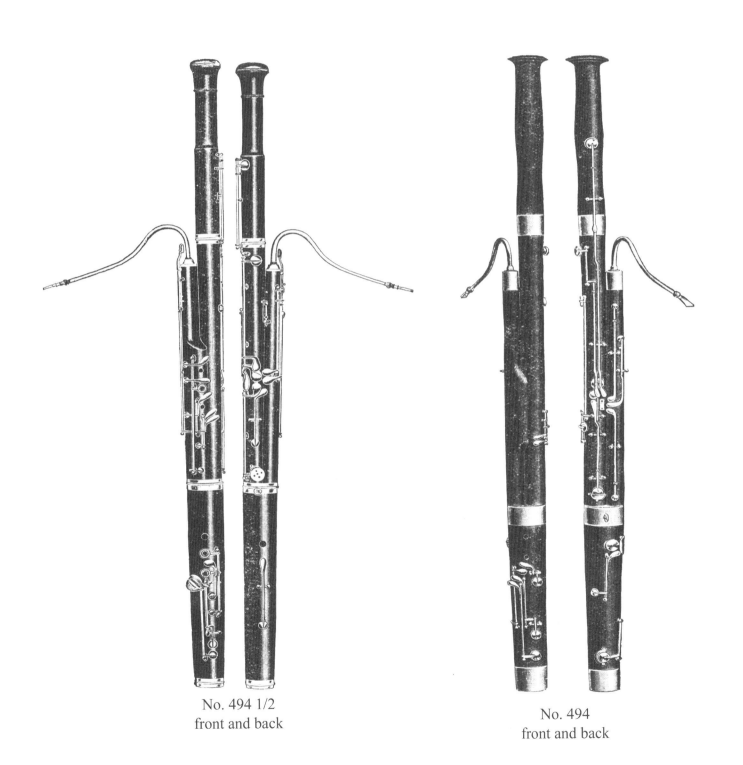

No. 494 1/2
front and back

No. 494
front and back

Penzel and Mueller

This company made some of the finest professional-quality clarinets in its day. Some references give the company's name as Penzel & Müller. The company also made other woodwinds. However, today only the clarinets are actively collected. The company received at least one patent for clarinet key improvements. *NLI* (p. 298) states that the company operated from 1899 to at least 1950. The company was evidently proceeded by G.L. Penzel & Bro. The following information is from a 1925 trade catalog. All instruments appear to have been equipped with keys made using the drop forge technique. All instruments appear to have been pitched in A=440, which the catalog describes as low pitch!

Albert system clarinet, Penzel & Mueller, key of B flat, A, E flat, and C, 15 keys, 4 rings, roller keys, Perfection trade mark

3	Grenadilla, quadruple silver plated over nickel silver keys, burnished fingertips	$77.00

Albert system clarinets, Penzel & Mueller, grenadilla, key of B flat, A, E flat, and C, quadruple silver plated over nickel silver keys, burnished finger tips, Artist trade mark. Arranged to produce the trills from Low E flat to F sharp, and from F sharp to G sharp in the lower register, and from B natural to C sharp, and from C sharp to D sharp in the middle register. The clarinets also have a fifth ring to produce a corrected forked B flat in the staff.

5	Solo clarinet, 16 keys, 5 rings	$81.00
6	Solo clarinet, 17 keys, 5 rings, extra double E flat key for the little finger of the left hand	$90.00
9	Solo clarinet, 18 keys, 5 rings, Penzel & Muller new system with 4 trill keys for the right hand	$100.00

The Penzel & Muller new system clarinet is described as being a blending of the Albert system and the Boehm system. To quote from the catalog (p. 10) "We consequently invented a mechanism, which consist of a new G sharp key in two parts with connection for the other keys. This key is moved by the B natural and C sharp keys, and permits the easy playing of ordinarily difficult passages without displacing the little finger of the heft hand, but by lifting the right hand, thus the habitual fingering of the Albert system is fully maintained." The catalog also states that this design is patented.

Clarinets, grenadilla, trimmed with quadruple silver plated over nickel silver keys, and burnished finger tips. Available in the keys of B flat, A, E flat, and C

10	Albert system, Improved "Artist model," 18 keys, 6 rings, two-piece design	$115.00
10½	Albert system, Improved "Artist model," 18 keys, 6 rings, 1-piece design	$117.00

Boehm system clarinets, Artist model, grenadilla, trimmed with quadruple silver plated over nickel silver keys, and burnished finger tips.

11	17 keys, 6 rings	$110.00
11½	17 keys, 7 rings, key for the forking E flat-B flat	$125.00
17½	17 keys, 7 rings, key for the forking E flat-B flat, extra articulated C sharp-G sharp key	$145.00
18¼	Same as 17½ with additional E flat key for little finger of left hand	$150.00

Numbers 11 and 11½ are furnished in the keys of B flat, A, E flat, and C. Numbers 17½ and 18¼ are furnished in B flat, A, and C only.

Boehm system clarinet, Penzel & Mueller, Artist model, 2 joints, forked E flat-B flat key, articulated C sharp-G sharp key, extra trill lever for the right hand second finger, extra lever for the left hand little finger used to produce A flat below the staff and E flat fourth space, extra key for the right little finger, extending the register to low E flat.

20½	Key of B flat, A, or C	$160.00

Meyer system flutes, Penzel & Mueller, Artist model, designed for concert use

58	Key of C, grenadilla, 11 keys, quadruple silver plated over nickel silver keys, register extends to low B natural	$40.00
59	Key of C, grenadilla, 13 keys, G.S. keys, register extends to low B natural	$45.00

Boehm system flutes, Penzel & Mueller, Artist model, designed for concert use

60	Key of C, grenadilla, closed G sharp key, G.S. keys	$110.00
61	Same as No. 61, quadruple silver plated throughout	$130.00

Simple system piccolo, Penzel and Mueller

4	Key of D flat for band use, grenadilla, 6 G.S. keys	$12.50

Boehm system piccolos, Penzel and Mueller, Artist model

62	Key of D flat for band or C for orchestra, grenadilla, G.S. keys	$60.00
62½	Key of D flat, extra head for C, can be used in band or orchestra	$70.00

Large clarinets and bassoon

Alto clarinets, Penzel and Mueller, full Boehm system, Artist model

I	Key of E flat alto clarinet, grenadilla, G.S. keys	$175.00
II	Key of B flat bass clarinet, grenadilla, G.S. keys	$250.00
III	Improved Heckel system bassoon, 21 keys, [wood not identified], F and G sharp keys, F sharp-G sharp trill keys, and C sharp and D sharp trill keys with rings on the wings	$250.00

G. L. PENZEL & E. MÜLLER.

CLARINET.

(Application filed Oct. 29, 1898.)

(No Model.)

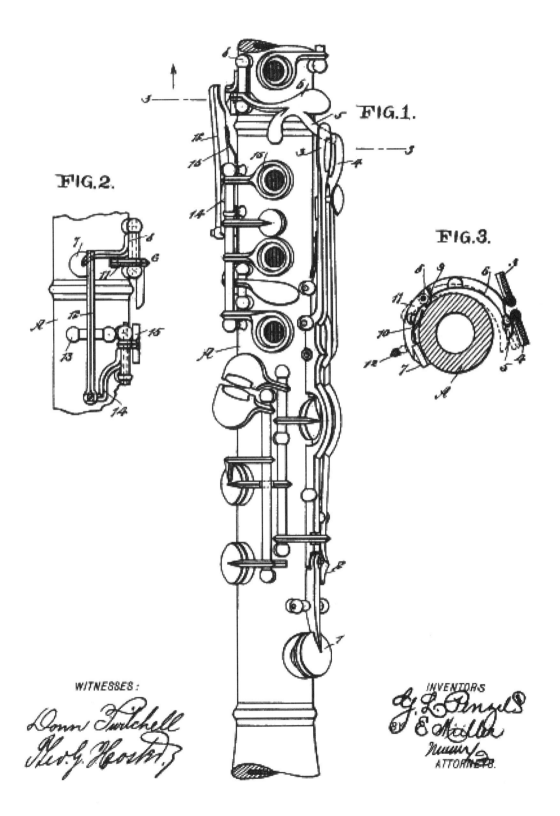

FIG.1.

FIG.2.

FIG.3.

WITNESSES :

INVENTORS

ATTORNEYS.

Clarinets made by Penzel & Mueller

No. 3

No. 5

No. 6

No. 9

Clarinets made by Penzel & Mueller

No. 10   No. 10 1/2   No. 11 1/2   No. 11   No. 17 1/2   No. 18 /14

J.W. Pepper

James Welsch Pepper began J.W. Pepper in 1876 in Philadelphia. The company continues to this day as one of the country's major music publishers. J.W. Pepper continued to make instruments until 1910 (*NLI*, p. 298), at which time the company changed its name to J.W. Pepper and Son. All instruments stamped J.W. Pepper and Son were imported for the company. J.W. Pepper was also the first U.S. company to import brass wind instruments from Europe. This action so angered Charles G. Conn that Conn instigated a protracted legal battle against Pepper that reached almost comical heights. Conn eventually had to recant his libelous accusations. J.W. Pepper had its own trade names: American Climax, American Favorite, Conqueror (not to be confused with the Connqueror), Excelsior, Imperial, Premier, Specialty, Surprise, Standard, and Twentieth Century. One feature that makes researching J.W. Pepper somewhat difficult is that Pepper preferred to publish his catalogs in the form of periodicals. True J.W. Pepper catalogs are difficult to locate because of poor-quality paper. The periodicals do provide some information, but not as much as one would like, as can be seen below. The following information is from *J.W. Pepper's Musical Times and Band Journal* Vol. XV, No. 174, 1898.

"Premier" military band flutes

1	Key of B or C, nickel plated, nickel plated embouchure and banding between finger holes	$1.00
2	Key of B or C, nickel plated, rubber embouchure hole	$1.25

These instruments were evidently stamped "Premier"

Imported flutes

19	Key of D, 6 keys, grenadilla, G.S. mounts, tuning slide, cork joints	$3.75
20	Key of D, 6 keys, grenadilla, G.S. mounts, tuning slide, cork joints	$5.80
23	Key of D, 8 keys, grenadilla, G.S. mounts, tuning slide, cork joints	$7.85

Imitation Meyer flutes

28	Key of D, 8 keys, grenadilla, tuning slide, cork joints	$10.85
29	Key of D, 8 keys, grenadilla, tuning slide cork joints, ivory head	$17.95
30	Key of D, 10 keys, grenadilla, tuning slide, cork joints	$16.35
31	Key of D, 10 keys, grenadilla, tuning slide, cork joints, ivory head	$24.50
32	Key of D, 13 keys, grenadilla, tuning slide, cork joints	$19.57
33	Key of D, 13 keys, grenadilla, tuning slide, cork joints, ivory head	$27.55

English model flute, Meyer system [Pratton? system]

50	8 G.S. covered keys, grenadilla, G.S. mounts	$26.70

These flutes were made in Germany, and were described as "somewhat similar in appearance to the Boehm flutes, but the system is the same as the Meyer. The holes are covered with pads which work automatically, …"

Clark's Flageolets, made in London, 11 inches long

1	Key of D, tin body	$0.10
2	Key of D, brass	$0.15
3	Key of D, nickel plated	$0.20

Eagle model

4	Key of B, nickel plated	$0.20
5	Key of C, nickel plated	$0.20
6	Key of D, nickel plated	$0.20
7	Key of E, nickel plated	$0.20
8	Key of F, nickel plated	$0.20
9	Key of G, nickel plated	$0.20
10	Key of D, French make, nickel plated, regular flageolet model	$0.60

Saxophones, Evette & Schaeffer. All examples have G-sharp trill key, extra F-sharp trill key, and extra key for producing low B-flat.

1	Brass	$58.30	$66.15	$68.40	$72.85
2	Nickel plated	$66.15	$76.55	$81.45	$87.00
3	Silver plated, satin finish, burnished points	$69.60	$81.80	$85.95	$97.25
4	Silver plated, satin finish, gold mounted	$76.50	$85.20	$97.40	$108.50
5	Silver plated, burnished	$73.10	$86.15	$91.00	$100.70
6	Silver plated, burnished, gold mounted	$79.75	$93.25	$100.40	$111.70

[Column 1 is the price for B flat sopranos. Column 2 is for E flat altos. Column 3 is for B flat tenors. Column 4 is for E flat baritones. No other saxophones were offered in this publication.]

Albert system "Premier" clarinets, [C.A. Mouchel], superior grade, reeds, etc.

1	Key of A, grenadilla, 13 keys, 2 rings	$18.75
2	Key of B flat, grenadilla, 13 keys, 2 rings	$18.75
3	Key of C, grenadilla, 13 keys, 2 rings	$18.75
4	Key of E flat, grenadilla, 13 keys, 2 rings	$18.75
5	Key of A, grenadilla, 15 keys, 2 rings	$21.75
6	Key of B flat, grenadilla, 15 keys, 2 rings	$21.75
7	Key of C, grenadilla, 15 keys, 2 rings	$21.75
8	Key of E flat, grenadilla, 15 keys, 2 rings	$21.75
9	Key of A, grenadilla, 15 keys, 4 rings	$26.75
10	Key of B flat, grenadilla, 15 keys, 4 rings	$26.75
11	Key of C, grenadilla, 15 keys, 4 rings	$26.75
12	Key of E flat, grenadilla, 15 keys, 4 rings	$26.75

[The maker's name is obtained from "J.W. Pepper's Musical Times and Band Journal" Vol. XV, No. 171, 1897. This earlier catalog only included 8 clarinets from this maker, at a price of about $4 less per clarinet.]

Albert system Excelsior clarinets, imported, medium grade, no accessories

26	Key of A, ebony, 13 G.S. keys, 2 rings, G.S. mounts	$12.00
27	Key of B flat, ebony, 13 G.S. keys, 2 rings, G.S. mounts	$12.00
28	Key of C, ebony, 13 G.S. keys, 2 rings, G.S. mounts	$12.00
29	Key of E flat, ebony, 13 G.S. keys, 2 rings, G.S. mounts	$12.00
30	Key of A, ebony, 15 G.S. keys, 3 rings, G.S. mounts	$15.00
31	Key of B flat, ebony, 15 G.S. keys, 3 rings, G.S. mounts	$15.00
32	Key of C, ebony, 15 G.S. keys, 3 rings, G.S. mounts	$15.00
33	Key of E flat, ebony, 15 G.S. keys, 3 rings, G.S. mounts	$15.00

J.W. Campaign piccolos, no maker given, sold as overstock, no catalog numbers

Key of D, grenadilla, 6 G.S. keys and mounts, tuning slide, cork joints
$2.20

Key of E flat, grenadilla, 6 G.S. keys and mounts, tuning slide, cork joints
$2.20

Piccolos, J. Thibouville-Lamy, stamped "Specialty," superior grade

1	Key of D or E flat, ebony, 6 keys, G.S. mounts, tuning slide, cork joints	$6.75
3	Key of D or E flat, ebony, 6 keys, G.S. mounts, tuning slide, cork joints	$10.75
5	Key of D or E flat, Boehm system, ebony	$40.45

"Premier" concert flutes, American made [possibly made by J.W. Pepper but not specifically stated as such], presumably in D, Meyer system

1	Grenadilla, 8 G.S. keys and mounts, tuning slide, cork joints	$18.70
2	Grenadilla, 8 G.S. keys and mounts, ivory head, tuning slide, cork joints	$27.65
3	Grenadilla, 10 G.S. keys and mounts, tuning slide, cork joints	$31.75
4	Grenadilla, 11 G.S. keys and mounts, ivory head, tuning slide, cork joints	$37.50
5	Grenadilla, 13 G.S. keys and mounts, tuning slide, cork joints	$35.00
6	Grenadilla, 13 G.S. keys and mounts, ivory head, tuning slide, cork joints	$43.85

"Premier" piccolo, American made, no maker identified, presumably in D or E flat, Meyer system

9	Grenadilla, 6 G.S. keys and mounts, tuning slide, cork joints	$9.00
10	Grenadilla, 6 G.S. keys and mounts, ivory head, tuning slide, cork joints	$12.00

Clarinets sold by J.W. Pepper

13 keys, 2 rings   15 keys, 2 rings   15 keys, 2 rings

Henry August Pollmann

NLI (p. 306) states that Henry August Pollmann began the company in 1880 in New York City. The company operated as a maker and importer of wind instruments until 1905. The company had a sizeable factory in Saxony. The following information and illustrations appear in an 1894 catalog. Note that descriptions for instruments vary in completeness. All but a few instruments came with tuning slides, and most had cork joints. Information in brackets is editorial. The catalog often described the instruments as having been made of ebony grenadilla. These are two different woods, according to modern usage. The catalog provided no explanation.

Note that some catalog numbers were not included, as the instrument included a fancy case that is not relevant to the price of the instrument. Other catalog numbers were not offered.

Albert system clarinets, made in Paris, boxwood, black, 6 brass keys, tuning slide, horn mounts

2000	Key of A	$6.50
2001	Key of B flat	$6.50
2002	Key of C	$6.50
2003	Key of D	$6.50
2010	Key of E flat	$6.50

Albert system clarinets, made in Paris, boxwood, black, 10 brass keys, tuning slide, horn mounts

2016	Key of A	$10.50
2017	Key of B flat	$10.50
2018	Key of C	$10.50
2019	Key of E flat	$10.50

Clarinets, made in Paris, cocus, black, 10 G.S. keys, tuning slide, horn mounts

2020	Key of A	$18.00
2021	Key of B flat	$18.00
2023	Key of C	$18.00
2024	Key of D	$18.00
2025	Key of E flat	$18.00

Albert system clarinets, Martin frères, Paris. Ebony grenadilla, 13 G.S. keys, G.S. mounts, 2 rings for right hand, cork joints

2036	Key of A	$25.00
2037	Key of B flat	$25.00
2038	Key of C	$25.00
2039	Key of D	$25.00
2040	Key of E flat	$25.00

Albert system clarinets, Martin frères, Paris. Ebony grenadilla, 13 G.S. keys, G.S. mounts, 2 rings for right hand, cork joints, C and B keys for trilling, medium grade

2042	Key of A	$32.00
2043	Key of B flat	$32.00
2044	Key of C	$32.00
2045	Key of D	$32.00
2046	Key of E flat	$32.00

Albert system clarinets, Martin frères, Paris. bony grenadilla, 15 G.S. keys, G.S. mounts, 2 rings for right hand, cork joints, C and B keys for trilling, leather bag, cleaner, extra mouthpiece, better grade

2056	Key of A	$42.00
2057	Key of B flat	$42.00
2058	Key of C	$42.00
2058½	Key of D	$42.00
2059	Key of E flat	$42.00

Albert system clarinets, Martin frères, Paris. Ebonite, 15 G.S. keys, G.S. mounts, 2 rings for right hand, cork joints, C and B keys for trilling, leather bag, cleaner, extra mouthpiece

2061	Key of A	$52.00
2062	Key of B flat	$52.00
2063	Key of C	$52.00
2064	Key of D	$52.00
2065	Key of E flat	$52.00

Albert system clarinets, ebony grenadilla, 15 G.S. keys, 2 rings for the right hand and 2 rings for the left hand, cork joints, one extra upper joint, arranged to produce the trills from low E to F#, from F# to G# (in the lower register) from B natural to C# and from C# to D# (in the middle register), roller keys, cork joints. [Possibly stamped Pollmann Professional]

2070	Key of A	$85.00
2071	Key of B flat	$85.00
2072	Key of C	$85.00
2073	Key of D	$85.00
2074	Key of E flat	$85.00

Clarinets, Berteling, New York. Grenadilla, ebony trimmed, 14 G.S. keys, 2 rings for right hand (double E flat and B flat), cork joints, roller keys, arranged to produce the trills from low E to F#, from F# to G# (in the lower register) from B natural to C# and from C# to D# (in the middle register)

2083	Key of A	$72.00
2083	Key of B flat	$72.00
2083	Key of C	$72.00
2083	Key of D	$72.00
2083	Key of E flat	$72.00

Clarinets, Berteling, New York. Grenadilla, ebony trimmed, 15 G.S. keys, 2 rings for right hand (double E flat and B flat), cork joints, roller keys, arranged to produce the trills from low E to F#, from F# to G# (in the lower register) from B natural to C# and from C# to D# (in the middle register)

2084	Key of A	$85.00
2084	Key of B flat	$85.00
2084	Key of C	$85.00
2084	Key of D	$85.00
2084	Key of E flat	$85.00

Clarinets, Berteling, New York. Grenadilla, ebony trimmed, 15 G.S. keys, 2 rings for right hand (double E flat and B flat), 2 rings for the left hand (F# and C#), cork joints, roller keys, arranged to produce the trills from low E to F#, from F# to G# (in the lower register) from B natural to C# and from C# to D# (in the middle register)

2085	Key of A	$95.00
2085	Key of B flat	$95.00
2085	Key of C	$95.00
2085	Key of D	$95.00
2085	Key of E flat	$95.00

Clarinets, Berteling, New York. Grenadilla, 15 G.S. keys, 2 rings for right hand, 2 for the left hand, cork joints, roller keys, arranged to produce the trills from low E to F#, from F# to G# (in the lower register) from B natural to C# and from C# to D# (in the middle register). Described as Berteling's combination clarinet

2086	Key of A	$110.00
2086	Key of B flat	$110.00
2086	Key of C	$110.00
2086	Key of D	$110.00
2086	Key of E flat	$110.00

Clarinets, Berteling, New York. No material given, full Boehm system, roller keys, cork joints, best grade

2087	Key of A	$140.00
2087	Key of B flat	$140.00
2087	Key of C	$140.00
2087	Key of D	$140.00
2087	Key of E flat	$140.00

The above clarinets made of ebonite $155.00.

Clarinets, Berteling, New York. No material given, tuning slide, B flat solo clarinet three inches longer than conventional instrument with low E flat, D keys. [The key system is suggestive of half Boehm clarinet]

2095	Key of B flat	$140.00
02095	Key of B flat, made of ebonite	$150.00

Musettes

2126	Cocus, no mounts	$3.00
2127	Boxwood, 1 key	$5.00
2131	Boxwood, 6 keys	$12.00

Oboes, Martin frere's, Paris, France. 15 keys, 2 rings, G.S. mounts

2148	Ebony-grenadilla	$65.00
2149	Ebonite	$75.00

Oboes, Berteling, New York. Ebony-grenadilla, described as artist model

2151	9 Silver keys, G.S. mounts	$60.00
2153	12 Silver keys, G.S. mounts	$66.00

2155	15 Silver keys, G.S. mounts, 2 rings for right hand	$80.00
2157	15 Silver keys, G.S. mounts, 2 rings for right hand, 2 for the left hand	$97.00
2159	Boehm system, 13 Silver keys, G.S. mounts, 5 rings	$110.00

English horns (cor anglais), Berteling, New York. Ebony grenadilla, 15 G.S. keys, 2 rings for the right hand, G.S. mounts

2165	2 rings for right hand	$110.00
2166	2 rings for the right hand, 2 rings for the left hand, G.S. mounts	$125.00

English horn (cor anglais), Berteling, New York

2167	Boehm system, 13 G.S. keys, 5 rings, G.S. mounts	$150.00

Flageolets, key of C

2100	Imitation ebony, 1 key	$1.40
2102	Imitation ebony, 1 key, G.S. trimmed	$2.00
2104	Cocus, 1 key, G.S. trimmed	$2.75
2106	Cocus, 6 keys, G.S. trimmed	$4.50

Flageolets, key of B natural

2108	Imitation ebony, 1 key	$2.00
2110	Imitation ebony, 1 key, G.S. mounts	$2.50
2112	Cocus, 1 key, G.S. mounts	$3.50
2114	Cocus, 4 keys, G.S. mounts	$3.70

Bassoons, full keyed, all the latest improvements

2121	All wood	$125.00
2122	Same as above but with metal bell	$160.00

Penny whistles [described as tin fifes in the catalog]

2762	Tin, 10 inches. 3 dozen in a box	$0.50
2763	Tin, 12 inches. 3 dozen in a box	$0.76
2764	Tin, 14 inches. 3 dozen in a box	$0.90
2765	Tin, 14 inches, metal mouthpiece, fancy. 1 dozen in a box	$1.25

Penny whistle, Clark, London, England. Key of D, 11 inches

2819	Tin. 1 dozen in a box	$1.40
2820	Brass. 1 dozen in a box	$2.10
2821	Nickel plated. 1 dozen in box	$2.50

"Eagle" tin whistle, keys of B, C, D, E, and G.

2818	Copper, bronzed. 1 dozen in box	$3.00
2819	Nickel plated, bronzed. 1 dozen in box	$3.00

Fifes

2782	Key of C, imitation ebony, nickel plated mounts. 1 dozen	$4.00
2783	Key of B, imitation ebony, nickel plated mounts. 1 dozen	$4.00
2785	Key of C, rosewood, brass mounts. 1 dozen	$5.50
2786	Key of B, rosewood, brass mounts. 1 dozen	$5.50
2788	Key of C, cocus, G.S. mounts. 1 dozen	$9.00
2789	Key of B, cocus, G.S. mounts. 1 dozen	$9.00
2792	Key of C, ebony, G.S. mounts. 1 dozen	$11.00
2793	Key of B, ebony, G.S. mounts. 1 dozen	$11.00
2794	Key of C, ebony, G.S. embouchure, and mounts. 1 dozen	$18.50
2796	Key of B, ebony, G.S. embouchure, and mounts. 1 dozen	$18.50

Fifes, 2 joints and tuning slide, G.S. mounts

2788½	Key of C, cocus. 1 dozen	$9.60

2789½	Key of B, cocus. 1 dozen	$9.60
2792½	Key of C, ebony. 1 dozen	$12.50
2793½	Key of B, ebony. 1 dozen	$12.50

Fifes, ebony, extra long G.S. mounts, square embouchure hole, finger holes of varying diameter [for improved intonation]

| 2797 | Key of C. 1 dozen | $19.00 |
| 02797 | Key of B. 1 dozen | $19.00 |

Fifes, ebony, 1 G.S. mounts and key

| 2804 | Key of C, long G.S. ferrules | $21.00 |
| 0205 | Key of B, long G.S. ferrules | $21.00 |

Fifes

2798	Key of C, G.S. body, raised finger holes, fancy trimmings. 1 Dozen	$21.00
2799	Key of B, G.S. body, raised finger holes, fancy trimmings. 1 Dozen	$21.00
2800	Key of C, nickel plated, G.S. body, raised finger holes, rubber embouchure, fancy trimmings. 1 Dozen	$14.50
2801	Key of B, nickel plated, G.S. body, raised finger holes, rubber embouchure, fancy trimmings. 1 Dozen	$14.50
2802	Key of C, G.S. body, nickel plated, raised finger holes, rubber embouchure, rubber lined holes. 1 Dozen	$26.00
2803	Key of B, G.S. body, nickel plated, raised finger holes, rubber lined holes, rubber embouchure, fancy trimming. 1 Dozen	$26.00
2806	Key of C, G.S. metal body, nickel plated, wide bore, rubber lined holes, rubber embouchure, holes not raised. 1 Dozen	$18.50
2809	Key of B, metal body, nickel plated, wide bore, rubber lined holes, rubber embouchure, holes not raised. 1 Dozen	$18.50

Fife, ebony, extra long G.S. ferrules, fine quality

| 2805 | Key of C. 1 dozen | $14.00 |
| 2807 | Key of B. 1 dozen | $14.00 |

Piccolo, cocus, G.S. keys and mounts

5534	Key of B flat, 1 G.S. key, and mounts	$1.40
5536	Key of B flat, 1 G.S. key, and mounts, tuning slide, cork joints	$1.75
5538	Key of B flat, 4 G.S. keys, and mounts, tuning slide, cork joints	$3.25
5540	Key of B flat, 6 G.S. keys, and mounts, tuning slide, cork joints	$3.75

Fife and piccolo mouthpieces (cheaters), Britannia brand

2828	Best quality, adjustable screw for metal fife. 1 Dozen	$1.25
2829	Best quality, adjustable screw for regular wood fifes. 1 Dozen	$1.25
2830	Best quality, adjustable screw for piccolo. 1 Dozen	$1.25

Simple system flutes, key of D, cork joints

2920	Imitation ebony, 1 G.S. key, bone mounts	$1.25
2921	Imitation ebony, 1 G.S. key, G.S. mounts	$1.50
2922	Boxwood stained black, 1 G.S. key, G.S. mounts	$2.50
2923	Boxwood stained black, 4 G.S. keys, G.S. mounts	$3.15
2924	Boxwood stained black, 4 G.S. keys, G.S. mounts, tuning slide	$4.00
2926	Boxwood stained black, 6 G.S. keys, G.S. mounts, tuning slide	$5.00
2930	Cocus, 1 G.S. key, G.S. mounts, finely polished	$2.80
2930	Cocus, 1 G.S. key, G.S. mounts, tuning slide, finely polished	$3.20
2934	Grenadilla, 4 G.S. keys, G.S. mounts, tuning slide, finely polished	$4.25
2936	Grenadilla, 6 G.S. keys, G.S. mounts, tuning slide, finely polished	$5.25
2938	Grenadilla, 8 G.S. keys, G.S. mounts, tuning slide, finely polished	$7.25

Simple system flutes, key of D, imported, grenadilla stained black, G.S. mounts, cork joints, tuning slide

2940	4 G.S. keys	$4.75
2942	6 G.S. keys	$5.75
2944	8 G.S. keys, Concert model	$8.00
2945	8 G.S. keys, Concert model	$9.25
2946	8 G.S. keys, G.S. head	$11.00
2947	8 G.S. keys, G.S. head, lined holes and lip plate, Concert model	$11.00
2948	8 G.S. keys, ivory head	$19.00
2949	8 G.S. keys, ivory head, Concert model	$22.50
2950	8 G.S. keys, G.S. head, and tuning slide	$14.00

Conservatory model, concert flutes, key of D, imported, grenadilla stained black, G.S. keys and mounts, cork joints, tuning slides

2982	9 keys to B	$16.00
2984	10 keys to B	$17.00
2986	10 keys to B, ivory head	$16.00
2986½	10 keys to B, extra quality finish, ivory head	$45.00
2939	Berteling, 11 keys to B, extra quality finish, ivory head	$75.00

Concert flutes, key of D, imported, grenadilla stained black, G.S. keys and mounts, cork joints, tuning slides, Conservatory model.
[The illustration accompanying these prices includes an ivory head joint stamped "Nach Meyer Hanover."]

2985	13 keys to B	$19.00
2987	13 keys to B, ivory head	$32.00
2988	14 keys to B, ivory head	$33.00
2987¼	13 keys, to B, ivory head	$36.00
2989¼	13 keys to B, extra quality, ivory head	$50.00
2989½	14 keys to B, extra quality, ivory head	$55.00
2989¾	13 keys to B, roller keys, extra quality, ivory embouchure	$90.00

Flute, key of D, grenadilla wood, ebonized, G.S. keys and mounts, cork joints

2944	8 G.S. keys and mounts	$8.00
2945	8 G.S. keys, Concert model, better quality	$9.25
2947	8 G.S. keys, metal inserts around embouchure and finger holes	$11.00
2949	Same as above, ivory head joint	$22.50
2950	Same as above, G.S. head, G.S. slide joint and name plate	14.00

Pollmann concert flutes, key of D, grenadilla, ebonized, G.S. keys and mounts

2954	11 keys, to B	$40.00
2956	11 keys, to B, ivory head	$53.00
2958	13 keys, to B	$50.00
2960	13 keys, to B, ivory head	$63.00
2989¾	13 keys, to B, roller keys, ivory head	$90.00

Concert flutes, key of D, George Cloos, grenadilla wood, trimmed with G.S., artistic finish (large bore, easy to blow, reliable in scale and voluminous in tone)

2962	8 keys to C	$33.00
2963	8 keys to C, ivory head	$45.00
2964	11 keys to B	$50.00
2965	11 keys to B, ivory head	$60.00
2966	13 keys to B	$60.00
2967	13 keys to B, ivory head	$72.00

"Improved flute", George Cloos, grenadilla wood, G.S. keys and mounts. [Flutes of similar design were sold by other makers of the time, but described as being half Boehm as it incorporates some of the improvements found on Boehm system flutes, such as post and pillars, covered keys, and a cylinder bore. However, this flute is fingered like a simple system flute. Note the rods on both side of the flute. Pollmann offered only this one model.]

2970	Key of D, 8 keys with extra keys for covering holes	$125.00

Concert flutes, key of D, Berteling, G.S. keys and mounts
[All flutes except number 38 were custom order only.]

10	8 keys	$45.00
11	10 keys	$50.00
16	8, G.S. head	$52.00
18	10 keys, G.S. head	$60.00
28	8 keys, extra finish, ivory head	$65.00
38	10 keys, extra finish, ivory head, finest artists' flute	$72.00
40	13 keys, extra finish, ivory head, finest artists' flute	$80.00

Berteling's improved flute to B natural, patented September 19th, 1882. The following comments apply to Numbers 45 to 48. "The 3 F first, second, and third octaves can be taken by fork fingering, which is convenient in a great many passages; by means of a double ring attachment the 3 F sharp first, second, and third octaves are produced correct. The ring attachment on left hand piece will produce second and third octaves of C sharp open then the trill from C natural to D is correct in both octaves, and the trill from high F sharp to high G sharp is readily performed. The second key from above will produce a fine and elegant trill from C to D also from C sharp to D also the same key will produce the trill from high G to high A and G sharp to A."

45	13 keys, complete to C natural, plain head, Best in existence	$115.00
46	13 keys, complete to C natural, ivory head, Best in existence	$125.00
47	14 keys, complete to B natural, plain head, Best in existence	$125.00
48	14 keys, complete to B natural, ivory head, Best in existence	$135.00

Boehm system flutes, Berteling, made to order only. All flutes furnished with closed G# keys, unless specifically ordered

50	Wood body, G.S. keys to C natural	$166.00
51	Wood body, G.S. keys to B natural	$185.00
52	Wood body, G.S. keys to B flat	$200.00
53	Wood body, silver keys to C natural	$235.00
54	Wood body, silver keys to B natural	$250.00
55	Wood body, silver keys to B flat	$265.00
56	G.S. body and keys, heavy plated and ornamental engravings, to C natural	$235.00
57	G.S. body and keys, heavy plated and ornamental engravings, to B natural	$250.00
58	G.S. body and keys, heavy plated and ornamental engravings, to B flat	$265.00
59	Silver body and keys, ornamental engravings, to C	$350.00
60	Silver body and keys, ornamental engravings, to B	$367.00
61	Silver body and keys, ornamental engravings, to B flat	$375.00

Flutes, key of F, imported

2990	Imitation ebony, 1 G.S. key, bone rings, no tuning slide	$1.10
2991	Boxwood, ebonized, 4 G.S. key, and mounts, no tuning slide	$3.00
2994	Cocus, 1 G.S. key and mounts, no tuning slide	$2.40
2995	Cocus, 1 G.S. key and mounts, tuning slide	$3.00
2996	Cocus, 4 G.S. key and mounts, tuning slide	$4.00
2997	Grenadilla, ebonized, 6 keys and mounts, tuning slide, and cork joints	$5.25

Ocarinas, American make, clay body

4901	Soprano, key of C, size about 4 1/2 by 1 3/8	$0.35
4902	Soprano, key of B, size about 4 1/2 by 3 3/8	$0.35
4903	Soprano, key of B flat, size about 4 1/2 by 1 3/8	$0.35
4904	Soprano, key of G, size about 5 by 1 ¾	$0.40
4905	Soprano, key of G flat, size about 5 by 1 3/8	$0.40
4906	Soprano, key of F, size about 5 1/2 by 1 ¾	$0.40
4907	Soprano, key of E, size about 5 1/2 by 1 ¾	$0.40
4908	Alto, key of D, size about 5 5/8 by 1 ½	$0.50
4909	Alto, key of D flat, size about 5 5/8 by 1 ½	$0.50
4910	Alto, key of E flat, size about 5 5/8 by 1 ½	$0.50
4911	Alto, key of E, size about 5 5/8 by 1 ½	$0.50
4912	Alto, key of C, size about 6 by 1 5/8	$0.50
4913	Alto, key of B flat, size about 6 by 1 ¾	$0.60
4914	Alto, key of A, size about 6 by 1 ¾	$0.60
4915	Alto, key of A flat, size about 6 1/2 by 2	$0.60
4916	Alto, key of G, size about 6 1/2 by 2	$0.60
4917	Alto, key of G flat, size about 6 1/2 by 2 ¼	$0.90
4918	Alto, key of F, size about 6 1/2 by 1 ½	$0.90
4919	Alto, key of E, size about 7 by 3 ¼	$1.50
4920	Alto, key of E flat, size about 7 by 3 ¼	$1.50
4921	Bass, key of D, size about 7 1/2 by 3 ½	$1.75
4922	Bass, key of C, size about 8 by 3 ½	$2.25
4923	Bass, key of B, size about 8 by 3 ½	$2.25
4924	Bass, key of A, size about 8 by 3 ½	$3.25
4925	Bass, key of G, size about 8 by 3 ½	$3.25
4926	Contra bass, key of E, size about 10 by 5 ¼	$3.75
4927	Contra bass, key of E flat, size about 10 by 5 ¼	$5.00
4928	Contra bass, key of D, size about 10 by 5 ½	$5.00
4930	Duet in key of C	$1.20
4932	Trio in key of C, 1st and 2nd tenor and bass	$4.00
4934	Quintet, key of C, 1st and 2nd tenor and 1st and 2nd bass	$6.00

Ocarinas, Mathieu, Paris, metal body, nickel plated

4881	Soprano, key of C	$0.35
4882	Soprano, key of A	$0.45
4883	Soprano, key of F	$0.60
4884	Soprano, key of D	$0.75
4885	Alto, key of C	$0.90
4886	Alto, key of A	$1.25
4891	Alto, key of C, tuning slide	$1.50

Saxophones, Buffet, Crampon & Co. Paris, France. [Brass body]

1553	B flat soprano, full keyed	$125.00
1554	E flat alto, full keyed	$140.00
1555	B flat tenor, full keyed	$140.00
1556	B flat baritone, full keyed	$150.00
01553	B flat soprano, full keyed, silver plate	$153.75
01554	E flat alto, full keyed, silver plate	$182.75
01555	B flat tenor, full keyed, silver plate	$191.60
01556	B flat baritone, full keyed, silver plate	$212.50

Simple system flutes

F flute
No. 2995

D flute
with C foot
No. 2947

D flute with
C foot, pewter
plug keys for
lowest keys
No. 2950

D concert
flute with
B foot
No number

D flute
No. 2970

BERTELING'S IMPROVED FLUTE TO "B NATURAL." Patented September 19th, 1882.

The Improvements in this Flute are as follows:—The 3 "F" first, second and third Octaves can be taken by fork Fingering, which is convenient in a great many passages ; by means of a Double Ring Attachment the 3 "F" sharp first, second and third Octaves are produced correct. The Ring Attachment on left hand piece will produce second and third Octaves of "C" sharp, **open**, then the trill from "C" natural to "D" is correct in both Octaves, and the trill from high "F" sharp to high "G" sharp is readily performed. The second key from above will produce a fine and elegant trill from "C to D," also from "C" sharp to "D," also the same key will produce the trill from high "G" to high "A" and "G" sharp to "A."

BERTELING'S IMPROVED BOEHM FLUTE, TO "C NATURAL," WOOD BODY, CYLINDER BORE.

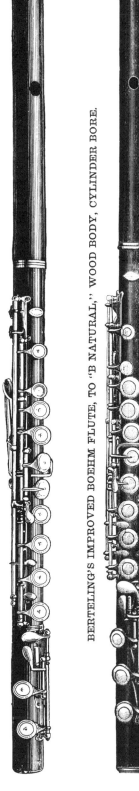

BERTELING'S IMPROVED BOEHM FLUTE, TO "B NATURAL," WOOD BODY, CYLINDER BORE.

BERTELING'S IMPROVED BOEHM FLUTE, TO "B FLAT," SILVER BODY, CYLINDER BORE.

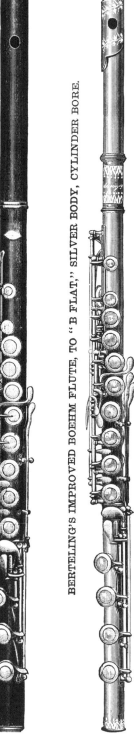

Berteling's
Improved
Concert flute
Nos. 10, 16, 28

Berteling's
Concert flute
Nos. 45 to 48

Berteling's
Boehm flute
Nos. 50 and 53

Berteling's
Boehm flute
Nos. 51 and 54

Berteling's
Boehm flute
Nos. 58 and 61

Albert system clarinets
made by Martin frères

Note that the D and E flat
clarinets appear to be similar,
with wooden ferrules at the
top of the instrument, an
older style for the lowest keys

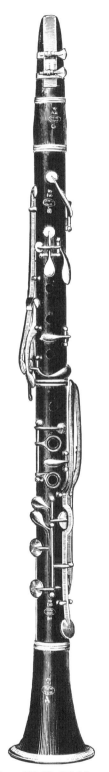

Nos. 2042-2046,
Nos. 2056-2065,
Nos. 2070-2074

Nos. 2036-2040

Nos. 2026-2029
[not found in
the catalog]

Nos. 2016-
2025

Nos. 2000-
2010

Clarinets sold by Pollmann
Numbers 2083-2085, 2070-2085
are Berteling's B flat solo clarinets

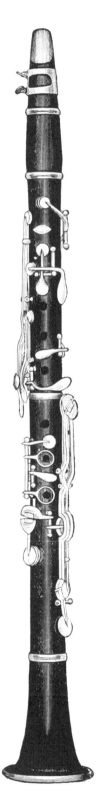

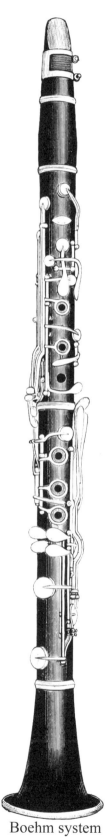

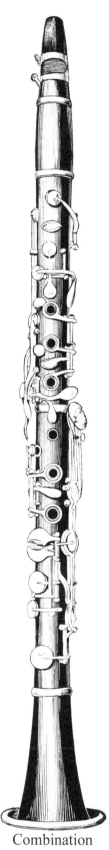

No. 2083

Nos. 2084-2085

Nos. 2070-2074-2085

Boehm system
Nos. 136-137

Combination
No. 2086

Instruments sold by Pollmann
Woodwinds made by
Berteling

Clarinet	Oboe	Oboe	Oboe	English horn
No. 2095	Nos. 2151-2153	No. 2155	Nos. 2157-2159	No. 2166

Alto Saxophone made by Buffet, Crampon & Co.

Rampone

This company is one of Italy's major makers of musical instruments. *NLI* (p. 318), states that the company began operations in Quarna in 1847. Around 1850, the company expanded, and opened a factory in Milan. Rampone stayed in both locations until 1912 when the company changed its name to Rampone & Cazzani. This company is still in operation, evidently making many of the instruments listed here. The following information comes from an undated catalog surely printed around 1900. The catalog is in private hands, and only available as a poor-quality photocopy. So, some of the information presented here is uncertain. All prices in this section are in Italian Lira. The catalog shows that this company was very experimental. However, this company is not well known in the U.S. It is hoped that this untranslated information will help value instruments by this company.

Clarinetti La-Si*b*-Do-Mi*b*-La*b*. Ebano o granatiglia – Chiavi in alpacca, prima qualità

1	13 chiavi senza anella	36
2	13 chiavi con due anella del Fa diesis	38
3	14 chiavi con due anella e colla doppia di Si*b* pezzo superiore	40
4	14 chiavi con due anella e colla doppia del Ebano	45
5	14 chiavi due anella e col doppio do, fra l'indice e il medio mano sinistra	40
6	15 chiavi due anella, colla doppia chiave del ebano e doppia chiave di Si*b*, pezzo superiore	50
7	15 chiavi con due anella, doppia di Si*b* pezzo superiore e leva di Mi*b*	50
8	16 chiavi due anella, doppia chiave di ebano, doppia di Si*b*, pezzo superiore e leva di Mi*b* (tipo ministeriale)	58
9	17 chiavi con due anella, doppia chiave di ebano, doppia di Si*b* pezzo superiore, leva di Mi*b* e key lunga del trillo La-Do	62

Desiderandosi I clarinetti sistema Albert e cioè colla key di Si*b* (portavoce) a tortiglione, colla canetta sporgente e la key di La diesis (prima ottava) diritta, invece di essere a cavalletto, il prezzo è invariabile.

Clarinets in La, Si*b*, C, Mi*b*, and La*b*, ebano or granadilla, chiave in alpacca, lucidatura dei legni naturale e brillante, Lavorazione accurate

10	13 chiavi senza anella	46
11	13 chiavi con due anella di Fa diesis	48
12	14 chiavi con due anella e doppia di Si*b*, pezzo superiore	50
13	14 chiavi con due anella e doppia del C diesis	55
14	15 chiavi con due anella, doppia del Ebano e leva di Mi*b*	60
15	15 chiavi con due anella, doppia del Ebano e leva di Mi*b*	60
16	16 chiavi con due anella e doppia di Si*b*, pezzo superoire, doppia Ebano e leva di Mi*b* (tipo ministeriale)	70
17	17 chiavi con due anella, doppia chiavi di Ebano, doppia di Si*b*, pezzo superiore, leva di Mi*b* e chiave lunga per il trillo di La-Do	75
18	18 chiavi con due anella, doppio Ebano, doppia chiavi di Si*b*, pezzo superiore, leva di Mi*b* e chiave lunga per il trillo La-Do, discendente al grave Mi*b*	85
19	Come il numero 18, in più, la chiave di doppio Do fra l'indice e il medio mano sinistra	90

Desiderandosi i tenoni foderati e le spine filettate in alpacca il prezzo aumenta di L. 20 per ogni clarinetto. – Volendosi il fusto in ebanite (caoutchouc) L. 25 in più. – Le rolletta alle chiavi dei due mignoli aumentano il prezzo di L. 2 per rolletta.

Clarinetto a La, Si*b*, C, Mi*b*, and La*b*, ebano, granadilla, alpacca chiavi, ludicatura dei jegni naturale e brillante. Tipi per Esportazione – qualità extra superiore.

20	13 chiavi, due anella di Fa diesis	65
21	14 chiavi, due anella e doppia di Si*b* pezzo superiore	70
22	14 chiavi, due anella e doppia chiavi di Do diesis	75
23	14 chiavi, due anella e leva di Mi*b*	75
24	14 chiavi, due anella e doppio C fra l'indice e il medio della mano sinistra	75
25	15 chiavi, due anella, doppia di La*b* e doppia di C sharp	80
26	15 chiavi, due anella, doppia di La*b* e leva di Mi*b*	85
27	15 chiavi, due anella, doppia Ebano e leva di Mi*b*	85
28	16 chiavi, due anella, doppia Ebano, leva di Mi*b*, doppia di Si*b* (tipo minister.)	90
29	17 chiavi, due anella, doppia Ebano, leva di Mi*b*, doppia Si*b* e chiave lunga per il trillo La-Do	95
30	19 chiavi, come il numero 30 e col Sol diesis articolato	105
31	19 chiavi, come il numero 30 e col Sol diesis articolato	110

N.B. Desiderandosi I tenori dedreati e le spine filettate in alpaca il prezzo aumenta di L. 20. – per ogni clarineto. – Le relette alle chiavi dei due mignoli aumentano il prezzo di L. 2. – per reletta. – Col fusto in ebanite (caoutchouc) L. 25 in più.

Clarinetti per Solista – di vari sistema

In due pezzi oppure in un sol pezzo – Con 3-4-5 anella – In ebano o granatiglia chiavi alpacca

32	13 chiavi e 3 anella, per ottenere il trillo di Fa diesis e Sol diesis	100
33	14 chiavi e 3 anella, per ottenere il trillo di Fa diesis e Sol diesis con chiave del doppio Do diesis	115
34	15 chiavi e 3 anella, come il N. 33 e in più la doppia di Si*b* pezzo superiore	122
35	16 chiavi e 3 anella, come il N. 34 e leva di Mi*b*	130
36	16 chiavi e 4 anella, per ottenere il Si*b* a forchetta	140
37	17 chiavi e 4 anella, come il N. 36 e chiave lunga per trillo di La-Do	150
38	18 chiavi e 4 anella, come il N. 37 e discendente al Mi*b* grave	165
39	16 chiavi e 4 anella, per ottenere il trillo di Si e Do diesis acuto	140
40	17 chiavi e 4 anella, come il N. 39 e chiave lunga per trillo di La-Do	150

41	18 chiavi e 4 anella, come il N. 40 3 discendente al Mib grave	165
42	16 chiavi e 5 anella, per ottenere il trillo di Do e Do diesis acuto e Sol diesis artic.	175
43	17 chiavi e 5 anella, come il N. 42, e chiave lunga per il trillo di La-Do	175
44	18 chiavi e 5 anella, come il N. 43 e discendente al Mib grave	185

N.B. Desiderandosi i tenoni foderati e le spine filettate in alpacca il prezzo aumenta di L. 20 per ogni Clarinette. – Le relette alle chiavi dei due mignoli aumentano il prezzo di L. 2 per roletta – Per chi desiderasse il fusto in ebanite (caoutchouc) in prezzo aumenta di L. 25 per I Clarinetti in due pezzi e Di L. 40 per quelli in un sol pezzo – Per l'argentatura alle chiavi (che per questi Clarineti è molto consigliabile) L. 25 in più.

Clarinetti per solista di vari sistema

In due pezzi oppure in un sol pezzo – modello Barret

45	13 chiavi 4 anella col trillo di La e Do	110
46	14 chiavi 4 anella doppio Do diesis	120
47	14 chiavi 5 anella doppio Do diesis e Sol diesis articolato	130
48	15 chiavi 4 anella doppio Do diesis e leva di Mib	125
49	15 chiavi 5 anella doppio Do diesis, leva di Mib e Sol diesis articolato	135
50	16 chiavi 4 anella doppio Do diesis, leva di Mib e trillo La-Do	135
51	16 chiavi 5 anella doppio Do diesis, leva di Mib, trillo La-Do e Sol diesis articolato	145
52	17 chiavi 4 anella doppio Do diesis, leva di Mib e trillo La-Do discendente al Mib grave	160
53	17 chiavi 5 anella doppio Do diesis, leva di Mib, trillo La-Do e discendente al Mib grave con Sol diesis articolato	175
54	col pezzo inferiore sistema pezza Boehm e pezzo sup. Modello Barret a 4 anella	160
55	come il N. 54 più il Sol diesis articolato a 5 anella	175
56	come il N. 55 più la leva del Mib a 5 anella	185
57	come il N. 56 più la leva del Mib a 5 anella e chiave lunga del trillo La e Do	185
58	come il N. 57 colla chiave degli aruti a tortiglione	195
59	come il N. 58 in un sol pezzo	200
60	come il N. 59 discendente Mib grave	215
61	come il N. 60 con barilotto a pompa	225

Questo tipo di Clarinetto è molto consigliabile ai solisti perchè conservando la medesima digitazione del Clarinetto a 13 chiavi possono ottenere vantaggi indiscutibili nei vari passaggi, trilli e tremoli.

Il Cliente soddisfatto nelle sue ordinazioni renderà sincero e gradito omaggio alla mia Casa, raccomandandola a Colleghi ed Amici.

Clarinetti finissimi per Solista, sistema Boehm. La-Sib-Do-Mib

[The first column of prices is for brass keys. The second price is for silver keys.]

62	Mezzo Boehm a 2 anella, doppia chiave di Sib	125	225
63	Mezzo Boehm a 2 anella, colla chiave lunga per trillo di La-Do	125	225
64	Mezzo Boehm a 3 anella, colla chiave lunga per trillo di La-Do, e Sol diesis articolato	130	230
65	Mezzo Boehm come il N. 64 più la chiave del doppio Sib	135	235
66	Mezzo Boehm come il N. 65, con leva di Mib	138	238
67	Mezzo Boehm come il N. 66, e dicendente al Mib grave	145	245
68	Sistema Boehm completo in due pezzi	170	270
69	Sistema Boehm completo in due pezzi colla leva di Mib	180	280
70	Sistema Boehm completo in due pezzi colla leva di Mib discendente al Mib grave	195	300
71	Sistema Boehm completo il No. 70, con Sol diesis articolato	215	330
72	Sistema Boehm completo il N. 71, col meccanismo per il Sib a forchetta	230	345
73	Sistema Boehm completo in un sol pezzo	190	290
74	Sistema Boehm completo in un sol pezzo, col doppio Sol diesis	200	300
75	Sistema Boehm completo come il N. 74, e Sol diesis articolato	215	325
76	Sistema Boehm completo come il N. 75, e leva di Mib	225	335
77	Sistema Boehm completo come il N. 76, discendente al Mib grave	240	350
78	Sistema Boehm completo come il N. 77, col meccanismo per il Sib a forchetta	225	370
79	Sistema Boehm completo come il N. 78, col meccanismo per la leva alle chiavi di Sol diesis e La, da digitarsi coll'indice della mano destra	285	400

N.B. Nessun Clarinetto sistema Boehm sorte dalla mia Casa, se non prima scrupolosamente provato e collaudato dal Disintissimo Sig. Prof. Ulderico Perilli, primo Clarinetto (solista) del Teatro dell'Opera alla Scala di Milano. – I suddetti Clarinetti sono garantiti per la loro solidità, finezza di lavoro, precisione di meccanica, bontà di voce ed intonazione perfettissima.

Per la maggiore conservazione della meccanica si consiglia l'argentatura a forte alle chiavi (per quelli col meccanismo in alpacca) il che facendo il prezzo aumenta di L. 20 per ciascun Clarinetto mezzo Boehm e L. 25 per ciascun Clarinetto sistema Boehm completo.

Disiderandosi I Clarinetti in ebanite il prezzo aumenta di L. 25 per quelli in due pezzi e L. 40 per quelli in un sol pezzo.

I Clarinetti sistema Boehm a tamponatura chiusa come la figura N. 74 bis costano in più L. 35 cad.

Clarinetti La-Sib-Do a voce rinforzata. Con campana ricurva (Sistema Brevettato Rampone).

Primo Qualità, in ebano o granatiglia – chiavi alpacca

80	13 chiavi, due anella	50
81	14 chiavi, due anella colla doppia di Sib, przzo superiore	55
82	14 chiavi, due anella col doppio Do diesis	60
83	15 chiavi, due anella col doppio Do diesis e leva di Mib	65
84	15 chiavi, due anella col doppio Do diesis e colla doppia di Sib	65
85	16 chiavi, due anella col doppio Do diesis, leva di Mib, e doppia di Sib	70

Lacorazione Accurata, Chiavi alpacca

86	13 chiavi, due anella	65
87	14 chiavi, due anella colla doppia di Sib, pezzo superiore	70
88	14 chiavi, due anella col doppio Do diesis	75
89	15 chiavi, due anella col doppio Do diesis e leva di Mib	80
90	15 chiavi, due anella col doppio Do diesis e colla doppia di Sib	80
91	16 chiavi, due anella col doppio Do diesis, leva di Mib, e doppia di Sib	85

Qualità extra superiore, chiavi alpacca

92	13 chiavi, due anella	80
93	14 chiavi, due anella colla doppia di Sib, pezzo superiore	85
94	14 chiavi, due anella col doppio Do diesis	90
95	15 chiavi, due anella col doppio Do diesis e leva di Mib	95
96	15 chiavi, due anella col doppio Do diesis e colla doppia di Sib	95
97	16 chiavi, due anella col doppio Do diesis, leva di Mib, e doppia di Sib	100

Aumenti

Per chi desidera le rolette ai mignoli L. 2 per roletta in più – Per chi desidera I tenoni foderati in alpacca e spine filettate L. 20 in più. – Per chi desidera I fusti in ebanite (caoutchouc) L. 25 in più.

Avvertenza importante

Riguardo ai prezzi è d'uopo tener presente che di questi non si debbono fare nudi confronti, fra una Casa e l'altra, senza prendere in seria considerazione, la ben studiata ed accurate costruzione, il materiale di assoluta prima qualità di controllo, ecc.

Fatiche e spese non vengono risparmiate per la costruzione dei miei strumenti. Mi lustingo quindi che I Signori Maestri e Dilettanti di musica, tenuto calcolo delle suesposte ragioni, mi riserberanno la preferenza in ogni loro occasione.

Lunghi anni di lavoro, continui studi, diligenza di controllo, mi permettono di fregiarmi del motto: "Lealtà ed onestà sino allo scrupolo.

Clarinetti Contralti (Claroni in Fa o Mi*b*) chiavi e guarnizioni alpacca, prima qualità

98	13 chiavi, 3 anella	90
99	14 chiavi, 3 anella doppio Do diesis o doppio Si*b*	100
100	15 chiavi, 3 anella doppio Do diesis e doppio Si*b*	110
101	16 chiavi, 3 anella, tipo Ministeriale	120

Clarinetti Contralti in Fa o Mi*b* in ebano o granatiglia, chivai alpacca, qualità extra, Lavorazione accurate

102	13 chiavi, 3 anella	110

103	14 chiavi, 3 anella, doppio Do diesis o doppio Si*b*	120
104	15 chiavi, 3 anella, doppio Do diesis o doppio Si*b*	130
105	15 chiavi, 3 anella, tipo Minsteriale	140

Aumenti

N.B. Per chi desidera le rolette ai mignoli, l'aumento è di L. 2. – per ogni roletta.

Clarinetti Contralito in Fa o Mi*b*, qualità extra superiore = Lavorazione finissima, in ebano scelto o granatiglia – chivi alpacca

106	13 chiavi, 3 anella	125
107	14 chiavi, 3 anella, doppio Do diesis o doppio Si*b*	135
108	15 chiavi, 3 anella, doppio Do diesis e doppio Si*b*	145
109	16 chiavi, 3 anella, doppio Do diesis e doppio Si*b* con leva di Mi*b*	155
110	17 chiavi, 3 anella, come il N. 109, in più il trillo di La-Do	165
111	18 chiavi, come il N. 110, discendente al Mi*b* grave	175

Clarinetti Contralti in Mi*b*, Sistema Boehm (tipo unico)

112	in Mi*b*, Sistema Boehm	215
113	in Mi*b*, Sistema Boehm discendente al Mi*b* grave	235

N.B. Per chi desidera ai Clarinetti Contralti I tenoni foderati e le spine filettate in alpacca, il pezzo aumenta di L. 20. – per ciascun istrumento.

Zeigler system flutes made by Rampone

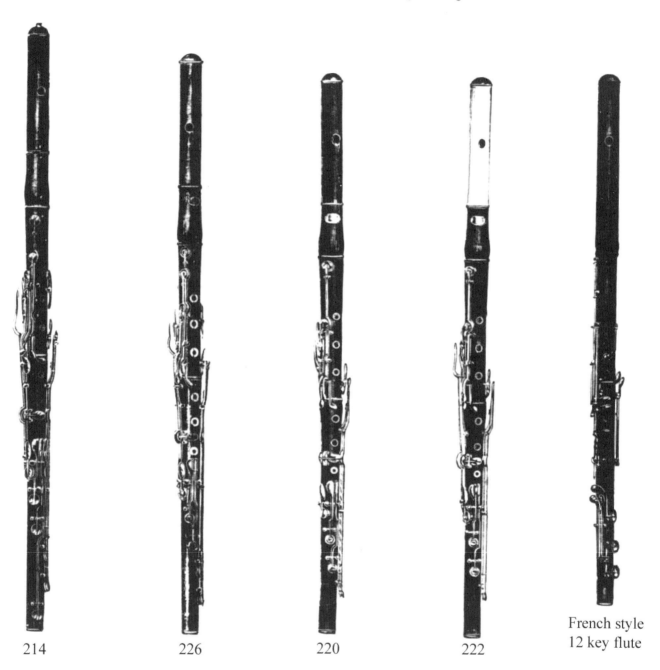

214   226   220   222   French style
12 key flute

Piccolos made by Rampone

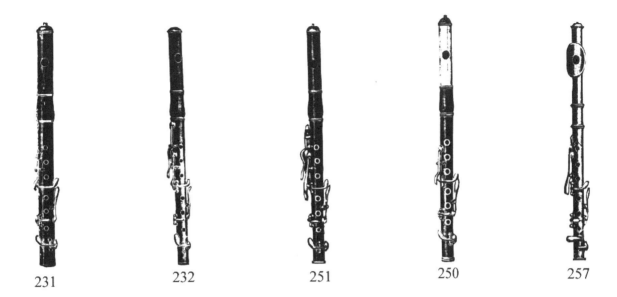

231   232   251   250   257

Ziegler system flutes made by Rampone

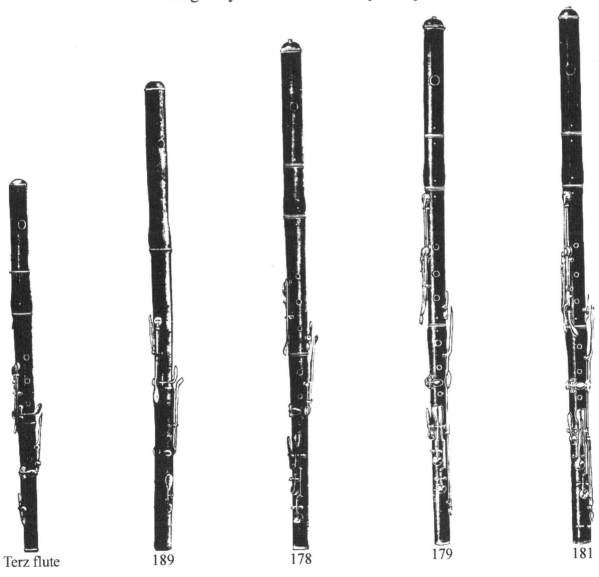

Terz flute   189   178   179   181

Clarinets sold by Rampone

1   2   2   4   6   16   6   6

17   16   28   30   31   28

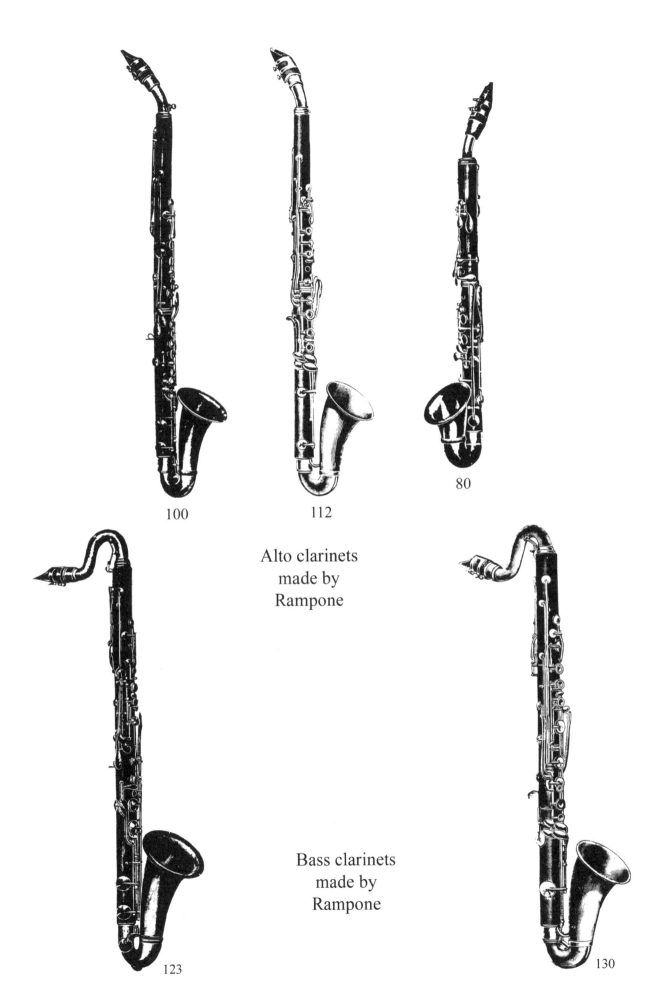

100

112

80

Alto clarinets
made by
Rampone

123

Bass clarinets
made by
Rampone

130

Oboes and English horns
made by Rampone

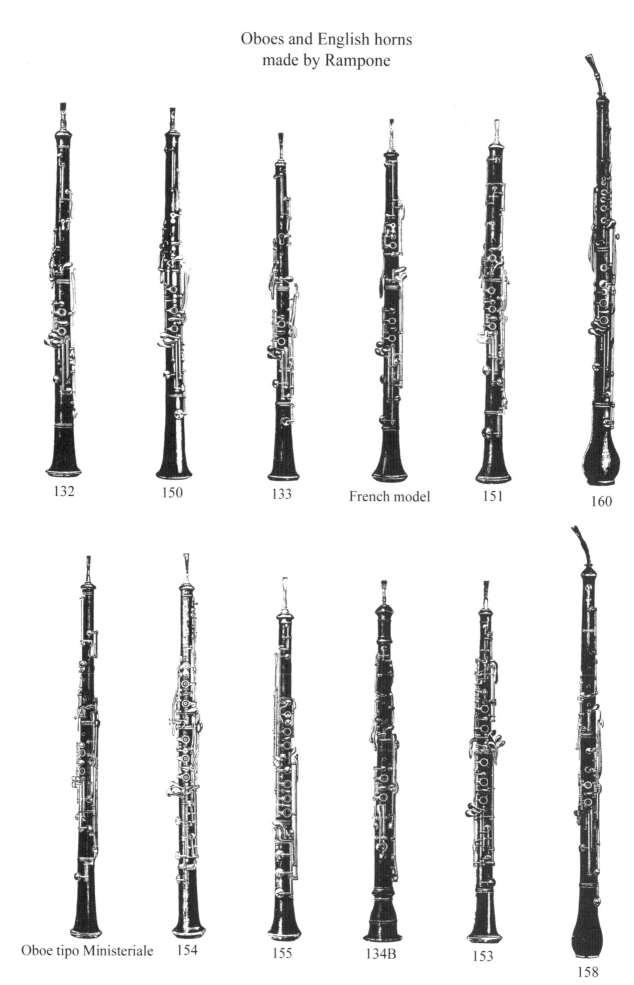

132   150   133   French model   151   160

Oboe tipo Ministeriale   154   155   134B   153   158

Bassoons made
by Rampone

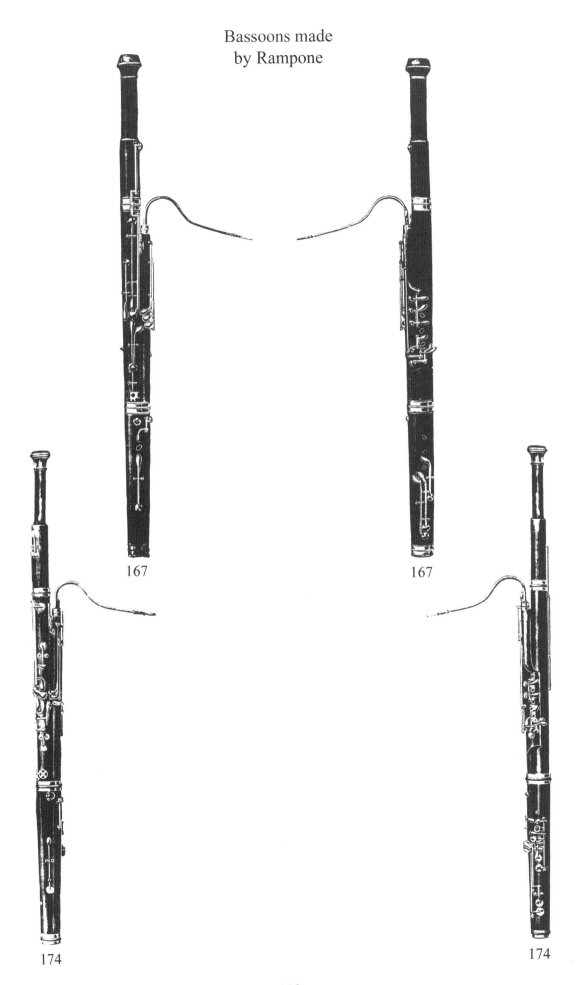

167

167

174

174

Sarrousophones made by Rampone

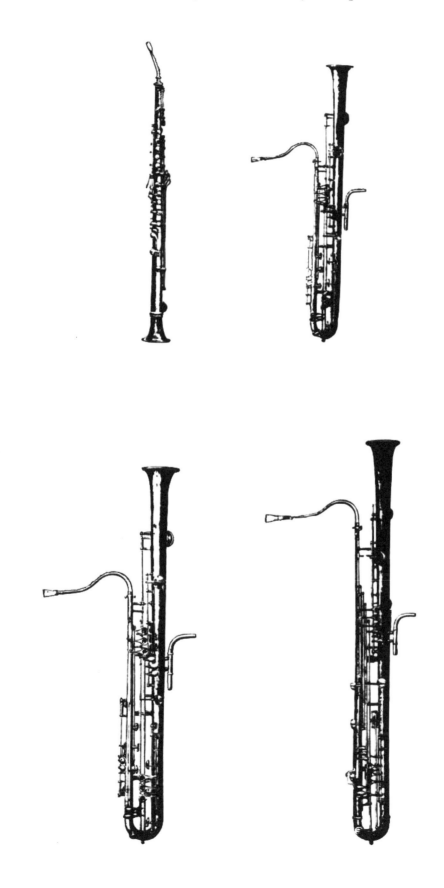

Rudall, Carte & Co., Ltd.

Rudall, Carte & Co., Ltd. was and still is one of the U.K.'s most important maker of woodwind instruments. The company is also very important as an innovator, making major improvements to the modern flute. The company even manufactured its own Rudall-Boehm system flute. Instruments from this company appear in many collections. However, some instruments have fingering systems little known to most players, which affects the value. *NLI* (p. 339) states that the company began operation in 1872 in London. The following information is from a photocopy of an undated and incomplete catalog. The catalog states that high pitch A=452.4 and low pitch A=439, and also that the company was "established over a century and a half." Instruments at high or low pitch made to any specification." All prices are in English pounds.

The Premier Class Instruments are the highest grade, followed by the Imperial Class Instruments.

Imperial Class clarinets		Pound	shilling
77	Cocus, 13 keys and rings	11	0
78	Cocus, 14 keys and rings (14th being extra C#)	12	0
79	Cocus, 15 keys and rings	12	10
80	Cocus, 14 keys and rings and Barret action	15	0
	Double action G sharp to any of the above, extra	2	2
81	Cocus, Carte's Patent, 1st modification	18	0
82	African black wood, Boehm's system	23	0
	Any of the above clarinets can be made of ebonite at an extra	1	1

Premier Class clarinets			
83	Cocus, 13 keys and rings	8	0
84	Cocus, 14 keys and rings (14th being extra C#)	9	0
85	Cocus, 15 keys and rings	9	10
86	African black wood, Boehm's system	18	18

Special Class clarinets			
87	Cocus or black wood, 13 keys	7	10
88	Cocus or black wood, 14 keys (14th being extra C#)	8	5
89	Cocus or black wood, 15 keys and rings	9	0

Tenor clarinets			
91	Cocus, 15 nickel silver keys and rings	13	0
92	Ebonite, 15 nickel silver keys and rings	15	0

Bass clarinets			
93	Cocus, 15 nickel silver keys and rings	29	0
94	Ebonite, 15 nickel silver keys and rings	30	0
	Quotation given for Boehm's system		

Basset horns in F			
95	Cocus, 13 nickel silver keys and rings	28	0
96	Ditto, 15 nickel silver keys and rings	30	0
	Eight rollers to either of above, extra	4	4
	Extra for ebonite	1	1

Imperial Class, oboes, rosewood, black wood or ebonite			
97	Rosewood, 13 nickel silver keys and rings down to B natural	12	0
98	Rosewood, 13 nickel silver keys and rings, and thumb-plate down to B natural	18	0
99	Rosewood, 17 nickel silver keys, rings, and thumb-plate down to B natural	22	0
100	Rosewood or black wood, 17 nickel silver keys and ring, F sharp and G shake, down to B flat	24	0
101	Same as above, silver plated keys	26	0
102	Ditto, with self-acting octave keys, nickel silver keys	27	0
103	Same as above	29	0
104	Barret system, rosewood or black wood, down to B flat silver plated keys	38	0
105	Conservatoire Model, rosewood or black wood, silver plated keys	40	0
106	Boehm system, rosewood or black wood, descends to B natural, nickel silver keys	24	0
107	Boehm system, rosewood or black wood, descends to B flat, nickel silver keys	28	0
	Any of the above can be supplied in ebonite	1	1
	Quotations given for silver mechanisms		
108	Rosewood, 13 nickel silver keys and rings, down to B natural	10	0
109	Rosewood, 13 nickel silver keys and rings, and thumb-plate down to B natural	14	0
110	Rosewood, 17 nickel silver keys and rings, and thumb-plate, down to B flat		

English horn, rosewood or black wood, nickel silver keys, Imperial Class

111	Fingering corresponding to that of 13 keyed oboe, down to B natural	30	0
112	Same as above with vented F	32	0
113	Same as above with thumb-plate	33	10
114	Fingering corresponding to that of 17 keyed oboe, vented F down to B flat with thumb-plate	38	0

Oboe d'Amore (in A)

115 Rosewood, with 17 nickel silver keys, double action F sharp and G
     sharp keys, with thumb-plate   36   0

Improved Savary model bassoons, maple, rosewood, and ebonite

116 Maple with rosewood tenor joint, 17 nickel silver keys   32   0
117 Maple with ebonite tenor joint, 17 nickel silver keys   33   0
118 Rosewood, with 17 nickel silver keys   36   0
119 Rosewood, with ebonite tenor joint, 17 nickel silver keys 37 0
120 Rosewood, with 19 nickel silver keys C sharp shake, and third right
     hand covered   38   0
121 Rosewood, with 22 nickel silver keys   40   0
122 Rosewood, with 22 nickel silver keys, with ebonite tenor joint
                                                 41   10
123 Ebonite, with 17 nickel silver keys   41   0

124 Ebonite, with 22 nickel silver keys   44   0

Contra bassoon

125 Maple, with nickel sliver keys, same fingering as bassoon   55   0

Saxophones

[The following is a restructuring of the original table]
Types of instruments, all are brass bodied:
1 Simple form
2 Perfected system, extra B flat, F# and G# shakes, rollers, etc.
3 Perfected system with automatic octave keys
4 Extra, down to B flat
5 Nickel plating
6 Best silver plating

#	instrument	type 1	type 2	type 3	type 4	type 5	type 6
126	B flat, Soprano	18 18	20 0	24 0	2 0	1 15	3 15
127	E flat, Alto	23 0	25 0	29 0	2 10	2 0	5 0
128	B flat, Tenor	27 0	28 0	32 10	3 0	2 10	6 10
129	C, Melody	27 0	28 10	32 10	3 0	2 10	6 10
130	E flat, Baritone	34 0	36 0	40 0	3 10	4 0	7 10

Clarinets made by Rudall, Carte & Co.

Fifteen key clarinet

Carte's patent clarinet

Boehm system clarinet

No. 81

No. 82

Barret action
No. 80

Tenor (or alto)
clarinet
No. 91

Bass clarinet
No. 93

Double reed instrument
made by Rudall, Carte & Co.

17 key oboe
No. 99

Barret system
oboe
No. 104

Oboe d'amore
No. 111

17 key Savary model bassoon
front and back views
Number 116 to 119

Soprano saxophone
in B flat, perfected
system, with Automatic
octave keys. No. 126

Alto saxophone
in E flat, perfected
system, with Automatic
octave keys. No. 127

Tenor saxophone
in B flat, perfected
system. No. 128

Moses Slater

Moses Slater was founded in New York City as a manufacturer of quality brass wind instruments. *NLI* (p. 375) states that the company operated between about 1865 and about 1920. The following information is from a 1915 catalog. Note that catalog numbers are reused throughout. While some instruments were probably made by Slater, not all were. Some makers' names are given. Slater's woodwind instruments were generally of average quality.

Simple system flutes

1	Key of D, cocus, 1 G.S. key and mounts	$1.60
2	Key of D, cocus, 1 G.S. key and mounts, tuning slide	$1.80
3	Key of F, cocus, 1 G.S. key and mounts	$1.50
4	Key of F, cocus, 1 G.S. key and mounts, tuning slide	$1.60
5	Key of G, cocus, 1 G.S. key and mounts	$1.40
10	Key of D, grenadilla, 4 G.S. key and mounts, tuning slide	$2.50
11	Key of D, grenadilla, 4 G.S. key and mounts, tuning slide, tuning slide, cork joints, etc.	$2.60
12	Key of F, grenadilla, 4 G.S. key and mounts, tuning slide	$2.40
15	Key of D, grenadilla, 6 G.S. key and mounts, tuning slide, tuning slide	$3.00
16	Key of D, grenadilla, 6 G.S. key and mounts, tuning slide, tuning slide, cork joints, etc.	$3.15
17	Key of F, grenadilla, 6 G.S. key and mounts, tuning slide, tuning slide, cork joints, etc.	$2.00
20	Key of D, grenadilla, 8 G.S. keys and mounts, tuning slide, cork joints, etc.	$4.25
21	Key of D, grenadilla, 8 G.S. keys and mounts, tuning slide, G.S. embouchure	$4.75
22	Key of D, grenadilla, 8 G.S. keys and mounts, tuning slide, G.S. lip plate and lined tone holes	$6.25
23	Key of D, grenadilla, 8 G.S. keys and mounts, tuning slide G.S. head and slide joint	$8.00
15	Key of D, grenadilla, 8 G.S. keys and mounts, tuning slide, American ivory head, cork joints, etc.	$10.50

[The reuse of this catalog number is as it appears in the catalog.]

30	Key of D, grenadilla, 8 G.S. keys and mounts, aluminum head, tuning slide, ebonite embouchure hole	$12.00
35	Key of D, grenadilla, 8 G.S. keys and mounts, celluloid covered head, G.S. lip plate	$6.50

Simple system flutes, H.F. Meyer

100	Key of D, 11 G.S. keys and mounts, grenadilla, ivory head	$75.00

Boehm system flute, Evette & Schaeffer

110	Grenadilla, G.S. keys	$102.50
125	Key of D, grenadilla, 8 G.S. keys and mounts, covered finger holes, English model (suggestive of Rudall & Carte's Radcliff model)	$25.00

Meyer system flutes

150	Grenadilla, 8 G.S. keys and mounts, with tuning slide	$7.25
151	Same as above, but with American ivory head joint	$13.50
152D	Grenadilla, 10 G.S. keys and mounts	$11.40
153	Same as above, with American ivory head joint	$17.50
154D	Grenadilla, 13 G.S. keys and mounts	$12.60
155	Same as above, with American ivory head joint	$19.20

Meyer system flutes, extra quality

160D	Grenadilla, 10 G.S. keys and mounts, tuning slide	$21.60
161	Same as above, with American ivory head joint	$28.20
162D	Grenadilla, 13 G.S. keys and mounts, tuning slide	$25.20
163	Same as above, with American ivory head joint	$31.80

Albert system clarinets available in A, B flat, C, or D, French make, American concert pitch

12	Ebony, 10 G.S. keys and mounts	$7.25
49	Ebony, 13 G.S. keys and mounts, 2 ring keys	$13.50
54	Ebony, 15 G.S. keys and mounts, 2 ring keys, C and B trill keys	$15.00
54½	Same as 54 but in International pitch (low pitch)	$15.00
55	Ebony, 15 G.S. keys and mounts, 4 ring keys, C and B trill keys, and 4 roller keys	$20.00

Albert system clarinets, marked Henry Pourcelle [trade name of unidentified maker], key of A, B flat, C, D, and E, American concert pitch, metal finger holes

59	Ebony, 15 G.S. keys and mounts, 2 rings (double C and B flat keys for trilling)	$19.80
59½	Ebony, 15 G.S. keys and mounts, 2 rings, roller keys	$23.40
59¼	Same as above in international pitch	$23.40

Albert system clarinets, Evette & Schaeffer, key of A, B flat, C, D, and E, American concert pitch

80	Ebony, 15 G.S. keys and mounts, 2 ring keys, double C and B keys	$35.00
80¼	Ebony, 15 G.S. keys and mounts, 2 ring keys, double C and B keys, International pitch	$35.00
83	Ebony, 15 G.S. keys and mounts, 4 ring keys, 4 roller keys, C and B keys	$43.00

Albert system clarinets, George Cloos, key of A, B flat, C, D, and E flat, American pitch

67	Grenadilla, 13 G.S. keys and mounts, 2 rings	$28.00
69	Grenadilla, 15 G.S. keys and mounts, 2 rings (double C and B keys for trilling)	$32.00
71	Grenadilla, 15 G.S. keys and mounts, 4 rings, roller keys (double C and B keys for trilling)	$40.00

Saxophones, Evette & Schaeffer, additional F sharp trill key also a plate for the first finger of the heft hand for the new B flat, and a new patent system at the G sharp key for the trill, and extra patent key for going down to low B flat, and a new E flat key, and with double C sharp, B natural, and B flat keys for the middle finger of the right hand. The alto and tenor, with new E and F natural keys.

B flat Soprano

No. 50	Brass	$75.00
No. 51	Brass, silver plated, satin finish	$85.00
No. 52	Brass, silver plated, burnished	$87.50

E flat altos

No. 53	Brass	$85.00
No. 54	Brass, silver plated, satin finish	$92.50
No. 55	Brass, silver plated, burnished	$102.50

B flat tenors

No. 56	Brass	$85.00
No. 57	Brass, silver plated, satin finish	$102.95
No. 58	brass, silver plated, burnished	$109.00

E flat baritones

No. 59	Brass	$90.00
No. 60	Brass, silver plated, satin finish	$112.00
No. 61	Brass, silver plated, burnished	$119.00

Bassoon

No. 1	Rosewood, 17 keys	$87.00

Oboe

No. 1	Ebony, 15 keys, 2 rings	$32.00

Musettes

No. 1	Boxwood, 1 key	$3.40
No. 2	Ebony, 7 keys	$10.25

Octavin [described in the catalog as an entirely new instrument with the tone between a saxophone and clarinet, with the fingering of a clarinet, three octaves from G sharp to high G; see page 17 for illustration]

No. 1	B flat, grenadilla, G.S. keys and mounts	$30.00

Piccolos, grenadilla, G.S. keys and mounts

No. 103	Key of B flat, 1 key	$0.85
No. 106	Key of B flat, 1 key, tuning slide	$1.05
No. 121½	Key of B flat, 6 keys, tuning slide	$2.20
No. 3	Key of D, 1 key	$0.60
No. 6	Key of D, 1 key, tuning slide	$0.75
No. 18	Key of D, 4 keys, tuning slide, cork joint	$1.35
No. 21	Key of D, 6 keys, tuning slide, cork joint	$1.65
No. 24	Key of D, 6 keys, tuning slide, cork joint, G.S. embouchure	$2.25
No. 26	Key of D, 6 keys, tuning slide, cork joint, G.S. head joint	$2.40
No. 37	Key of D, 6 keys, tuning slide, cork joint, G.S. lip plate and holes	$2.70

No. 27	Key of D, 6 keys, tuning slide, cork joint, American ivory head joint	$4.80
No. 28	Key of D, 6 keys, tuning slide, cork joint, celluloid covered head, G.S. lip plate	$3.15
No. 19	Key of D, 8 keys, tuning slide	$4.20
No. 158	Key of D, 6 keys, Meyer model	$3.00
No. 178	Key of D, 6 keys, Meyer model, American ivory head joint	$5.75
No. 3¼	Key of E flat, 1 key	$0.60
No. 6¼	Key of E flat, tuning slide	$0.75
No. 18¼	Key of e flat, 4 keys, tuning slide, cork joint	$1.35
No. 21¼	Key of E flat, 6 keys, tuning slide, cork joint	$1.65
No. 24¼	Key of E flat, 6 keys, tuning slide, G.S. embouchure	$2.25
No. 26¼	Key of E flat, 6 keys, tuning slide, G.S. head joint	$2.40
No. 37¼	Key of E flat, 6 keys, tuning slide, G.S. lip plate and holes	$2.70
No. 27¼	Key of E flat, 6 keys, tuning slide, cork joint, American ivory head joint	$4.80
No. 28¼	Key of E flat, 6 keys, tuning slide, cork joint, celluloid covered head, G.S. lip plate	$3.15
No. 158¼	Key of E flat, 6 keys, Meyer model	$3.00
No. 178¼	Key of E flat, 6 keys, Meyer model, American ivory head joint	$5.75

Piccolos, H.F. Meyer, Hanover

No. 9	Key of D, 6 keys, ivory head joint	$22.50
No. 9¼	Key of E flat, 6 keys, ivory head joint	$22.50

Piccolos, George Cloos, American

No. 406	Key of D, 6 keys, cocus	$9.60
No. 407	Key of D, 6 keys, cocus, ivory head joint	$11.75
No. 406¼	Key of E flat, 6 keys, cocus	$9.60
No. 407¼	Key of E flat, 6 keys, cocus, ivory head joint	$11.75
No. 506	Key of B flat, 6 keys, cocus	$10.25

Piccolos, cylinder bore, covered finger hole, no maker given

No. 410	Key of D, grenadilla, 6 keys	$9.30
No. 410¼	Key of E flat, grenadilla, 6 keys	$9.30

Boehm system piccolos, Evette & Schaeffer

No. 17	Key of D, cocus, with connecting rings	$42.00
No. 17 ¼	Key of E flat, cocus, with connecting rings	$42.00

Boehm system piccolos, George Cloos, high or low pitch

No. 60	Key of D, grenadilla, G.S. keys	$55.00
No. 60¼	Key of E flat, grenadilla, G.S. keys	$55.00
No. 70	Key of D, grenadilla, solid silver keys	$66.50
No. 70¼	Key of E flat, grenadilla, solid silver keys	$66.50

Fifes

No. 100	Key of B flat, rosewood, brass ferrules	$0.25
No. 101	Key of C, rosewood, brass ferrules	$0.25
No. 102	Key of B flat, cocus, G.S. ferrules	$0.45
No. 103	Key of C, cocus, G.S. ferrules	$0.45
No. 104	Key of B flat, ebony, G.S. ferrules	$0.60
No. 105	Key of C, ebony, G.S. ferrules	$0.60
No. 106	Key of B flat, "Crosby Model", cocus, very long ferrules	$0.85
No. 107	Key of C, "Crosby Model", cocus, very long ferrules	$0.85
No. 108	Key of B flat, "Crosby Model", ebony, very long ferrules	$0.85
No. 109	Key of C, "Crosby Model", ebony, very long ferrules	$0.85

No. 110	Key of B flat, ebony, long G.S. ferrules, extra quality	$0.75
No. 111	Key of C, ebony, long G.S. ferrules, extra quality	$0.75
No. 112	Key of B flat, grenadilla, long G.S. ferrules, extra quality	$1.25
No. 113	Key of C, grenadilla, long G.S. ferrules, extra quality	$1.25
No. 116	Key of B flat, ebony, G.S. ferrules, and band	$1.00
No. 117	Key of C, ebony, G.S. ferrules, and band	$1.00
No. 118	Key of B flat, nickel plated, raised finger holes, gutta percha blow hole	$0.75
No. 119	Key of C, nickel plated, raised finger holes, gutta percha blow hole	$0.75
No. 120	Key of B flat, nickel plated, flush finger holes gutta percha blow hole	$1.00
No. 121	Key of C, nickel plated, flush finger holes gutta percha blow hole	$1.00

Flageolets

No. 125	Key of B, cocus, 1 G.S. key and rings	$1.55
No. 126	Key of C, cocus, 1 G.S. key and rings	$1.55
No. 127	Key of C, cocus, 4 G.S. keys and rings	$2.10
No. 128	Key of C, cocus, 6 G.S. keys and rings	$2.30
No. 129	Key of D. cast model, nickel plated, French make	$0.50
No. 140	Key of B, C, D, E, F, or G, nickel plated, U.S. Eagle model	$0.15
No. 141	Key of D, tin, Clark model, 11 inches long	$0.10
No. 142	Key of D, brass, Clark model, 11 inches long	$0.15
No. 143	Key of D, nickel, Clark model, 11 inches long	$0.18

Albert system clarinets, French make, in A, B flat, C, D, or E flat, American concert pitch

No. 12	Ebony, 10 G.S. keys and mounts	$7.25
No. 49	Ebony, 13 G.S. keys and mounts, 2 rings	$13.50
No. 54	Ebony, 15 G.S. keys and mounts, 2 rings, C and B trill keys	$15.00
No. 55	Ebony, 15 G.S. keys and mounts, 2 rings, C and B trill keys, 4 rollers	$20.00
No. 54¼	Same as No. 54, but in International pitch (low pitch)	$15.00

Albert system clarinets, Henry Pourcelle, Paris, in A, B flat, C, D, or E flat, American concert pitch with metal finger holes

No. 59	Ebony, 15 G.S. keys and mounts, 2 rings (double C and B flat keys for trilling)	$19.80
No. 59½	Ebony, 15 G.S. keys and mounts, 2 rings, roller keys	$23.40
No. 59¼	Ebony, 15 G.S. keys and mounts, 2 rings, roller keys, International pitch (low pitch)	$23.40

Albert system clarinets, Evette & Schaeffer, Paris, in A, B flat, C, D, or E flat

No. 80	Ebony, 15 G.S. keys and mounts, 2 rings, double C and B keys	$35.00
No. 83	Ebony, 15 G.S. keys and mounts, 4 rings, 4 roller keys, double C and B keys	$43.00
No. 80¼	Ebony, 15 G.S. keys and mounts, 2 rings, double C and B keys, International pitch (low pitch)	$35.00

Albert system clarinets, George Cloos, American, in A, B flat, C, D, and E flat, American pitch

No. 67	Grenadilla, 13 G.S. keys and mounts, 2 rings	$28.00
No. 69	Grenadilla, 15 G.S. keys and mounts, 4 rings (double C and B keys for trilling)	$32.00
No. 71	Grenadilla, 13 G.S. keys and mounts, 2 rings, 4 rings, roller keys (double C and B flat keys for trilling)	$40.00

Simple system flutes, 1 G.S. key and mounts

No. 1	Key of D, cocus	$1.60
No. 2	Key of D, cocus, tuning slide	$1.80
No. 3	Key of F, cocus	$1.50
No. 4	Key of F, cocus, tuning slide	$1.60
No. 5	Key of G, cocus	$1.40

Simple system flutes, 4 G.S. keys and mounts

No. 10	Key of D, grenadilla, tuning slide	$2.50
No. 11	Key of D, grenadilla, tuning slide, cork joints	$2.80
No. 12	Key of F, grenadilla, tuning slide	$2.40

Simple system flutes, 6 keys, G.S. keys and mounts

No. 15	Key of D, grenadilla, tuning slide	$2.50
No. 16	Key of D, grenadilla, tuning slide, cork joints	$3.15
No. 17	Key of F, grenadilla, tuning slide, cork joints	$3.00

Simple system flutes, 8 keys

No. 20	Key of D, grenadilla, tuning slide, cork joints	$4.25
No. 21	Key of D, grenadilla, tuning slide, G.S. embouchure	$4.75
No. 22	Key of D, grenadilla, tuning slide, G.S. lip plate and holes	$6.25
No. 23	Key of D, grenadilla, tuning slide, G.S. head joint, and slide joint	$8.00

Simple system flute, 8 keys, ivory head

| No. 15 | Key of D, grenadilla, tuning slide, American ivory head joint, cork joints | $10.50 |

Simple system flute, 8 keys, aluminum head joint

| No. 30 | Key of D, grenadilla, tuning slide, ebonite blow hole | $12.00 |

[This is the only woodwind instrument listed in this book that is made with aluminum.]

Simple system flute, 8 keys, celluloid covered head joint

| No. 25 | Key of D, grenadilla, G.S. lip plate | $6.50 |

Simple system flute, H.F. Meyer, Hanover, Germany

| No. 100 | Key of D, grenadilla, 11 keys, ivory head joint, to low B | $75.00 |

Boehm system flute, Evette & Schaeffer, Paris

| No. 110 | Grenadilla, G.S. covered keys | $102.50 |

[Pratton system (?) flute]

| No. 125 | Key of D, 8 keys, English model, covered keys | $25.00 |

Eugène Thibouville

This French company was part of a very well known family of musical instrument makers that began early in the 19th century and is still making instruments today. Eugène managed the company from 1856 until his death in 1891. Then Les files d'Eugène Thibouville operated until at least 1893. The company was also associated with the Noblet family, and later Thibouville Lamy. See *NLI* (397) for a fuller history of this complex but important company. Prices listed below are in 1893 francs. The following information is from an 1893 trade catalog, and is a free translation by the author.

Boehm system clarinets

1	Ebony, or grenadilla, silver keys and ferrules	250
2	Ebony, or grenadilla, G.S. keys and ferrules	110
3	Ebony, or grenadilla, copper (more likely brass) keys and ferrules	105
4	Boxwood or grenadilla, G.S. keys and ferrules	105
5	Boxwood or grenadilla, copper (brass) keys and ferrules	100

Non-Boehm system clarinets

6	Ebony or grenadilla, 13 silver keys and ferrules, 2 ring keys	125
7	Ebony or grenadilla, 13 G.S. keys and ferrules, 2 ring keys	44
8	Ebony or grenadilla, 13 G.S. keys and ferrules, no ring keys	40
9	Boxwood or grenadilla, 13 G.S. keys, 2 ring keys	38
10	Boxwood or grenadilla, 13 G.S. keys, no ring keys	33
11	Boxwood or grenadilla, 10 G.S. keys, genre 13 keys	29
12	Boxwood or grenadilla, 8 G.S. keys, genre 13 keys	27
13	Boxwood or grenadilla, 7 G.S. keys, genre 13 keys	26
14	Boxwood or grenadilla, 7 G.S. keys, T. genre 13 keys	22
15	Boxwood or grenadilla, 6 G.S. keys, T. genre 13 keys	20
16	Boxwood or grenadilla, 7 G.S. keys, with swab	17 50
17	Boxwood or grenadilla, 6 G.S. keys, with swab	16 50
18	Boxwood or grenadilla, 13 brass keys and ferrules, ring keys	33
19	Boxwood or grenadilla, 13 brass keys and ferrules, no ring keys	27
20	Boxwood or grenadilla, 10 brass keys and ferrules, no ring keys, 13 key systems	24
21	Boxwood or grenadilla, 8 brass keys and ferrules, no ring keys, 13 key systems	22
22	Boxwood or grenadilla, 7 brass keys and ferrules, no ring keys, 13 key systems	21
23	Boxwood or grenadilla, 7 brass keys and ferrules, no ring keys, 13 key systems	19
24	Boxwood or grenadilla, 6 brass keys and ferrules, no ring keys, 13 key systems	18
25	Boxwood or grenadilla, 7 brass keys and ferrules, with swab	14 50
26	Boxwood or grenadilla, 6 brass keys and ferrules, with swab	13
	Ebony or grenadilla, omitonique 15 G.S. keys, 5 G.S. ferrules	60

Albert system clarinet

G.S. body?, 14 keys G.S. keys, 2 G.S. key rings, double C key (?)	60

Large clarinets

Alto in E flat, grenadilla wood, 13 G.S. key	175
Bass in A flat, grenadilla wood, 13 G.S. key	200

Boehm system (both alto and bass?)	360

Skeletonized metal clarinets

	13 key model G.S.	G.S., silver plate	G.S., silver plate, heavily polished
	80	95	105
Buffet model			
	85	100	110
Albert model			
	90	105	115
14 key model	95	110	120
Boehm system			
	200	215	225

Oboes

	Ebony or grenadilla, Boehm system, G.S. keys	150
	Ebony or grenadilla, Triébert system, 15 keys G.S. keys, 3 G.S. key rings	110
29	Ebony or grenadilla, 13 silver keys and ferrules, 2 key rings	175
30	Ebony or grenadilla, 13 silver keys and ferrules, no key rings	140
31	Ebony or grenadilla, 10 silver keys and ferrules, no key rings	110
32	Ebony or grenadilla, 13 G.S. keys and ferrules, 2 key rings	75
33	Ebony or grenadilla, 13 G.S. keys and ferrules, no key rings	60
34	Ebony or grenadilla, 10 G.S. keys and ferrules, no key rings	55
35	B flat, boxwood, 13 G.S. keys, ring keys, ferrules	60
36	B flat, boxwood, 10 G.S. keys, no key rings	55
37	B flat, boxwood, 13 brass keys, no key rings	48
38	B flat, boxwood, 10 brass keys, no key rings	40
Burnished finish for an additional 1 25		

Skeletonized metal oboes

13 key model	100	110	120
Conservatory model 15 keys			
	120	130	150

Musettes

39	Boxwood, 7 G.S. keys	18
39	B flat, boxwood, 6 G.S. keys	16
40	B flat, boxwood, 4 G.S. keys	12
41	B flat, boxwood, 3 G.S. keys	10
42	B flat, boxwood, 2 G.S. keys	8
43	B flat, boxwood, 1 G.S. key	6

44	B flat, boxwood, no keys	5
45	B flat, boxwood, 6 brass keys	14
46	B flat, boxwood, 4 brass keys	10
47	B flat, boxwood, 3 brass keys	9 50
48	B flat, boxwood, 2 brass keys	6 50
49	B flat, boxwood, 1 brass key	5 50
50	B flat, boxwood, no keys	4 50

Boehm system flutes

	Grenadilla, silver keys and ferrules	290
	Grenadilla, G.S. keys and ferrules	200
	Silver body and keys	400
	G.S. body and keys	200
	G.S. body and keys	180
51	Ebony or grenadilla, silver keys and ferrules	225
52	Ebony or grenadilla, G.S. keys and ferrules	110

Non-Boehm system flutes

53	Ebony or grenadilla, 10 silver keys and ferrules	75
54	Ebony or grenadilla, 9 silver keys and ferrules	70
55	Ebony or grenadilla, 8 silver keys and ferrules	60
56	Ebony or grenadilla, 10 G.S. keys and ferrules	36
57	Ebony or grenadilla, 9 G.S. keys and ferrules	34
58	Ebony or grenadilla, 8 G.S. keys and ferrules	30
59	Ebony or grenadilla, 6 silver keys and ferrules	40
60	Ebony or grenadilla, 5 silver keys and ferrules	35
61	Ebony or grenadilla, 4 silver keys and ferrules	30
62	Ebony or grenadilla, 6 G.S. keys and ferrules	18
63	Ebony or grenadilla, 5 G.S. keys and ferrules	17
64	Ebony or grenadilla, 4 G.S. keys and ferrules	16
65	Ebony or grenadilla, 1 G.S. key and ferrules	11
66	Boxwood, 6 G.S. keys and ferrules	12
67	Boxwood, 5 G.S. keys and ferrules	11
68	Boxwood, 4 G.S. keys and ferrules	10
69	Boxwood, 1 G.S. key and ferrules	7
70	Boxwood, 1 G.S. key and ferrules	4
71	Boxwood, 6 brass keys and ferrules	11
72	Boxwood, 5 brass keys and ferrules	10
73	Boxwood, 4 brass keys and ferrules	9
74	Boxwood, 1 brass key and ferrules	3 50
75	Boxwood, 1 brass key and ferrules	3 50

Boehm system piccolos

76	Ebony or grenadilla, silver keys and ferrules	105
77	Ebony or grenadilla, G.S. keys and ferrules	80

Non-Boehm system piccolos

78	Ebony or grenadilla, 6 silver keys and ferrules	25
79	Ebony or grenadilla, 5 silver keys and ferrules	20
80	Ebony or grenadilla, 4 silver keys and ferrules	19
81	Ebony or grenadilla, 6 G.S. keys and ferrules	12
82	Ebony or grenadilla, 5 G.S. keys and ferrules	11
83	Ebony or grenadilla, 4 G.S. keys and ferrules	10
85	Boxwood or grenadilla, 6 G.S. keys and ferrules	11
86	Boxwood or grenadilla, 5 G.S. keys and ferrules	10
87	Boxwood or grenadilla, 4 G.S. keys and ferrules	9
88	Boxwood or grenadilla, 1 G.S. key and metal ferrules	4 50
89	Boxwood or grenadilla, 1 G.S. key and ferrules	2 50

90	Boxwood or grenadilla, 5 brass keys and ferrules	9
91	Boxwood or grenadilla, 4 brass keys and ferrules	8
92	Boxwood or grenadilla, 1 brass key and metal ferrules	3 50
93	Boxwood or grenadilla, 1 brass key and wood ferrules	2 25

The above instrument could be had with ivory or animal horn ferrules for the same prices

Boehm system flageolets

	Ebony or grenadilla, silver keys and mounts	150
	Ebony or grenadilla, G.S. keys and mounts	90

Non-Boehm system flageolets

94	Ebony or grenadilla, 5 silver keys and ferrules	35
95	Ebony or grenadilla, 4 silver keys and ferrules	31
96	Ebony or grenadilla, 3 silver keys and ferrules	22
96	B flat, ebony or grenadilla, 6 G.S. keys and ferrules	19
97	B flat, ebony or grenadilla, 5 G.S. keys and ferrules	17
98	B flat, ebony or grenadilla, 4 G.S. keys and ferrules	15 50
99	B flat, ebony or grenadilla, 3 G.S. keys and ferrules	11
100	B flat, ebony or grenadilla, 2 G.S. keys and ferrules	10
101	B flat, ebony or grenadilla, 1 G.S. key and ferrules	9
102	B flat, ebony or grenadilla, no key, G.S. ferrules	6 50
103	Boxwood, 5 brass keys	12
104	Boxwood, 4 brass keys	11
105	Boxwood, 3 brass keys	7
106	Boxwood, 2 brass keys	5 50
107	Boxwood, 1 brass key	3 25
108	Boxwood, no keys	2 25

The above instruments could be had with ivory ferrules for the same prices.

109	Boxwood, 3 brass keys, horn ferrules	6
110	Boxwood, 2 brass keys, horn ferrules	5

Extra fine instruments, with many accessories (swabs, lyres, etc.)

Clarinet, Boehm system, ebony or grenadilla, G.S. keys and mounts	130
Clarinet, omnitonic, ebony or grenadilla, G.S. keys and mounts	75
Clarinet, Buffet model, ebony or grenadilla, 13 G.S. keys, mounts, and 2 key rings	60
Clarinet, ebony or grenadilla, 13 G.S. keys, mounts, and 2 ring keys	52
Clarinet, ebony or grenadilla, 13 G.S. keys and mounts. No ring keys	48
Oboe, Boehm system, ebony or grenadilla, G.S. keys and mounts	175
Oboe, Triébert conservatoire model, ebony or grenadilla, 15 G.S. keys and 2 ring keys	120
Oboe, ebony or grenadilla, 13 G.S. keys and 2 ring keys	85
Boehm system flute, cylindrical model, ebony or grenadilla, G.S. keys and mounts	220
Boehm system flute, conical model, ebony or grenadilla, G.S. keys and mounts	125
Simple system flute, 10 G.S. keys and mounts	45
Simple system flute, 6 G.S. keys and mounts	22
Simple system flute, 5 G.S. keys and mounts	20
Boehm system piccolo, ebony or grenadilla, G.S. keys and mounts	105
Simple system piccolo, ebony or grenadilla, 6 G.S. keys and mounts	18
Simple system piccolo, ebony or grenadilla, 5 G.S. keys and mounts	16
Boehm system flageolet, ebony or grenadilla, G.S. keys and mounts	125
Flageolet, ebony or grenadilla, 7 G.S. keys	25
Flageolet, ebony or grenadilla, 6 G.S. keys	22
Flageolet, ebony or grenadilla, 5 G.S. keys	20

Cane flutes

Ebony or grenadilla, 5 G.S. keys, black varnish	40
Ebony or grenadilla, 1 G.S. key, black varnish	32

Cylindrical metal flutes. Note that the first two flutes are not offered with silver plated over G.S., extra polish, or in solid silver

	G.S.	Silver plate over G.S.	Silver plate over G.S., extra polish, solid silver
5 keys	28	36	40
7 keys	30	38 50	42 50
7 keys, Boehm system, C foot	38 50	46 50	50 50
8 keys, Boehm system, C foot	43	51	55
8 keys, Boehm system, C foot	45	56	60
9 keys, Boehm system, C foot	50	61	65
10 keys, Boehm system, C foot	55	66	70

12 keys, Boehm system, C foot	75	82	90
8 keys, American plateau model	12	18	20

Cylindrical metal piccolos

5 keys	22 50	30	33
6 keys	24 50	32 50	35 50
8 keys, C foot	32	40	43 50
10 keys, C foot	38	45	48
Student fife, municipal model, 1 key	7	10	11

Cylindrical Boehm system flutes

Perfection model, C foot	180	195	200	375
Perfection model, B foot	195	210	215	400

Rudolph Wurlitzer

NLI (p. 437-438) documents the history of this company and family. Rudolph Wurlitzer emigrated from Germany to Cincinnati in 1853 and became an importer of instruments. The company is not known for having made woodwind instruments.

Changes in the company's name can help date instruments. The following information is from p. 53 of a fragment of an undated Wurlitzer trade catalog owned by the author.

Simple system flutes in D

1714   Grenadilla, 6 nickel silver keys, rings, caps, tuning slide, cork joints
$12.50

1715   Grenadilla, 8 nickel silver keys, rings, caps, tuning slide, cork joints
$15.00

Wurlitzer-Meyer System flutes. Low pitch only

1779   Grenadilla, nickel silver keys $20.00

1782   Same as above but with 11 keys $25.00

1783   Same as above but with 13 keys $27.50

Half Boehm-Meyer System Flute. [This short-lived and comparatively rare flute type was an effort to combine the post and pillar key system and closed tone holes found on Boehm system flutes with the fingering system of the Meyer system flute. This hybrid looks very much like the Pratton system, and never gained much popularity.]

1809   Grenadilla, 14 covered keys C foot, cylinder bore, joint caps $60.00

Schwedler-Kruspe model flute

1820   Low B-flat, Grenadilla, keys and trimmings nickel silver, 14 keys, 3 of them having rubber rollers, conical bore, built in low pitch joint caps
$65.00

Metal Boehm-system flute, Luigi Vanotti

1830   Open G-sharp key, open tone holes $110.00

1831   Same as above, but with closed G-sharp key $110.00

1813   Wurlitzer-Boehm system flute, low pitch only, open or closed G-sharp, solid silver body, mechanism and trimmings, gold springs, made with tone holes drawn from the main tube and not soldered
$160.00

Bibliography

The following bibliography is intended to serve two purposes. First, it documents the resources that were used to prepare this book. Second, this bibliography is intended to form a beginning point for more in depth research. Critically important authors in their areas of expertise are subjectively included here. An exhaustive bibliography of reference material about woodwind instrument books could easily fill this book twice over. Trade catalogs housed in the Library of Congress or in the author's collection are so identified. Additional trade catalogs can often be found in major museums and sizable university music department libraries, often under the Library of Congress call number beginning with ML155 or occasionally within libraries special collections divisions, such as the University of Maryland's Howe Collection covering keyboard instruments, Oberlin's Herbert Goodkind collection covering bowed string instruments, or the National Music Museum (formerly the Shrine to Music Museum) covering a wide subject range.

General (general history of instruments, catalogs of collections, and auction houses and manufacturers' catalogs)

Baines, Anthony. *Woodwind Instruments and their History.* London: Faber & Faber, 1957. Essential reference book.

Banks, Margaret Downie and James W. Jordan. "C.G. Conn: The Man (1844-1931) and His Company (1874-1915)." *Journal of the American Musical Instrument Society* 14 (1988): 61-113.

Bauer, George. *Illustrated Catalogue.* Philadelphia: George Bauer, [c.1900]. [Trade catalog owned by the Library of Congress].

Borders, James M. *European and American Wind and Percussion Instruments: Catalogue of the Stearns Collection of Musical Instruments.* Ann Arbor, Michigan: University of Michigan, 1988.

Buegeleisen & Jacobson Inc. *Musical Merchandise. Catalog No. 160. 1930-1931.* New York: Buegeleisen & Jacobson; 1930. [Trade catalog owned by the author].

Carse, Adam. *Musical Wind Instruments. A History of the Wind Instrument used in European Orchestras and Wind-Bands from the later Middle Ages up to the Present time.* London: MacMillan and Co., Ltd., 1939. Essential reference book.

Couesnon & Cie. *Catalogue Pochette.* Paris: Couesnon & Cie, 1900. [Trade catalog, photocopy in author's collection]

Cundy-Bettoney. *Silva-Bet and Wood-Winds. The Artists' Choice.* Boston, Massachusetts: Cundy-Bettoney, 1932. [Trade catalog owned by the author].

Czechoslovak Music Co. *Musical Merchandise. Wholesale Catalogue No. 6.* New York: Czechoslovak Music Co., [c.1931]. Printed by J. Schmidt, Marneukirchen, Germany. [Trade catalog owned by the author].

Foote, J. Howard. *Catalogue of Musical Instruments, Strings, Musical Boxes, and General Musical Merchandise. Part I.* New York: J. Howard Foote, 1893. [Trade catalog, photocopy in author's collection].

Haynes, John C. & Co. *Catalogue.* Boston: John C. Haynes, 1889. [Trade catalog owned by the author].

Die Holzblasinstrumente im Oberösterreichischen Landesmuseum = Woodwind instruments of the Oberösterreichisches Landesmuseum. Linz: Das Museum, 1997.

Leblanc. G. *Wood Winds.* Paris and New York: G. Leblanc, [c.1922]. [Trade catalog owned by the author].

Lyon & Healy. *Lyon & Healy Campaign Edition.* Chicago: Lyon & Healy, 1896. [Trade catalog owned by the Library of Congress].

Klemm, G. & A. *Musikinstrumente und Saiten.* Markneukirchen: G. & A. Klemm, [c.1895]. [Trade catalog owned by the author].

Meinl, William. [Catalog. New York: William Meinl; c.1901]. [Trade catalog owned by the author].

Montague, Jeremy. *The World of Romantic & Modern Musical Instruments.* London: David & Charles, 1981.

The New Encyclopaedia Britannica. 15th Edition. Chicago: Encyclopaedia Britannica Inc., 2002.

Penzel, Mueller & Co. *Woodwind Instruments, 1925-6.* Long Island City: Penzel, Mueller & Co., 1925. [Trade catalog owned by the author].

Pepper, J.W. *Musical Times and Band Journal.* Philadelphia: J.W. Pepper; 1897, Vol. XV, No. 171. Christmas Number. [Trade catalog owned by the author].

Pepper, J.W. *Musical Times and Band Journal.* Philadelphia: J.W. Pepper; 1898, Vol. XV, No. 174. Decoration Day. [Trade catalog owned by the author].

Pollmann, August. *Catalogue K. 1894'95.* New York: August Pollmann, 1894. [Trade catalog owned by the author].

Rampone, Agostino. *Instrumenti Musicai/Catalogo N. 1223.* Milan: Agostino Rampone, [n.d.]. [Trade catalog, photocopy in author's collection].

Rudall, Carte & Co., Ltd. [Catalogue]. London: Rudall, Carte & Co., [n.d.]. [Trade catalog, photocopy in author's collection].

Slater, M. *M. Slater's Illustrated Catalogue and Net Price List of Musical Instruments and Trimmings for Bands and Orchestras.* New York: M. Slater; 1915. [Trade catalog owned by the author].

Thibouville, Les Files d'Eugène. *Prix Courant. Manufacture Generale d'Instruments de Musique.* Paris: Les Files d'Eugène Thibouville, 1893. [Trade catalog, photocopy in author's collection].

Voorhees, Jerry L. *The Development of Woodwind Fingering Systems in the Nineteenth and Twentieth Centuries.* Hammond, LA: Jerry L. Voorhees, 2003. Valuable reference.

Waterhouse, William. *The New Langwill Index. A Dictionary of Musical Wind-Instrument Makers and Inventors.* London: Tony Bingham, 1993. Essential reference book. An absolute must for serious collectors and researchers.

Zimmermann, August. *Catalogue of "Own Make" Musical Instruments. Brass, Woodwind and Percussion Instruments for Band Use.* Leipzig: August, Zimmermann, 1925. [Trade catalog owned by the author].

Young, Philip T. *4900 Historical Woodwind Instruments.* London: Tony Bingham, 1993. Only in-depth listing of known woodwind instruments from before the Baroque era.

Dictionaries

The New Grove Dictionary of Music and Musicians. Stanley Sadie, editor; executive editor, John Tyrrell. 2nd ed. New York: Grove, 2001. Essential reference book.

Bassoon

Jansen, Will. *The Bassoon, its History, Construction, Makers, Players and Music.* Buren, The Netherlands: Uitgeverij F. Knuf, [c.1978]. 5 v.

Kopp, James B. "Notes on the Bassoon in Seventeenth-Century France." *Journal of the American Musical Instrument Society* 17 (1991): 85-114. Addresses the complex terms for early bassoons.

Semmens, Richard. "The Bassoons in Marin Mersenne's *Harmonie Universelle* (1636)." *Journal of the American Musical Instrument Society* 10 (1984): 22-31. Discusses the complex use of terms related to the early bassoon.

See also Reed instruments, general (below)

Clarinet

Klosé, Hyacinthe. *Complete Method for the Clarinet.* London: Hawkes and Co., [n.d.]. English translation of book published by E. Gerard in Paris.

Rendall, F. Geoffrey. *The Clarinet. Some Notes on Its History and Construction.* London: Ernest Benn Ltd., New York: W. Norton & Co. Inc., 1954.

Rice, Albert R. *The Baroque Clarinet.* Oxford: Clarendon Press; New York: Oxford University Press, 1992.

Rice, Albert R. *The Clarinet in the Classical Period.* Oxford: Oxford University Press, 2003.

Van der Meer, John Henry. "The Typology and History of the Bass Clarinet." *Journal of the American Musical Instrument Society* 13 (1987): 65-88.

Flute

Bates, Philip. *The Flute.* London: Philip Bates, 1969. Page 140 contains a diagram of Siccama's one-keyed flute, and Siccama's adaptation of Boehm's rings, circa 1845. Page 141 contains a diagram of Siccama's 'Diatonic' flute, circa 1847.

Bowers, Jane. "New Light on the Development of the Transverse Flute between about 1650 and about 1770." *Journal of the American Musical Instrument Society* 3 (1977): 5-56. Discusses artwork depicting flutes and the few surviving instruments.

Coltman, John W. "Theobald Boehm and the Scale of the Modern Flute." *Journal of the American Musical Instrument Society* 9 (1983): 89-111.

Lenski, Karl and Karl Ventzke. *Das goldene Zeitalter des Flote. Die Boehmflote in Frankreich 1832-1932.* Celle, Germany: Moeck, 1992. Includes on page 215 the diagram of the 'Systeme Borne-Julliot' patent flute key design.

Powell, Ardal. *The Flute.* New Haven: Yale University Press, 2002.

Rockstro, Richard Shepherd. *A Treatise on the Construction the History and the Practice of the Flute, Including a Sketch of the Elements of Acoustics and Critical Notes of Sixty Celebrated Flute-Players.* Reprint: Buren, Netherlands: Fritz Knuf, 1986. Essential reference book.

Rudall, Carte & Co. *An Essay of the Construction of Flutes, ...* London: Rudall, Carte & Co., 1882.

Seyfrit, Michael. *Musical Instruments in the Dayton C. Miller Flute Collection at the Library of Congress. A Catalog. Volume 1: Recorders, Fifes, and Simple System Transverse Flutes of One Key.* Washington, D.C.: Library of Congress, 1982. Subsequent volumes are unlikely.

Solum, John. *The Early Flute. Early Music Series 15.* Oxford: Clarendon Press, 1992. Though mainly concerned with performance, this is a valuable book, especially for its discussion of historical publications, how to buy and maintain flutes, etc.

Spohr, Peter. "Some Early American Boehm Flutes." *Journal of the American Musical Instrument Society* 25 (1999): 5-30.

Toff, Nancy. *The Development of the Modern Flute.* New York: Taplinger Pub. Co., 1979. Paperback reprint Urbana, Illinois: University of Illinois Press, 1986. This book includes a very extensive discussion of variant flute systems, with illustrations. Essential reference book.

Vance, Stuart-Morgan. "Carte's Flute Patents of the Mid-Nineteenth Century and Related Systems." *Journal of the American Musical Instrument Society* 13 (1987): 89-106

Vanotti, Luigi. *Catalogo N. 14 ditta Luigi Vanotti.* Milano: Sala & Ceppetelli for Luigi Vanotti, circa 1920. [Trade catalog owned by the Library of Congress, Dayton Miller Flute Collection].

Welch, Christopher. *Six Lectures on the Recorder and other Flutes in Relation to Literature.* London: Oxford University Press, 1911. Page 102 includes illustrations of an 8-key simple system flute, and a bass recorder (not to scale). Page 90 includes illustrations of two German one-key baroque flutes. Page 25 includes an illustration of the elaborate yet rather awkward renaissance-era key commonly found on large recorders.

Recorder

See Welch, Christopher under flute category

Oboe

Adkins, Cecil. "William Milhouse and the English Classical Oboe." *Journal of the American Musical Instrument Society* 22 (1996): 42-88.

Adkins, Cecil. "The German Oboe in the Eighteenth Century." *Journal of the American Musical Instrument Society* 37 (2001): 5-47. This article discusses creating a mathematical system for identifying German oboes of the eighteenth century.

Adkins, Cecil. " Proportions and Architectural Motives in the Design of the Eighteenth-Century Oboe." *Journal of the American Musical Instrument Society* 25 (1999): 95-132. Page 128 includes a diagram of a baroque oboe with possibly the most detailed nomenclature for this instrument.

Halfpenny, Eric. "The English Two-and Three-Keyed Hautboy." *Galpin Society Journal* 2 (1949): 10-26.

Haynes, Bruce. *The Eloquent Oboe: A History of the Hautboy from 1640 to 1760.* Oxford University Press, 2001.

Other woodwind instruments

Joppig, Gunther. "Sarrusophone, Rothphone (Saxorusophone) and Reed Contrabass." *Journal of the American Musical Instrument Society* 12 (1986): 5-39.

Reed instruments, general

Heckel, Wilhelm. *Preisliste uber fine Instrumente.* Biebrich am Rhein, Germany: Wilhelm Heckel, [before 1930]. [Trade catalog owned by the Library of Congress, Dayton Miller Flute Collection].

Saxophone

Buescher. *The Origin of the Saxophone.* Elkhart, IN: Buescher, [c.1910]. [Trade catalog, incomplete photocopy in the author's collection].

Non-European woodwind instruments

Bryant, Wanda. "The Keyless Double Reed Aerophone: Its Usage, Construction, and Worldwide Distribution." *Journal of the American Musical Instrument Society* 16 (1990): 132-176. Discusses non-European instruments of the oboe family.

Payne, Richard W. "Indian Flutes of the Southwest." *Journal of the American Musical Instrument Society* 115 (1989): 5-31. This is one of a few works that discusses and illustrates the various types of flutes made by the indigenous people of the U.S.

Payne, Richard and John D. Hartley. "Pre-Columbian Flutes of Mesoamerica." *Journal of the American Musical Instrument Society* 18 (1992): 22-61.

Preservation and conservation

Watson, John R. "Historical Musical Instruments: A Claim to Use, an Obligation to Preserve." *Journal of the American Musical Instrument Society* 17 (1991): 69-82.

Flute and Clarinet Systems of the 18ᵗʰ, 19ᵗʰ, and 20ᵗʰ Centuries

The following list is a sampling of flute systems and approximate dates of usage, all of which are documented in Toff's book. Today, only the Boehm system is widely used.

Alberti, early 20ᵗʰ century
Barrett, late 19ᵗʰ century
Boehm, 1832
Boehm, (modern flute) 1847-present
Burghley, mid 19ᵗʰ century
Carte, late 19ᵗʰ century
Clinton, mid 19ᵗʰ century
Equisonant, mid 19ᵗʰ century
Giorgi, late 19ᵗʰ century
Gordon, early 19ᵗʰ century
McAvoy, early 20ᵗʰ century
Meyer (see simple system)
Murray, after 1948
Pratten Perfected, late 19ᵗʰ century
Radcliff, late 19ᵗʰ century
Rockstro, late 19ᵗʰ century
Schwedler, 19ᵗʰ century-early 20ᵗʰ century
Siccama, 19ᵗʰ century
Simple system late 19ᵗʰ century-circa 1930
Tulou, late 19ᵗʰ century
Ward, mid 19ᵗʰ century

This list of clarinet systems was generated from Rendall's *The Clarinet*. Of the systems, the Boehm system is still in use, and is the most commonly found system followed by the Albert system, which is rarely used today. Some of these systems are basically Boehm systems with varying levels of modification.

Albert, 19ᵗʰ-early 20th century
Alberti, patented 1914
Bärmann, 1860-early 20ᵗʰ century?
Barret, late 19ᵗʰ-early 20ᵗʰ century
Binda, patented 1884 (transposing clarinet)
Boehm, late 19ᵗʰ century-present
    Full Boehm, late 19ᵗʰ century-present
    Half Boehm, late 19ᵗʰ century-early 20ᵗʰ century
    Plain Boehm, late 19ᵗʰ century-present
Child key, patented 1924
Clinton-Boehm, 19ᵗʰ century
Müller system 19ᵗʰ-early 20ᵗʰ century
Oehler, late 19ᵗʰ century-early 20ᵗʰ century
Pupeschi, 19ᵗʰ century
Romer, late 19ᵗʰ century-early 20ᵗʰ century
Sax, mid 19ᵗʰ century-?
Schaffner, 20ᵗʰ century (also applied to oboes and flutes, *see* Rendall, p. 107)
Thirteen key, mid to late 19ᵗʰ century (also called Klosè or Klosè-Boehm system)

Appendix 3
Glossary of Terms

Albert system clarinets: a misnomer evidently first used in the U.S. to designate a Müller system clarinet, and is still used today. Albert was one of the most important late 1800s makers of these clarinets. Arguably, most of the 19th century clarinets were made in this key system. Later in the 19th century, this system often has roller keys for the right little finger. Albert system clarinets are also easily distinguished from Boehm system clarinets as Albert system clarinets do not have more than two keys for the right and for the left hand little fingers (see illustrations in the makers section for examples of both). Both systems use Post and pillars, causing some confusion.

Aluminum: a relatively soft silvery elemental metal rarely used to make anything prior to the late 19th century due to the extreme cost of production. After widespread electrification of the U.S. and Western Europe during the early 20th century, aluminum production increased. Aluminum, however, had limited uses in the production of woodwind instruments due to difficulties in working the metal.

Amateur instruments: instruments intended for use by non-professional musicians. This class of instruments has two subclasses within it. Dilettante instruments are instruments of exceptional quality, and artistry well above the needs of professional musicians. These instruments can be highly carved, or made of exotic shapes or materials, and were made for rich customers, such as nobility. These instruments sell quite well, and tend to be sought by museums, and very serious collectors. The second class of amateur instruments is the more common instruments of modest workmanship and/or material. These instruments are quite numerous, and of very modest value. See also student-quality instruments.

AMIS: The American Musical Instrument Society.

Antique instrument: according to United States importation laws, any object made at least one hundred years ago is an antique. Semi-antique instruments were made at least fifty years ago. An exact date for antiquities is somewhat subjective, but such objects surely date from before the Middle Ages. Examples of such woodwind instrument instruments, though rare, do exist, generally in the form of very simple bone flutes, but are seldom found outside of museums because of stringent laws restricting ownership.

Bell joint: the extreme end of the clarinets, oboes, and bassoons. This joint includes a flared end, and is often where the marker's mark, city of manufacture, and additional information is most likely to be found. Rare examples of highly ornamented clarinet and oboe bell joints made between circa 1600-1800 exist and are generally quite valuable, if only for their artistic quality. Clarinet and oboe bell joints prior to about 1800 were occasionally made with a flare it that changed its outward curve resulting in what appears to be a stepped flare.

Bocal: see crook.

Boehm key systems: a term used to describe three distinct (1831, 1832, and 1847) designs by Theobold Boehm to improve the intonation and playability of the flute. The 1847 system is the basis of the modern flute. The use of post and pillars, and ring keys, though not inventions of Boehm, were critical to his systems. This method for mounting keys was quickly applied to other instruments with varying success. The clarinet benefited from Boehm's research, and by the late 19th century, Boehm system clarinets replaced Albert system clarinets as the preferred system for professional quality clarinets. Two other features that characterize the Boehm system are a high degree of metal workmanship and a recalculation of the proper positioning of finger holes to improve intonation. A few Boehm system bassoons and oboes have been made, and are sought by collectors. See the bibliography of this book for further reading, especially in *NGDMM*, Second edition, and Nancy Toff's book.

Brass wind instruments: instruments that are made exclusively of metal, use a mouthpiece, and generally have valves. Examples include: trumpets, cornets, trombones, and tubas. As saxophones are made of brass, some people mistakenly assume that saxophones are brass wind instruments. Saxophones are woodwind instruments as they use a reed to produce sound, and have no valves only fingerholes. See woodwind instruments.

Bushing: the process of applying a material (generally ivory, bone, or metal) around the embouchure or finger holes to either limit or correct wear. Often, this bushing can be found on the thumb hole of recorders where the performer's thumb nail has cut into the wood requiring this repair. Additionally, many makers during the later part of the 19th century made flutes with bushings. Examples of pre-19th century instruments surely exist with bushings.

Conservatory model: a term generally found on French instruments beginning around the middle of the 1800s, especially appearing on flutes and oboes, and later on U.S.-made instruments. This term means that the instrument conforms to the specifications in use by the French Conservatoire for pre-professional instruments. These instruments are substantially better than student-grade instruments.

Cork setting device: a means for adjusting the position of the cork at the upper most end of a flute. Moving the cork can greatly affect the flute's playability and intonation. This device dates from at least 1780, and is generally a mark of a professional-quality instrument. Currently, this device is rarely encountered, as all-metal flutes generally do not have a cork in the end of the head joint.

Corps de rechange: an invention of the classic era that allowed a musician to exchange a joint of an instrument so that the musician could play in tune with other instruments that had different pitches. This concept disappeared around 1800, partly with the introduction of extended tuning slides built into flutes and clarinets, and because pitch more-or-less standardized on high pitch and low pitch. Instruments that retain their corps de rechange (generally 2 or 3) are sought by museums and serious collectors, and even anonymous examples tend to sell well.

Covered key: see plateau key.

Crook: a metal S-shaped tube used mainly on bassoons, also called a bocal. A double reed fits into one end. The crook is then fitted into the instrument. Pulling in and pushing out the crook allows the musician to tune the instrument. Bassoons that do not have their original crooks tend to sell for less than bassoons with crooks. However, professional musicians will often exchange crooks to improve tone quality. Missing crooks can be manufactured by specialists. Crooks are also found on large woodwind instruments of the Renaissance.

Cross fingering: also called forked fingering as tone holes were either covered or opened to produce chromatic pitches. Boehm and others devised many key systems to reduce the reliance upon cross fingerings that tended to produce notes that were not in tune or had a muffled tone color.

Ebonite: a synthetic material made of vulcanized rubber, invented by Mr. Goodyear around 1850. It is identified by having a slick black look on new instruments. On old instruments, it takes on a greenish-yellow look, as the sulfur begins to appear. The earliest known use of this material is a flute dated 1851 made by A.G. Badger. In the 1880s, makers began making clarinets from ebonite. Initially, ebonite was quite expensive and only used to make professional instruments. Later, presumably after Mr. Goodyear's patent expired, ebonite was used increasingly for student-quality instruments. One important feature of ebonite is that it does not split unless dropped.

Ebony: a black hardwood (Diospyros reticulate) that grows mainly along the west coast of Africa. The wood was evidently first used to make woodwind instruments in the last quarter of the 18th century. It is very dense and less prone to splitting than many other woods. When first used, only high-quality instruments were made from it because of its cost. In the 18th century, this changed, as mass deforestation began. Today, this wood is increasingly difficult to obtain, and some countries have altogether prohibited its export. So, once again, because of cost, ebony is used to make mainly high-quality woodwind instruments. During the late 19th century, methods were developed to dye other woods to simulate ebony, as was very common on pianos, and inexpensive woodwind instruments. Ebony also grows in Asia and is generally a light red color but with attractive black patterns, suggestive of smoke. It is used for ornamental turnings, but rarely for musical instruments.

Electroplating: Beginning around 1880, keys and instruments were being electroplated with either silver or G.S. The exact date is uncertain. Therefore, any woodwind instrument with plated keys probably dates from around the turn of the 20th century (or later), or else the keys were plated after leaving the factory. One complication here is that repairers often salvage keys from other instruments, or plate worn out keys. Therefore, dating woodwind instruments based upon metals used to make keys must be done with great care. The same can be said for dating instruments based upon techniques used to manufacturer keys. Even so, applying mass-produced cast or stamped keys to pre-1840 era instruments seems unlikely due to a general lack of uniformity common among hand-made instruments of the time.

Embouchure hole (on piccolos, fifes, and flutes): the hole into which the player blows. On early flutes (Renaissance through late Classical period), this hole was circular and relatively small, about the size of a finger hole. Around 1810, Nicholson devised a flute that had an oval embouchure hole (not his invention) that produced a louder tone than previous flutes. Some difference of opinion exists regarding when this development occurred, as many early flutes have evidently had their embouchure holes modified, most notably since the early 19th century. Many flutes made before this time have been modified, often reducing their value, but possibly improving intonation and playability. Some makers during the 19th century (especially later part) even produced embouchure holes that were almost rectangular in shape. During the early 19th century, embouchure holes were sometimes lined with ivory. During that century, embouchure holes were lined with ivory or later metal, all in order to limit the head joint from splitting.

Equisonant flute: A system devised by Clinton around 1855. Toff, p. 92-94, describes and illustrates this rather rare keys system that is based upon the simple system flute. It has ring keys for the top two fingers of the left hand and bottom two fingers of the right hand. All other keys are plateau keys.

Ethnographic instruments: instruments designed for use by musicians in non-western music settings, often professional quality. Examples are generally of higher quality than tourist-quality instruments. See also folk instruments.

Experimental instruments: instruments that were made to help identify/solve a specific problem, such as a means to correct poor intonation or eliminate an awkward fingering. Some experimental instruments were incomplete, consisting only of a joint, not a complete instrument. All experimental instruments should be examined by a specialist to determine value, as some instruments can sell for considerable amounts.

Ferrule: a ring that is found between joints, as on a fife, piccolo, flute, clarinet, etc. The purpose of this ring is to strengthen the wood and reduce wear. Ferrules can be made of metal, ivory, bone, or animal horn. Ivory ferrules became popular during the classical period, and eventually died out around 1900. Some makers are known to have elaborately engraved the silver or gold ferrules of expensive instruments. Metal ferrules came into wide use mid 19th century. See also mounts.

Flageolet: a wind instrument consisting of a small pipe blown at the end like a whistle, the tones of which are sweet, shrill, and clear. It is an instrument of but little power, hence is used chiefly as a solo instrument. It forms a good accompaniment for the voice. Its scale is nearly the same as that of a D flute. The above description is from "Musical Cyclopedia: Principles of Music," Boston: James Loring, 1834, p. 151-2. Double flageolets were also made, especially by Bainbridge. Boehm system flageolets were produced for a limited time during the late 19th century and are relatively rare, as they never really became popular. A fair number of flageolets were also made in France. Many late 18th century flageolets have ivory or bone finger studs, which some experts call teets.

Finger numbering system: the method of abbreviating fingers that operate keys. As an example, L1 means the index finger of the left hand. This method is used in many of the more technical books about woodwind instruments.

Folk instruments: instruments made for use by non-professional musicians. These instruments can occasionally have value. The tone quality of these instruments varies, as does their workmanship. They are of superior quality to tourist-grade instruments. They are intended to be played, while tourist-grade instruments are intended to be art objects, at best. See also ethnographic instruments.

G.S.: see German silver.

German silver: the term has been used without much precision. Some makers used the term German silver (G.S.), while others use nickel silver, or both. Less commonly, makers might use the term white bronze or simply white metal. G.S. is generally composed of copper, nickel, and zinc. It is has no silver, but has a dull silvery look. G.S. was introduced some time in the early 19ᵗʰ century, but was first developed many years earlier in China. Most keys and many instruments made during the late 19ᵗʰ century were plated with G.S. G.S. was often electroplated over brass keys beginning in the 19ᵗʰ century. Over time, G.S. can take on a green appearance especially if exposed for some time to humidity.

H.P.: high pitch. Generally, this means an instrument that plays at about A=440. Such instruments are quite usable today, as they sound in tune with current instruments. However, some high pitch instruments can be pitched well above 440 and have therefore limited use. This mark came into use around 1880 and persisted until about 1930. See makers mark.

Head joint: the upper most segment of a flute, piccolo, or fife (assuming it has more than one joint). This is the joint that contains the embouchure hole. Head joints have evolved over the centuries (conical, parabolic, and cylindrical, with or without tuning slides, etc). Some makers, especially late in the 19ᵗʰ century, also made head joints with a device to adjust the cork at the very top of the head joint in order to improve playability and intonation. Metal tuning slides came into wide use later in the 19ᵗʰ century. Some makers even made only head joints, as their tone quality could greatly influence the overall sound of a flute. Late in the 19ᵗʰ century, makers began to produce metal-lined head joints for flutes in order to reduce cracking. Examples were made as early as the first half of the 19ᵗʰ century. Dating an instrument by its head joint is problematical, especially as antique instruments can be found that are composites. Such composite instruments are of modest value. Modern Boehm system flutes with head joints made by prominent makers are an exception, but are out of the time range of this book. See Improved head joint, Embouchure hole, and Reform flute.

Improved head joint: a metal head joint made of metal that Schwedler developed prior to 1900. It was used on piccolos, but mainly flutes. The head joint is distinctive by being much thinner than most head joints. It is also thinner than the flute body. Most makers experimented with this design. A typical feature of this head joint is a built-up lip plate to facilitate playing. Often the lip plate is made of ebonite with two pearl buttons on either side of the embouchure. Many improved head joints are decorated with ornate turnings. This head joint disappeared soon after the beginning of the 20ᵗʰ century. Flutes with such head joints cannot be dated simply by this head joint, as such parts can easily be swapped with other flutes. See also Reform flute.

Ivory: the tusk of an elephant. Recently, imitation ivory has been produced with some success. However, it is still only available in thin sheets. Some makers of historic reproductions have been experimenting with this material. The best quality imitation ivory has the color of ivory, and a similar grain pattern. Ivory was first used to make wind instruments possibly as far back as ancient Egypt. In Europe, ivory gained popularity during the Renaissance, and continued to be used into the early 20ᵗʰ century, in ever decreasing quantity. Bone is often confused with ivory. Bone, however, has small black thread-like lines where veins formed in the bone. Bone is also closer to a chalk white rather than a creamy white. Bone

was often used on instruments of lesser quality. Mastodon and walrus ivory have not been used to any great extent by makers.

Joint: a section of the body of an instrument that detaches from another section. Traditionally, modern flutes, clarinets, and oboes have three joints: the head joint, the middle joint, and the foot joint. Bassoons have four joints: a wing joint, butt joint, middle joint (or long joint), and bell joint. Some flutes have four joints. Piccolos have two joints. Fifes generally have one or possibly two joints.

Key: this term has two meanings that can cause some confusion. An instrument is generally pitched in a key, such as A, B flat, C, D, E flat, or F for clarinets. The pitch of a clarinet is sometimes stamped on it to avoid confusion. The second definition is for the mechanical device used to cover a tone hole. Various key systems exist. Keys are often the main means for dating an instrument. Flat keys made from a single piece of metal are the earliest forms, and are usually pinned into a raised block or ornamental turning. The earliest known keys probably appeared on large recorders and shawms during the late Renaissance, and are fulcrum and lever key (see illustration, page 19). This key persisted on one key flutes until about 1930. Tromlitz (c.1780) invented a key that is attached to a post and pillar at one end. The touch piece is in the middle of the key, and the pad is at the end opposite the post. Potter (London, cx.1800) invented a key that consists of a pewter plug that fits into a metal tone hole. This key enjoyed wide use during most of the 19ᵗʰ century for non-Boehm system flutes. Other early keys were constructed by soldering a round or cup shape onto a metal shaft and were called salt spoon keys. Keys can be very plain or highly ornamented. Late in the 19ᵗʰ century, French factories were set up that only made keys. These keys are characterized by having a thin metal needle-like feature on the top of the key. The keys were mass produced by various mechanical techniques. While they usually lacked the elegance and refinement of hand-made keys, they were considerably less expensive and greatly reduced the price of instruments, thereby helping to popularize many instruments, including the saxophone that was invented at this time. Late in the 19ᵗʰ century, the roller key was invented. It gained considerable popularity on Meyer system flutes, Albert system clarinets, and saxophones. Some makers offered, upon special order, roller keys on Boehm system flutes. The roller key is easily identified by having a smaller tube that allows a finger to easily roll between adjacent keys. See also post and pillar, and plateau keys.

Key system: a term used to describe the mechanical keys on an instrument. Often the name of the inventor is applied, such as Boehm system, Meyer system, simple system, etc. Key systems are generally made of G.S. or brass plated with G.S. or some other metal.

Kinder orchestra instruments: instruments designed for use by young children in a structured setting, such as kindergarten, or elementary school. These are generally of higher quality than toy instruments, as they are intended to produce sounds.

L.P.: low pitch. Generally, this means an instrument that plays at about A=435. Such instruments are of limited value for performance today as they sound quite flat. Some performers are forming ensembles to play period 19ᵗʰ century music and are once again using these instruments. This mark came into use around 1880 and persisted until about 1930. See makers mark.

Labium: the integral reed structure found on recorders, flageolets, penny whistles, and ocarinas. Instruments that have heavily reworked labium are generally looked upon with some question about tone quality, and playability.

Lip plate: found on flutes, piccolos, and a few metal fifes made towards the end of the 19th century. This is a built-up section of the head joint that includes the embouchure hole. This plate allows the player to rest the instrument more easily against the player's lower lip and chin. One possible reason for the popularization of the lip plate was that during the later part of the 19th century, anecdotal reports appeared in *The Musical Courier* and surely other trade publications stating that cocuswood could cause allergic reactions to the skin, presumably due to the natural chemicals in the wood. All modern flutes and piccolos have lip plates. Any Boehm system flute that does not have a lip plate was most likely made before the 20th century.

Lyre: an attachment to wind instruments (often with a wing nut) invented some time during the mid 19th century that allowed music to be held in viewable position during parades. No reference books seem to discuss the introduction of this attachment. The lyre was never successfully applied to flutes or piccolos. It was applied to clarinets, often either mounted to the instrument, or to a removable ferrule. Almost all late 19th century brass wind instruments have an attachment for a lyre. Many thousands of lyres exist, and no collector has been identified who is collecting this small but significant attachment.

Makers mark: a mark either burned into the wooden body of an instrument, engraved into the metal body, or less commonly applied to an instrument as an ornamental plaque. Much confusion exists about marks on instruments. Some names are indeed makers' names. Other names are the name of the company that sold the instrument. For all wind instruments, the best information source is *The New Langwill Index*. If a name is not found in this book, chances are that the name is that of a retail company, not a maker. In a few cases, the name of an owner has been found on instruments. Note that L.P. (low pitch) and H.P. (high pitch) are not makers' marks. They indicate the relative pitch of an instrument. These designations were widely used between the late 19th and early 20th centuries. Exact dates of first/last uses are uncertain.

Meyer system flutes: also called simple system. Designed by Albert, but manufactured in quantity by Meyer of Hanover. Many flutes exist with the mark "Nach Meyer" indicating the Meyer flute system, but not the maker.

Mounts: all the materials applied to an instrument, such as keys, ferrules. Some authors also include the wooden blocks in which the keys are attached. For this book, mounts are defined as being all metal attachments, not including keys and key mechanisms. This generally means ferrules, metal bushings, and protective rings at the ends of instruments are classed as a subset of mounts.

Musette: a term used at various times for two distinct instruments. The first musette was a small bagpipe popular among the French autocracy just before the French revolution. Examples are rare and museum pieces. The second instrument was a double reed instrument that evidently was first produced in France in the 19th century, and was introduced into the U.S. at the Chicago World's Fair of 1893. The instrument was loud and much despised by professional musicians because of its raucous tone, and intonation problems. Examples were still being offered for sale into the 1920s, and are not rare.

Museum-quality instruments: instruments of some intrinsic importance, either because of workmanship, ornamentation, history, uniqueness or significant design. Museum quality instruments often sell for top dollar even in poor condition, but not always. Experimental instruments are often classed as museum pieces due to their potential historic significance. Additionally, any instrument over three hundred years old (Renaissance period or earlier) is a probable museum piece.

Penny whistle: also called tin fife. This instrument was made of sheet tin, and sold for only a penny. Because it is not tunable, and has a modest price, this instrument should be classed as a toy. However, it has become a staple of Celtic music. Examples are plentiful and are not actively collected by museums.

Plateau key: also called covered key. This is a key that does not have a hole in it, as opposed to an open hole or ring key. Plateau keys came into being after the Boehm 1847 improvements began gaining acceptance, and can be found on virtually all woodwinds, especially the larger woodwind instruments such as saxophones, as the finger cannot reach to cover the tone hole, or the tone hole is simply too large to be covered by a finger or both. Such keys invariably rest upon an outward extension of the tone hole. Without such an alteration, tone holes were recessed. Initially, these extensions to the tube were manufactured by welding small pieces of metal to the instrument. Towards the end of the 19th century, C.G. Conn and others developed methods for manufacturing the extensions by pulling the metal from the wall of the instrument. This created a seamless extension, and improved the instruments' quality. Rare examples of instruments exist with square covered keys, and are of high value. Clarinets and oboes with plateau keys are uncommon but not especially rare.

Post and pillar: a means for mounting key systems onto an instrument rather than mounting a key into a block of wood, as was common on pre-1800 instruments. A metal post is screwed or soldered to the body of an instrument. Then, metal rods can be attached to the post forming a lever. Keys and pads are then attached either to a lever or the rod, thereby allowing pressure put upon a key to be transferred some distance to cover a tone hole that might otherwise not be reachable. This technology was popularized by Boehm. Most woodwinds use some form of post and pillar (with or without rods). The use of wood blocks to mount keys persisted late into the 19th century on inexpensive clarinets.

Professional-quality instruments: instruments that were made for use by professional musicians. These instruments are usually of the highest workmanship possible. These instruments tend to also be museum pieces. See also Conservatory model. The term is not generally applied to non-western instruments intended for use by professional musicians, reflecting a Eurocentric attitude, especially instruments made during the colonial period.

Reform flute: Toff (p. 83-84) describes this variation of a simple flute and states that around 1855 Maximilian Schwedler developed the flute with a cone-shaped wind way. Friedrich Wilhelm Kruspe manufactured this flute. The flute has also been called the Schwedler-Kruspe flute. Schwedler developed this flute to retain the unique tone quality of the German simple system flute but incorporated some of Boehm's improvements. On flutes with metal heads and wood bodies, one of the more identifiable features of this flute is a metal head joint with a lip plate and a relatively narrow diameter head joint compared to the rest of the flute. Early reform flutes often have ring keys. Later examples often have covered keys. The instrument was still being manufactured into the 1930s by Moritz Max Monnig. See Improved head joint.

Ring key: a key that is a very thin ring of metal. When pressed, the key will cause a key pad to cover a tone hole some distance away, while also allowing the finger itself to cover a tone hole directly under the key ring. Key rings came into wide use with the developments of Boehm. Though not invented by Boehm, the ring key was an important feature of his early flute key systems. On flutes, two ring keys occasionally appear together and are called brill keys. Key rings can still be found on clarinets, and bassoons. Key rings were still available on flutes as late as circa 1930 and sold by A.G. Klemm of Germany, and surely other companies. This key is rarely found on new flutes.

Rollers: a small tube of metal or other material in the touch key that allows the finger to easily slide between adjacent keys. Rollers have been applied to the keys of almost all woodwind instruments to help fingers more easily slide between adjacent keys. Rollers have been used since the early 19th century. Instruments with such keys were probably made after about 1820, unless they have been altered. A 13-key clarinet in C, made by Jean Jacques Baumann of Paris circa 1825, contains rollers, and is an early example, assuming it has not been altered. The instrument is based on Ivan Müller's clarinet but with the addition of rollers for L4 and R5 now in the Fiske Museum. Late in the 19th century, rollers were offered as special features on Albert system clarinets, and Meyer system flutes.

Signal horn: an instrument invented in the late 19th century and, though resembling a brass instrument, is a woodwind instrument, as it has internal metal reeds. The reeds are brought into contact with an air column by use of what appear to be Perinet valve. Signal horns have been made in various sizes and may have as few as one bell or as many as seven. The instrument is very loud, and raucous. At various times, this instrument was offered in trade publications as a car horn. This instrument would be very suitable for use in George Gershwin's "An American in Paris" for the taxi part. The instrument also has a strong association with Nazi youth bands, as it is quite easy to play. The instrument was still being made as late as the 1980s.

Simple system: a term applied mainly to flutes and piccolos to identify a fingering system that did not rely to any great extent upon complex mechanical key systems. Cross fingering was used with limited success to produce chromatic notes. Simple system flutes were developed during the Middle Ages (though the term more specifically is applied to 19th century flutes). This type of flute was still being sold as late as 1930, and has been revised by makers of historical reproductions.

Spatula: that part of a non-ring key that is touched by the finger. The name is derived from the shape. This is also called touch key.

Student-quality instruments: instruments designed often for use by students deciding upon seriously taking up an instrument. These instruments are of inferior design/workmanship/material compared to professional-quality or even conserva-tory instruments. Examples of student-quality instruments are so numerous as to be usable for firewood for many years, without any fear of ever running out of examples. On any online auction website, at least 70 percent of all the antique instruments are of student quality.

Tenon: the term means to hold. For musical instruments, it is an extension of material that allows two joints to fit together while often allowing the musician to slightly pull apart the two joints in order to tune the instrument. Metal tenon joints date from about the middle of the 19th century. All wooden tenon joints can either be lined with cork (a late 19th century invention) or thread wound around the male part of the joint. This is the style that developed during the Renaissance. In the 19th century, less expensive instruments were sold with string joints, but could be easily lined with cork.

Tin fife: see penny whistle

Tone hole: the hole that is covered either by a finger or the pad of a key to change the pitch of an instrument. See also undercut tone hole.

Touch key: the part of a key that is designed to be put in motion by the pressure of a finger. Also called spatula by some experts.

Tourist-grade instruments: instruments whose design is based upon non-western instruments, and made exclusively for sale to tourists. These instruments have very modest value, if any. Tone quality is secondary to decorative value, and many such examples are utterly unplayable. Occasionally in the past, ethnographic instruments have been sold as tourist-grade instruments. Tourist-grade instruments are generally small enough to fit into luggage.

Toy instruments: instruments intended for use by children for unstructured play. Tone quality of this class of instruments is secondary to decoration. These instruments are almost always smaller than professional-quality instruments, and often have non-functional parts.

Undercut tone hole: a tone hole that has been modified to improve intonation, and tone color. Wood on the inside of the instrument is removed around the tone hole. This delicate modification probably dates from the Renaissance. It has also been applied to the embouchure hole on flutes. Improper undercutting can significantly reduce the playability of an instrument and should only be done by professionals or to student-grade instruments.

White bronze: also known as German silver and nickel silver.

Woodwind instruments: instruments that traditionally were made of wood, but as of the mid 19th century, have also been made of metal, glass, ceramic, plastic, and other man-made materials. These instruments use reeds rather than a cup-shaped mouthpiece. The flute has what is called by experts an air reed rather than a cane reed as is found on most woodwind instruments. Examples include: piccolo, flute, clarinet, oboe, bassoon, and saxophone. Non-experts listing instruments online often describe woodwind instruments as having valves. With the exception of the signal horn, valves are only found on brass wind instruments such as trumpets. Woodwind instruments have finger holes without keys or else finger holes with key(s).

A Brief List of Trade Names and Companies that Sold these Brands

Often, instruments are only marked with a trade name. While these trade names can be helpful in identifying a maker, little research has been conducted into this area. So, this list is by no means complete. The information provided here was obtained from musical instrument trade catalogs, *NLI*, and the Internet. Trade names appear first, followed by the company most likely to have made the instrument, followed by the company most likely to have sold the instrument, and, when known, the quality of the instruments is listed last. Trade names followed by an asterisk (*) were found via the Internet, and the information is uncertain. While it is clear from this list that most trade names were used for student grade instruments, trade names were also applied to some professional instruments.

The idea of using trade names seems to have begun in the late 1800s. Little research has been conducted into this important subject. Trade names have been reused by different makers. Identifying an instrument's maker just by the trade name, therefore, can be problematic. Identifying companies that made unmarked instruments could require a lifetime of research. *NLI* is the most definitive source of information about this complex subject. Based upon surviving trade catalogs and instruments, one might cautiously speculate either a Germanic origin, or in the case where a retailer had a strong relationship with a maker, the maker might have provided unsigned instruments to a retailer.

Abbott: Buegeleisen & Jacobson, student and professional grade
American*: Harry Pedler Co.
American Artist*: Progressive Musical Instrument Corp.
American Climax: J.W. Pepper
American Conservatory*: Lyon & Healy
American Excelsior*: Berteling
American Favorite: J.W. Pepper
American Standard*: H.N. White, student grade
American Star*: Lyon & Healy
Aristocrat*: professional quality Buescher sax, later student grade instrument by Selmer
Armee: Couesnon & Cie
Artist*: Blessing, sold by Sears, Penzel & Mueller, professional quality
Atlas*: C. Ullmann
Bandmaster*: Elkhart Band Instrument Co.
Barbieri, F.*: student grade clarinets by Selmer
Beau Ideal: Lyon & Healy (brass only?)
Belmont* (*NLI* states that this trade name is Beaumont): C. Meisel
Beaumont: medium grade metal clarinets
Boston Wonder: Cundy-Bettoney, intermediate grade, Buegeleisen & Jacobson
Buisson, F.*: V. Kohlert's Sohne

Bundy: H. & A. Selmer, student quality
Champion: C.G. Conn, student grade
Cadet: Cundy-Bettoney, student grade
Campaign: J.W. Pepper, medium grade?
Campus: C.G. Conn, student grade
Cavalier: C.G. Conn, student grade
Challenge: J. Howard Foote
Challenger: C.G. Conn, student grade
Classroom: C.G. Conn, student grade
Collegiate*: Holton, student grade
Conqueror: J.W. Pepper
Connqueor: C.G. Conn (especially brass instruments)
Continental Colonial*: C.G. Conn, student grade
Coudet & Cie: Buegeleisen & Jacobson
Dubois, Henry*: unknown, French, student grade
Excelsior: J.W. Pepper, medium grade
Feuillard, A.*: Progressive Musical Instrument Corp.
Fontaine, A.: unknown, [French?], student grade
Frat: C.G. Conn, student grade
Gladiator: H.N. White, student grade
Greville: made in Paris, medium grade
Imperial: J.W. Pepper
Laube, P.X.: Cundy-Bettoney, student grade
Liberty: C.G. Conn
Madelon: Cundy-Bettoney, student grade
Monopole: Couesnon & Cie
National: Couesnon & Cie
New Symphony: C.G. Conn, professional quality
New Wonder: C.G. Conn, professional quality
Noblet, D.: Leblanc, student grade
Opera: Couesnon & Cie
Own make: [Though technically not a trade name, this phrase was used by many companies to indicate that a line of instruments was made to the company's specifications by a second company whose identity was rarely provided.]
Pan American: C.G. Conn, student grade
Premier*: Harry Pedler Co., student grade
Premier: J.W. Pepper, highest grade
Rainbow: C.G. Conn, student grade
Renab: George Bauer, student grade?
Specialty: J.W. Pepper, superior grade
Standard: C.G. Conn, student grade
Surprise: J.W. Pepper
Regent*: Ohio Band Instrument, student grade
Silver King: H.N. White
Silver Tone: Blessing, sold by Sears, student grade
Silvertone: sold by Montgomery Ward Inc., student grade
Soloiste*: unknown, U.S.?, student grade
Standard: J.W. Pepper
Super Artist: Blessing, sold by Sears, student grade
Supertone: sold by Sears, student grade

Three Star: Cundy-Bettoney, student grade
Truetone*: Buescher, professional grade
Twentieth Century: J.W. Pepper
Universel: Couesnon & Cie
U.S. Army Standard: Cundy-Bettoney, student grade
Scolaires: Couesnon & Cie

Silva-Bet: Cundy-Bettoney, professional quality
Superior: made in Elkhart, Indiana, professional quality
Superior*: Paul Dupree, student grade
Symphony: R. Wurlitzer, student grade
Victory*: Oliver Ditson, student grade

A Brief List of Companies Who Sold Instruments By Known Makers

This list of instrument makers whose works were sold by other companies is by no means complete. Makers' names are listed first, following by the company known to have sold instruments from the maker. Again, this is a subject that has been little researched. While some of the makers are U.S., all of the retailers are U.S., because I have had access to mainly catalogs from U.S. companies. No information exists in this list about instruments from U.S. makers being sold by European companies, which will give a false sense of U.S. musical instrument exports.

Albert, Eugene (mainly clarinets): J. Howard Foote

Albert, Jacque (mainly clarinets): J. Howard Foote

Berteling (all woodwinds): Pollmann, Martin Brothers

Bertin, Charles (flute): J. Howard Foote

Buffet (all woodwinds): George Bauer, J. Howard Foote

Buffet, Crampon & Co. (all woodwinds): George Bauer, Haynes, Lyon & Healy, Buegeleisen & Jacobson

Clark (tin whistles): George Bauer, Pollmann, J.W. Pepper, William Meinl & Son

Cloos, George (mainly fifes, piccolos, and flutes): George Bauer, Haynes, Lyon & Healy, Pollmann

Crosby, Walter (fifes): Lyon & Healy

Delaure, F. & Co. (flutes and clarinets): Lyon & Healy

Evette & Schaeffer (all woodwinds): George Bauer, Lyon & Healy, J.W. Pepper

Fiehn, J.H. (ocarinas): J. Howard Foote, Lyon & Healy, William Meinl & Son

Godfroy (all woodwinds): J. Howard Foote

Gunkel, Henry (mainly clarinets): Haynes

Hilleron, A. (clarinets): Haynes

Jaubert, F. & Co.: Lyon & Healy (brass only?)

V. Kohlert and Sons (all woodwinds): Buegeleisen & Jacobson, Czechoslovak Music Co.

Mathieu, Ch. (ocarinas): Lyon & Healy, Pollmann

Martin frères (all woodwinds): J. Howard Foote, Martin Brothers, Pollmann, Buegeleisen & Jacobson

Meyer, H.F. (flutes): J. Howard Foote, Lyon & Healy

Mouchel, C.A.: J.W. Pepper

Thibouville-Lamy: J.W. Pepper

Biographical List of Woodwind Makers and Manufacturers

The following information is based upon information found in *NLI*, museum catalogs, trade catalogs, and catalogs from auction houses. Instrument makers' names that appear here are provided based upon the likelihood of encountering such instruments in the antique market and museums. Many highly important makers are not listed here. Consult the *NLI* for an extensive list of trade names.

Abbott Premier. Probably a trade name for an unidentified French company. Appeared on clarinets made of wood, metal (skeletonized), or ebonite, saxophones, and brasswinds. Instruments imported by Buegeleisen & Jacobson. All clarinets made with either Albert or Boehm system.

Adler. 1820-present. Markneukirchen. Family of makers known for bassoons and other woodwinds. One of the earliest companies to make student-grade recorders. Bassoons are better quality. Co-produced the octavin.

Albert. 19th century. Bruxelles. Family of makers, best known for developing the "Albert system" clarinet.

Almenräder, Carl. 1786-1843. Cöln, Mainz, Biebrich, and Darmstadt. Known for high-grade bassoons. Instruments found in museums. Briefly in business with J.A. Heckel.

Astor. 1778?-1831? London. The workshop produced woodwind instruments and keyboard instruments. This is the family that became rich in the U.S. trading in furs, and eventually owned the Waldorf Astoria hotel. Instruments are of good to better quality, and many can be found in museums. Occasionally, instruments can be found for sale.

Badger, Alfred G. 1814?-1892. Buffalo, Newark, and New York City. Innovative and highly important U.S. maker. Introduced the Boehm system flute in the U.S. Also first to use ebonite to make flutes. One ebonite flute dated 1858 is known. Rarely found even in museums, as few instruments survive.

Bainbridge, William. 1803?-1834. London. Well known for his flageolets, especially complicated double and triple flageolets. Instruments found in museums, and occasionally for sale.

Bercioux, Eugène. 1820?-1914. Paris, New York City. Mainly known for his clarinets. Did not make a large amount of instruments, but instruments do appear from time to time. Not well represented in museum collections.

Berteling, Theodore. 1821-1890. Boston, New York City. In 1905, Carl Fischer bought the company. Name ended in 1920. Berteling is best known for his flutes, and clarinets (both Boehm and Albert system). Made professional and student quality instruments. Made German system bassoons. In undated catalog added to the Library of Congress in 1915, improved Berteling key system woodwinds were offered for sale.

Besson. 1837-present. Paris, London. Complex history for this company. Many Besson instruments (woodwind and brasswind) exist in museums and on the market. Instruments range from professional to student in quality. See *NLI* p. 29-30. French-made instruments are prized more highly than U.K. instruments. Gustave Auguste made important improvement to Boehm's post and axel system for flutes.

Bettoney, Harry. 1867-1953. Boston. The company is best known as Cundy-Bettoney. Clarinets from this maker range from professional to student in quality. Evidently developed Bettonite, a type of ebonite, which was used to make flutes and clarinets as late as 1930.

Boehm (Böhm), Theobald Friedrich. 1794-1881. München. Began making instruments in 1810. Studied jewelry making, and applied those skills to woodwind instruments. Developed new fingering system in 1832 (few makers copied this design; instruments are rare and generally valuable), and 1843 (the system for which his is still famous and upon which most modern flutes and clarinets are now made). Instruments by Boehm, Boehm and Greve, and Boehm and Mendler are in many museums, and are quite rare. Forgeries might exist. Few instruments exist outside of museums.

Bohland & Fuchs. 1870-1945. Graslitz. Primarily known for their brasswinds and also saxophones. Not well represented in museums.

Boosey. 1851-1930. London. Complex history; see *NLI* p. 40. Later became Boosey & Hawkes. Made professional grade woodwinds. Baines (p. 137) states that this company made the first Clinton model clarinet. The company also made many student-grade instruments still common today. Also worked with many important musical instrument innovators (brasswind and woodwind).

Boston Wonder. Trade name used by a number of companies. Buegeleisen & Jacobson included metal clarinets, flutes, and piccolos in its 1930-1931 catalog.

Bressan, Peter. 1663-1730. London. Trained in Paris. Very well represented in museums. Instruments are rarely found outside of museums. Young reported only 51 recorders and 3 flutes.

Bruno, Charles. 1834-? New York City. After moving to the U.S. in 1868 from Saxony, Bruno established a company importing instruments. Placed various trade names such as Lafayette, Paris; Perfackton; Perfection; Henry Pourcelle, Paris; La Vesta; and Vocotone.

Buescher. 1894-present? Elkhart, Indiana. *NLI* p. 48-49 states that Ferdinand August Buescher was the first person in the U.S. to make saxophones. Also made many student-grade band instruments still plentiful today. As late as 1930, the company sold instruments made by Kohlert. Buescher preferred to make saxophones with soldered sockets rather than drawn sockets (tone holes).

Buffet. Paris. Family of makers. Instruments range in quality from professional to student. Clarinets stamped Buffet Paris, or Buffet Crampon Paris generally sell for more than instruments made in London or the U.S. See also Buffet-Crampon.

Buffet-Crampon. Circa 1839-present? France. Complex history; company changed its name to Evette & Schaeffer. Made many band instruments; especially known for clarinets, oboes, bassoons, and saxophones (student and professional quality). Best quality instruments can be found in museums.

Cahusac. 1800s-1816. London. Family of makers. Woodwind instruments from this family are well represented in museums and private collections. Some instruments approach being works of art. Difficult to distinguish who made what instrument as all members of the family used similar stamps.

Catlin, Gerorge. 1778-1850. Hartford, Ct., Philadelphia. *NLI* p. 59 quotes Eliason as being the first important U.S. maker of woodwind instruments, though he was not the first. Instruments are in major museums and a few private collections.

Clementi & Co. 1802-1831. London. Made all manner of instruments, especially pianos, harps, and also woodwind instruments. All instruments are well represented in museums and a few private collections.

Clinton, John. 1810-1864. London. Inventor who made significant contributions to the development of the flute. Also made flutes under the name Clinton & Co. Instruments are not common and appear in museums.

Cloos, George. Late 19th century. New York City. Little information exists, but the company is known for its clarinets and flutes. Instruments appear from time to time. Not well represented in museums. Many U.S. companies sold his instruments.

Conn, Charles Gerhard. 1879-present. Primarily Elkhart, Indiana. Complex history, see *NLI* p. 69-70 and Banks (listed in the bibliography). Made all manner of wind and stringed instruments. Detested imported instruments and companies who imported them. Even made reed organs. Best known for student-grade instruments; the company also made professional-grade instruments. The early brass instruments are especially collected and appear in U.S. museums. The largest collection of Conn instruments and related papers are in the Shrine to Music Museum in South Dakota. Only a few other museums have a significant number of this company's woodwind instruments.

Couesnon. 1882-present. Paris. Quite possibly the largest maker of wind instruments. The company used trade names to indicate quality of instruments. From the highest to the lowest quality, they are: Modèle Monopole, Opéra HN, Armée BN, Armée GNM, National BO, Universel CGO, and Modèle SO.

Cundy-Bettoney Co. See Bettoney.

D'Almaine & Co. 1834-1867. London. Mainly a keyboard maker, but woodwind instruments of medium quality appear from time to time. The company changed names several times, thereby helping to date instruments. See *NLI* (p. 80).

Denner. 17th and 18th centuries. Nürnberg. Family of woodwind makers. Complex history (see *NLI* p. 86-87); known to have made all manner of woodwinds, especially recorders and flutes. Instruments are very rarely found outside of museums.

Dolmetsch, Arnold. 1858-1940. Haslemere. One of the first to revive the art of making antique instruments; especially know for keyboards, viole da gamba, and recorders. Instruments are still available from the company. Woodwinds range from very high quality to student quality.

Dorus, Vincent Joseph van Steenkiste. 1812-1896. Paris. Inventor of important improvement to the Boehm system flute. Not a maker, but worked with Louis Lot.

Evette & Schaeffer. 1885-1929. Paris. Successor to Buffet-Crampon. Woodwind instrument making company, many instruments available on the antique market. Represented in some museums, partly due to the considerable number of innovations the company produced.

Firth, Hall & Pond. 1839-1967. Litchfield, Connecticut. Complex history. One of the first companies in the U.S. to make woodwind instruments. Also Firth & Hall (New York City); Firth Pond & Co. (New York City); and Firth, Son & Co. Instruments are found in museums mainly due to the early date of this company. Instruments are not particularly inspired work.

Fischer, Carl. 1872-present. New York City. Though this name appears on many instruments, *NLI* states that the company made no instruments. Primarily imported student-grade instruments from Germany. The company has been and continues to be a major U.S. music publisher.

Franciolini, Leopoldo. 1879-c.1925. Firenze. The most famous forger of antique musical instruments of all types. Also known for selling authentic instruments. Any instrument that passed through his hands must be considered carefully, but might be authentic.

Gautrot anié. 1845-c.1884. Many of this company's instruments still exist in private hands. Made both woodwind and brasswind instruments. Made instruments that other makers stamped with their own mark, such as Tulou, Kretzschmann, and Thibouville & Fils. Brasswind instruments were generally of cheap construction. Better quality instruments were also made.

Gemeinhardt. Early 20th century-present. Mainly Elkhart, Indiana. This family is best known for student-quality flutes of acceptable quality. Few instruments are antique and are therefore outside the time range of this book.

Giorgi, Carlo Tommaso. 1856-1953. Firenze. Inventor of an interesting vertical flute that was manufactured by Wallis. Made no instruments personally.

Glier. 19th century to present. Mainly Klingenthal. Complex history. Members of the family made brasswind and woodwind instruments. C.G. Glier was a major exporter from Markneukirchen before World War II.

Godfroy. 18th–19th century. Mainly La Couture, Paris. Complex history. Instruments from Clair Godfroy aîné are not rare, but range in quality. Some are found in museums.

Grenser. 18th-19th century. Mainly Thüringer, and Dresden. Complex history. Family members made all manner of woodwind instruments. Many instruments made by this family appear in museum collections.

Haka, Richard. Circa 1661-1699? Amsterdam. Instruments by this maker are some of the most highly ornamented woodwind instruments ever made. Few, if any instruments exist outside of museums.

Hall, William & Son. See Firth, Hall and Pond.

Haseneier. Circa 1835-1944. Coblenz. Family of makers best known for improvements to the bassoon, including a Boehm-system bassoon. Heckel made improvements to his design.

Haynes, George Winfield. 1886-1930. Boston, Los Angeles, and New York. Haynes is primarily known as a flute maker, and moved around frequently. This helps date his instruments. Instruments are of good quality.

Haynes, William Sherman. 1900-present. Boston. In 1888, he joined his brother (see above) to make flutes. Instruments from this company are found in many professional orchestras, and some museums, especially the Dayton C. Miller Flute Collection. The company is still in operation making professional-quality instruments.

Heckel. 19th-20th century. Adorf, and Biebrich. Family of woodwind makers. Wilhelm Hermann Heckel is best known of the family. He developed the Heckelphone, and made many improvements to the bassoon; many of these improvements are still in use. Instruments appear in professional orchestras and museums. The company is still making instruments, including Heckelphones and bassoons, but not some of the more unusual instruments, such as the German shalmai.

Hopkins, Asa. Early 19th century. Connecticut. One of the earliest significant makers of clarinets, flutes, etc. in the U.S. Hopkins clarinets are sought by collectors. Sold company to Firth, Hall and Pond.

Hotteterre. 17th-18th century. La Couture. One of the most prominent makers of woodwinds, members of this family helped to transform the oboe, flute, and recorder from their Renaissance forms. Instruments are probably found mainly in museums.

Jehring, Julius. Circa 1820-1905. Germany. *NLI* (p. 2) states he invented the octavin. The instrument was however patented by him and Adler.

Klemm and Bro. 1819-circa 1880. Philadelphia. Mainly known for brasswind instruments, but a few woodwinds appear with the name. See also G. & A. Klemm.

Klemm, G. & A. 19th century. Markneukirchen, Leipzig. George and August Klemm were a major exporter of instruments to the Americas (North and South). Klemm of Philadelphia is possibly related, and made quality brass and woodwind instruments.

Kohlert. 19th and early 20th centuries. Mainly based in Graslitz. Many members of the family made instruments ranging from student to professional quality. Many simple system flutes exist. Kohlert's Söhne made a wide range of woodwind instruments, some quite rare, including a quarter-tone clarinet. Most instruments in circulation are student quality. However, V. Kohlert's Sons (surely the same company) made professional quality instruments into the early 1930s.

Kruspe. 19th and 20th centuries. Mainly based in Thüingen, and Erfurt. Makers of student and professional quality woodwind and brasswind instruments, many of which are readily available today. Friedrich Kruspe, based in Erfurt, studied under Boehm and also Triébert, and his instruments often show great innovation. This was one of the most innovative instrument makers.

Laurent, Claude. 1805-1848. Paris. One of the most important French makers of woodwind instruments in the first half of the 19th century. He was especially known for his glass flutes. Most quality instruments are in museums. Instruments made of wood are still available. Instruments made of metal and glass are rare and usually expensive.

Linton. Circa 1925-present. Elkhart, Indiana. Maker of student-grade and professional grade oboes and bassoons. The company is currently making instruments using cast plastic. Most instruments in circulation are student quality.

Longman & Broderip. 1776-1798. London. Makers of woodwind and brasswind instruments. Made a wide range of instruments, some of which are in museums.

Lorée, F. 1881-present. Paris. Maker of professional quality French oboes.

Lot. 18th century-present. Mainly La Couture. Woodwinds appear in many museums. Louis Lot was one of the premiere makers of flutes in France. Metal flutes made by him are still sought by professional players. He is especially known for quality metal flute head joints.

Lyon & Healy. 1864-present. Chicago. Began as retail company selling to most of the western U.S. Many brasswind instruments stamped with company name. Only known to have made instruments during the early 20th century. Currently only making professional-grade concert harps.

Mahillon, C. 1836-1935. Bruxelles. Made a range of brasswind and woodwind instruments, which are well represented in major museum collections. Instruments still can be found. Very influential maker, and curator of musical instruments at the Brussels Conservatory.

Martin frères. Circa 1840-1927. Paris. Many instruments of average to better quality still exist in the antique market. Some instruments appear in museums. Also signed instruments with the trade name "Coudet."

Meacham. 1810-1832. Hartford, Connecticut. One of the earliest U.S. makers of quality woodwind instruments. Instruments can still be found occasionally. Used a stamp with a unicorn that looks much like Astor's stamp. Instruments appear in many museums.

Milhouse. 18th and 19th centuries. Mainly Newark, and London. Many instruments by this family exist in major museums, especially flutes and bassoons. The family made a range of instruments.

Meinl, William & Sons. 1899 to circa 1921. New York. The company was one of only a few U.S. makers of quality flutes, clarinets, etc. at this time. Instruments are not common, because the company was in business for such a short time. Instruments are generally of good quality.

Monzani. Circa 1807-1829. London. Maker of high-quality woodwind instruments, especially flutes. Instruments are in museums. The company often marked instruments "Monzani and Hill."

Nicholson, Charles. Early part of the 19th century. London. He designed a flute with large finger holes and oval embouchure hole. The sound is quite loud, though the tone quality is a bit airy. Boehm was much impressed with Nicholson's improvements, and was inspired to begin making his own improvements. Instruments by Nicholson are quite rare. He worked with many prominent English makers. Many pre-Nicholson flutes have been modified to incorporate his ideas. Such instruments, though potentially valuable, are less so because of the modifications.

Noblet. 19th century. Mainly in and around Paris. Makers of mainly student-quality instruments. Many of these instruments are still available, few are in museums.

Oberlender. 18th century. Mainly in Nürnberg. Clearly one of the most important makers of woodwind instruments. Instruments appear in many museums. Not generally found in private collections.

Orsi. Milan, Italy. The company is still active, making an unusual assortment of instruments that few, if any companies are still making, including sarrousophones, and metal clarinets.

Penzel and Mueller (Penzel & Müller). 1899-? New York City. Well known for professional-quality clarinets. Flutes from this maker are not as desired as clarinets. Stamped instruments with trade names: Laubin, Prufer, W.S. Richards.

Pepper, J.W. 1976-1919. Philadelphia. The company stopped making instruments in 1919, but continued to import instruments, and is today a major music publisher. Instruments range from student to professional. Not well represented in museum collections. Research is still underway to unravel the company's complex history, and the often libelous altercations with Mr. Charles G. Conn.

Potter. 18th and 19th centuries. Mainly London. Many instruments of various quality still exist in the antique market. George Potter & Co. worked until about 1839 in Aldership, and is credited by some with inventing the pewter plug key used by many other English flute makers during the early 19th century.

Pottgeisser, Heinrich Wilhelm Theodor. 1766-1829. Elberfeld. Mainly an inventor; made early flute improvements. Influential mainly through his writings.

Powell, Vern Q. 1926-present? Boston. Well respected maker of professional quality flutes, still used by professionals.

Qualtz, Johann Joachim. 1697-1773. Worked in and around Berlin. Composer, flute player, teacher, and inventor. Only a handful of this maker's flutes exist, and they are museum pieces of the highest quality.

Selmer. Paris, London, and Elkhart, Indiana (?). 18??-present. Family of primarily woodwind makers. Later also made brass wind instruments. The company made all range of wind instruments, from professional to student. Professional instruments are well made instruments. Bundy is the company's student line. These instruments rarely sell for as much as a new student instrument. The company made improvements to Boehm's system still in use today by this company.

Triébert. Paris. 1810-early 1900s. Family of makers, begun by George Ludwig Wilhelm Triébert. His oboes were, during his life, considered some of the finest French oboes. His family also made very high grade bassoons, and made significant improvements to both instruments. Instruments from this family are well represented in museums.

Tulou, Jean-Louis. Paris. Mid 19th century. Flute teacher at the French Conservatoire, instrument maker, innovator, composer, etc. Made important improvements to the flute, and is known for elegant hand-made keys. In 1915, Couesnon bought the company. Instruments are found in museums.

Ward, Cornelius. London. 19th century. *NLI* first mentions him as the foreman for Monzani. He then went on to work with many important English instrument makers. In 1842, he patented his own flute system, and was known for high quality workmanship. His instruments are found in public and private collections, and are not very common.

Price List of Instruments

A Guide Organized by Names of Makers and Manufacturers

The following appendix consists of a price list gathered from various musical instrument auction catalogs. Abbreviations and dates indicate the auction catalogs. When catalogs do not include page numbers, item numbers found are substituted instead. This list is alphabetical by maker or manufacturer's name. Unsigned works are listed first as "[Anon.]" with whatever information can be inferred based upon construction style placed within brackets. N.L. means no location was provided in the catalog. N.D. means no date was provided. Because few instruments can clearly be dated, "ca." is not placed within brackets, unless associated with an anonymous instrument. Specific dates and date ranges are provided based upon stylistic features, and additional features that appear upon instruments. Descriptions of instruments and prices are listed in U.S. dollars unless otherwise indicated. The prices listed here are merely intended to assist in determining approximate valuations. Not all catalogs are as complete in their description as one would like. No citations for groups of instruments appear in this list. No information is provided in this list from on-line auctions, as obtaining information after the auction has ended is problematic. Information has been abridged from the original catalogs. So, the reader is advised to consult the catalogs if questions remain.

If one compares prices provided here with new instruments, one will observe that, with the exception of instruments made before 1700, new instruments sell for more than most antique woodwind instruments of similar make. However, ornate instruments or instruments made of rare material such as gold or ivory will always command top prices, depending upon condition. In other words, with the exception of a few significant makers listed in Appendix 5, historic instruments rarely sell for as much as newly-constructed professional-quality instruments of comparable design and workmanship. This fact should cause one to carefully consider speculating in this field. If one wishes to explore the prices of modern used woodwind instruments at auction, the Sotheby's 1995 catalog is suggested.

Format of Citations
Makers' name. Country, date. Publication, date, page number. Instrument type and key system. Description beginning with material of body, keys, additional information. Missing date follows each item type. Estimated or realized price.

Abbreviations Used
B&B: Butterfield & Butterfield (name has subsequently been changed to Bonham and Butterfield)
BSL: W & F C Bonham & Sons Ltd.
CHR: Christie's
HVN: Hotel des Ventes de Neuilly
PHI: Phillips
SKI: Skinner Inc.
STH: Sotheby's

[Anon. Austrian, late 18th century]. Clarinet in C. Boxwood, stamped I.S., 5 brass keys, a 6th key later addition, horn mounts. STH, 1987, p. 38. Estimate 300-400 pounds.
[Anon. Dresden, first quarter of the 19th century]. Flute. Boxwood, 5 brass keys, salt spoon cups, ivory mounts, 2 corps de rechange. STH, 1987, p. 52. Estimate 300-500 pounds.
[Anon. Dresden, first quarter of the 19th century]. Flute in F. Boxwood, 1 brass key, ivory mounts. STH, 1995, p. 48. Estimate 400-600 pounds.
[Anon. Dutch?, first quarter of the 18th century]. Treble recorder. Ivory, with turned decoration on the bell, head joint tenon socket and above the labium. The lower end of the middle joint has been replaced. STH, 1995, p. 49. Estimate 500-700 pounds.
[Anon. England, c.1770]. Flute-flageolet. Rosewood, 6 nickel keys with nickel mounts, and flageolet head joint. STH, 1995, p. 12. Estimate 100-150 pounds.
[Anon. England, c.1830.] Clarinet in C. Boxwood, 6 brass keys with ivory mounts. STH, 1992, p. 195. Estimate 250-350 pounds.
[Anon. England, c.1930]. Swanee-sax or slide sax. B&B, 1998, p. 12. Metal body. Estimate $2,250-2,500.
[Anon. England, first quarter of the 19th century]. Flute. Boxwood, 8 silver keys, ivory mounts, the C and C sharp keys with pewter plugs. STH, 1987, p. 13. Estimate 400-600 pounds.
[Anon. England, late 18th century?]. Alto recorder in the style of Stanesby. Boxwood, no keys or mounts. STH, 1992, p. 200. Estimate 1,000-2,000 pounds.
[Anon. England, n.d.]. Piccolo. Rosewood with nickel mounts, stamped "London Improved" D. BSL, 1993, number 32. Estimate 50-60 pounds.
[Anon. England, n.d.]. Pitch pipe. Mahogany, and plunger marked with notes for middle C up to C. STH, 1995, p. 20. Estimate 100-200 pounds.
[Anon. England, second half of the 18th century]. Flute. Ivory, 1 silver key. STH, 1994, p. 12. Estimate 600-800 pounds.
[Anon. English?, mid-18th century]. Flute. Ivory, 1 silver key, replaced end cap. STH, 1987, p. 3. Estimate 500-1,000 pounds.
[Anon. English, c.1820]. Double flageolet. Boxwood, 5 silver keys, ivory mounts, 2 shut off keys, replaced mouthpiece. STH, 1987, p. 8. Estimate 100-200 pounds.
[Anon. English, early 19th century]. Fife in B flat. Boxwood, 1 brass key, and mounts. STH, 1987, p. 41. Estimate 40-60 pounds.
[Anon. English, n.d.]. Band flute in B flat. Cocus, 1 G.S. key and mounts, stamped "London Improved Military Band Flute". STH, 1987, p. 28. Estimate 10-15 pounds.
[Anon. English, second quarter of the 19th century]. Piccolo. Ivory, 6 silver keys, salt spoon cups, silver mounts. STH, 1987, p. 27. Estimate 300-500 pounds.
Anon. English, early 19th century]. Fife in E flat. Boxwood, 1 brass key, and mounts. STH, 1987, p. 41. Estimate 60-80 pounds.
[Anon. European, early 19th century]. Flute. Boxwood, 1 brass key, salt spoon cup, horn mounts. STH, 1987, p. 320. Estimate 40-60 pounds.

[Anon. France, 19th century]. Flageolet. Ivory. HVN, 1998, number 523. Estimate 800-1,000 Francs.

[Anon. France?, n.d.]. Fife. [Wood?], 1 key. BSL, 1993, number 32. Estimate 30-50 pounds.

[Anon. French, c.1825]. Flute. Ebony, 5 silver keys, ivory mounts. STH, 1987, p. 33. Estimate 150-250 pounds.

[Anon. French, early 19th century]. Flute. Fruitwood, 1 brass key, ivory mounts, 1 G.S. replacement. STH, 1987, p. 320. Estimate 20-30 pounds.

[Anon. French?, 18th century]. Flageolet. Ivory, 4 finger holes and 2 thumb holes. STH, 2001, p. 131. Estimate 5,000-8,000 pounds.

[Anon. French?, third quarter of the 18th century]. Flute. Ivory, 1 silver key. STH, 1995, p. 46. Estimate 2,000-3,000 pounds.

[Anon. German, c.1820]. Clarinet in B flat and A. Boxwood, 6 brass keys, alternate corps de rechange, the B and C sharp keys extendable, horn mounts. STH, 1987, p. 57. Estimate 600-800 pounds.

[Anon. German, c.1860]. Walking stick flute. Fruitwood, 1 wood key, 2 G.S. mounts, the knob with inset circular ivory plaque. STH, 1987, p. 3. Estimate 800-1,000 pounds.

[Anon. German, c.1880]. Conical Boehm system flute. Black wood, G.S. keys and mounts, B foot. STH, 1995, p. 48. Estimate 200-300 pounds.

[Anon. German, c.1900]. Clarinet in E flat. Stained boxwood, 14 G.S. keys, mounts, and 4 rings. STH, 1987, p. 33. Estimate 100-200 pounds.

[Anon. German, c.1900]. Flute. Boxwood, 6 brass keys and brass mounts, 1 missing. STH, 1987, p. 29. Estimate 20-30 pounds.

[Anon. German, c.1900]. Flute. Cocus, 6 G.S. keys and mounts. STH, 1987, p. 9. Estimate 30-40 pounds.

[Anon. German, c.1900]. Piccolo. Ebony, 6 G.S. keys, ivory head joint. STH, 1987, p. 9. Estimate 20-30 pounds.

[Anon. German, early 19th century]. Flute. Ebony, 6 silver keys, ivory mounts, a 7th key missing. STH, 1987, p. 3. Estimate 200-300 pounds.

[Anon. German, early 20th century]. Flute. Ebony, 12 nickel keys and mounts, 1 missing. STH, 1987, p. 36. Estimate 50-80 pounds.

[Anon. German, first half of 19th century]. Flute. Ivory, stamped Martin Metzler, London, 6 nickel keys set in removable ivory saddles, nickel mounts. STH, 1987, p. 42. Estimate 800-1,000 pounds.

[Anon. German, first half of the 19th century]. Flute. Ivory, 1 silver key, unmounted. STH, 1987, p. 42. Estimate 700-1,000 pounds.

[Anon. German, first quarter of the 19th century]. Flute. Boxwood, 5 brass keys, the F key with alternative touch piece, ivory mounts, 1 later horn replacement. STH, 1987, p. 28. Estimate 100-200 pounds.

[Anon. German, late 18th century.]. Flute. Boxwood, 4 brass keys, horn mounts, lacking end cap and G sharp touch piece. STH, 1987, p. 9. Estimate 500-700 pounds.

[Anon. German, late 19th century]. Clarinet in B flat. Boxwood, 13 brass keys and mounts. STH, 1987, p. 320. Estimate 150-200 pounds.

[Anon. German, late 19th century]. Flute. Boxwood, 12 silver keys, low B key, the B, C, and C sharp keys with pewter plugs, the right forefinger touch piece for the B flat key missing, silver mounts. STH, 1987, p. 36. Estimate 30-50 pounds.

[Anon. German, late 19th century]. Flute. Ebony, 12 G.S. keys and mounts, B foot, ivory head joint with raised lip guide. STH, 1987, p. 28. Estimate 60-80 pounds.

[Anon. German, n.d.]. Flute. Ebony, 13 G.S. keys, B foot. STH, 1987, p. 3. Estimate 30-50 pounds.

[Anon. German, stamped Dresden on the lower middle joint, c.1800]. Clarinet in B flat. Boxwood, 5 brass keys, horn mounts. STH, 1987, p. 23. Estimate 600-800 pounds.

[Anon. Germany or Austria, late 19th century]. Oboe. Black wood, 13 nickel silver keys and mounts. STH, 1997 p. 31. Estimate 600-800 pounds.

[Anon. Germany or Austria, n.d.]. Walking stick flute. Boxwood, 1 brass key, ivory and horn mounts. STH, 1994, p. 14. Estimate 1,000-1,500 pounds.

[Anon. Germany, 18th century]. Flute. Ivory, 1 silver key, 4 joints, HVN, 1998, 532. Estimate 20,000-25,000 Francs.

[Anon. Germany, c.1800]. Flute. Black wood, 1 brass key, bone mounts, and 3 corps de rechange. STH, 1995, p. 11. Estimate 600-800 pounds.

[Anon. Germany, c.1860]. Clarinet in b flat. Boxwood, 12 brass keys, horn mounts. STH, 1995, p. 20. Estimate 500-700 pounds.

[Anon. Germany, c.1860]. Pitch pipe. Boxwood, 1 horn mount, able to produce g1 to a2. STH, 1995, p. 48. Estimate 250-350 pounds. 300-500 pounds.

[Anon. Germany, first half of the 18th century]. Treble recorder. Boxwood, highly carved with faces, dolphins, and acanthus leaves. STH, 1997, p. 40. Estimate 5,000-7,000 pounds.

[Anon. Germany, first quarter of the 19th century]. Flute. Boxwood, 1 brass key, horn mounts. STH, 1995, p. 20. Estimate 300-500 pounds.

[Anon. Germany, mid 18th century]. Oboe. Boxwood, 3 brass keys (twin G holes), ivory mounts. STH, 1994, p. 30. Estimate 2,000-4,000 pounds.

[Anon. Germany?, c.1800]. Flute. Black wood, 1 silver key, ivory and horn mounts. STH, 1995, p. 49. Estimate 500-700 pounds.

[Anon. London, c.1860]. Flute. John Clinton model, nickel silver tube, keys on post and pillars. STH, 1995, p. 41. Estimate 500-700 pounds.

[Anon. n.d., third quarter of 19th century]. Flute. African black wood, G.S. keys. STH, 1987, p. 30. Estimate 20-30 pounds.

[Anon. n.l., c.1875]. Simple system flute. Cocus, G.S. keys and mounts [no key number provided]. STH, 1987, p. 30-50 pounds.

[Anon. n.l., first half of the 17th century]. Recorder in G. Fruitwood, twinned G holes, and later ivory beak. STH, 1997, p. 36. Estimate 3,000-6,000 pounds.

[Anon. n.l., late 18th century]. Flute in F. 1 brass key. STH, 1985, number 158. Estimate $200-400.

[Anon. n.l., late 19th century]. Flute. Cocus, 12 G.S. keys and mounts, B foot, metal head joint. STH, 1987, p. 28. Estimate 40-60 pounds.

[Anon. n.l., modern]. Renaissance style flute. Fruitwood, no keys. STH, 1987, p. 29. Estimate 30-50 pounds.

[Anon. n.l., n.d.]. Flute. 1 key. B&B, 1998, number 17. Estimate 20-30 pounds.

[Anon. Probably English, mid-19th century]. Clarinet in B flat. Boxwood, 6 brass keys, horn and ivory mounts. STH, 1987, p. 33. Estimate 150-200 pounds.

[Anon. probably German, early 19th century]. Flute. Boxwood, 4 brass keys, horn mounts. STH, 1987, p. 29. Estimate 70-100 pounds.

[Anon. South Germany, early 19th century]. Flute. Boxwood, 1 brass key, horn mounts, and 3 corps de rechange. STH, 1992, p. 191. Estimate 400-600 pounds.

[Anon. Swiss?, 18th century]. Bassoon. Pearwood, 1 brass key, repaired with butterfly touch piece stamped I. IR, brass mounts, engraved P.H.T., 3 missing. STH, 1987, p. 38. Estimate 800-1,200 pounds.

[Anon. Switzerland? 16th century]. Flute. Nut wood, no key, missing mounts, single body, sold with multiple flute case. [This is one of only a very few wood wind instruments from the Renaissance that survives, and is not in a museum. This fact accounts for the high estimate despite the instrument being damaged beyond repair.] STH, 1995, p. 18. Estimate 15,000-20,000 pounds.

[Anon. Vienna, c.1820]. Clarinet in B flat. Boxwood, 6 brass keys, horn mounts. STH, 1995, p. 49. Estimate 500-700 pounds.

[Anon.] France, early 20th century. Mellosax. Nickel-plated tubing and side mechanism, 2 octave keys. STH, 1999, p. 39. Realized 300 pounds.

[Anon.]. Hungary, early 20th century. Tarogato. STH, 1992, p. 194. [Unidentified wood body.] Estimate 500-700 pounds.

[Thibouville, Jérôme?] France, 19th century. Musette. Ebony, 2 joints, no keys. HVN, 1998, number 536. Estimate 1,000-1,500 Francs

Albert, E.J. Brussels, first quarter of the 20th century. Pair of Clinton system clarinets in B flat and A. Black wood, G.S. keys and mounts. STH, 1994, p. 11. Estimate 600-800 pounds.

Albert. Belgium, [n.d.] Boehm system flute. Silver, signature on plaque. HVN, 1998, number 525. Estimate 6,000-8,000 Francs.

Alrichter, Julius. Frankfurt, c.1920. Flute. Black wood, 9 G.S. keys and mounts. STH, 1987, p. 8. Estimate 50-70 pounds.

Amlingue, Michel. Paris, c.1800. Flute. Boxwood, 1 silver key, 3 corps de rechange. STH, 1987, p. 18. Estimate 1,500-2,000 pounds.

Amlingue, Michel. Paris, first quarter of the 19th century. Clarinet in B flat and A. Boxwood, 10 brass keys, ivory mounts, 2 sets of joints, 1 stamped B, the other stamped A. STH, 1987, p. 38. Estimate 800-1,200 pounds.

Ammann, Ulrich. Alt St. Johann, c.1830. Clarinet in B flat. Boxwood, 5 brass keys, ivory and horn mounts. The bell is equipped with a brass sliding vent hole key set in an ivory plate giving the alternative note C and B. STH, 1997, p. 36. Estimate 600-800 pounds.

Anciuti, Joannes Maria. Milan, 1715. Sopranino recorder. Ivory, no keys or mounts. STH, 1994, p. 14. Estimate 8,000-12,000 pounds.

Angot & Dubreuil. Ivry-la-Bataille, c.1875. Flute. Boxwood, 5 G.S. keys and mounts. STH, 1987, p. 34. Estimate 100-150 pounds.

Apelberg, Peter. Copenhagen, last quarter of the 18th century. Composite flute. Ebony, 1 silver key, ivory mounts. Only the head joint was made by Apelberg. STH, 1995, p. 46. Estimate 300-400 pounds.

Asté, Jean-Hilaire. This maker is also known as Halary. Paris, c.1820. Bass clarinet in C. Metal, 6 brass keys, raised finger holes. STH, 1987. p. 46. Estimate 500-800 pounds.

Astor & Co. London, c.1800. Clarinet in C. Boxwood, 8 brass keys, ivory mounts. STH, 1987, p. 18. Estimate 250-250 pounds.

Astor & Co. London, c.1820. Flute. Boxwood, 8 silver keys and ivory mounts, and pewter plugs. Includes alternate flageolet head joint. STH, 1999, p. 43. Realized 550 pounds.

Astor & Co. London, late 18th century. Flute. Ivory, 4 silver keys (2 replaced). STH, 1994, p. 14. Estimate 800-1,200 pounds.

Astor, G. & Co. London, c.1800. Flute. Boxwood, 6 silver keys, salt spoon cups, the C and C sharp with pewter plugs, ivory mounts. STH, 1987, p. 40. Estimate 250-400 pounds.

Astor, George. London, c.1800. Straight topped Oboe. Boxwood, 2 silver keys, ivory mounts. STH, 1997, p. 34. Estimate 1,800-2,500 pounds.

Bahram. Graslitz, late quarter of the 18th century. Oboe. Boxwood, 2 brass keys. STH, 1995, p. 12. Estimate 1,500-2,000 pounds.

Bainbridge & Wood. London, c.1810. Double flageolet. Boxwood, 5 silver keys, ivory mounts, 2 silver shut off keys, ivory mouthpiece. STH, 1987, p. 28. Estimate 220-300 pounds.

Bainbridge & Wood. London, c.1810. Single flageolet. Boxwood, 2 silver keys, ivory mount, ivory mouthpiece. STH, 1987, p. 57. Estimate 200-300 pounds.

Bainbridge & Wood. London, c.1815. Double flageolet. Boxwood, 3 silver keys, ivory mounts. STH, 1994, p. 12. Estimate 400-600 pounds.

Bainbridge & Wood. London, c.1815. Double flageolet. Boxwood, 5 silver keys, 2 silver wind-cutter keys, ivory mounts. STH, 2001, p. 134. Estimate 1,000-1,500 pounds.

Bainbridge, William. London, c.1810. Single flageolet. Boxwood, 2 silver keys, ivory mounts. STH, 1995, p. 48. Estimate 150-250 pounds.

Bainbridge, William. London, c.1820. Single flageolet. Rosewood, 5 silver keys, ivory mounts. STH, 1995, p. 20. Estimate 150-200 pounds.

Bainbridge, William. London, c.1825. Double flageolet. Boxwood, silver keys, 6 on the left pipe, 5 on the right pipe, later extensions of right foot, 2 silver wind cutter keys, ivory mounts. STH, 1987, p. 38. Estimate 150-250 pounds.

Bainbridge, William. London, c.1825. Double flageolet. Boxwood, 6 brass keys, ivory mounts. STH, 1987, p. 8. Estimate 280-350 pounds.

Bainbridge, William. London, c.1825. Double flageolet. Boxwood, 11 brass keys, no mounts. STH, 1994, p. 32. Estimate 400-600 pounds.

Bainbridge, William. London, c.1825. Double flageolet. Boxwood. STH, 1994, p. 32. Estimate 400-600 pounds.

Bainbridge, William. London, early 19th century. Double flageolet. 5 silver keys, 2 silver wind cutter keys, ivory mounts. STH, 2001, p. 134. Estimate 600-800 pounds.

Bainbridge. London, c.1830. Left-handed flute. Cocus, 8 silver keys, salt spoon cups, silver mounts, 1 later. STH, 1987, p. 36. Estimate 250-350 pounds.

Bainbridge & Wood. London, c.1810. Single flageolet. Ebony, 3 silver keys, 1 key raises the instrument's pitch a half step, ivory mounts, later ivory mouthpiece. STH, 1987, p. 64. Estimate 100-150 pounds.

Barfoot, Charles Smith. Blandford, c.1830. Clarinet. Boxwood, 6 brass keys, ivory mounts. STH, 1995, p. 48. Estimate 300-500 pounds.

Barrett & Grainer. [n.l., n.d.]. Boehm system flute. CHR, March 1994, p. 16. Estimate 200-300 pounds.

Bauer, J. Prague, c.1820. Oboe. Boxwood, 7 brass keys, stepped bell, no mounts. STH, 1997, p. 36. Estimate 2,500-3,500 pounds.

Bauer, Jakob. Vienna, c.1785. Oboe. Boxwood, 2 brass keys, horn mounts. STH, 1995, p. 12. Estimate 1,500-2,000 pounds.

Baumann, Joseph. Paris, early 19th century. Clarinet in C, boxwood, 5 brass keys, ivory mounts. STH, 2001, p. 132. Estimate 400-600 pounds.

Belles, Paul. Cologne, c.1820. Piccolo. Boxwood, 1 brass key, body in 3 joints, with duplicate center joints. STH, 1987, p. 27. Estimate 400-600 pounds.

Belles, Paul. Cologne, c.1825. Flute. Boxwood, 7 brass keys, salt spoon cups, horn mounts. STH, 1987, p. 37. Estimate 250-350 pounds.

Bellissent. Paris, c.1830. Flute. Cocus, 5 silver keys, ivory mounts. STH, 1987, p. 21. Estimate 200-300 pounds.

Bellissent. Paris, c.1835. Flute. Rosewood, 6 silver keys and mounts, silver keys on pillar mounts with crescent-shaped base plates, the circular covers carved with scallop shells, the touch pieces each carved with a different motif, the long F key absent. STH, 1987, p. 3. Estimate 1,000-1,500 pounds.

Bercioux, Eugene. Paris, c.1900. Boehm system flute. Silver body and keys. STH, 1997, p. 39. Estimate 1,000-1,500 pounds.

Bernareggi, Francisco. Barcelona, c.1827-1863. Walking stick flute. Possibly walnut, carved in imitation of bamboo, key absent, the knob and ferrule also absent. STH, 1995, p. 44. Estimate 800-1,200 pounds.

Berthold & Sohn. Speir-am-Rhein, late 19th century. Müller system clarinet in C. Ebony, G.S. keys and mounts, 4 ring keys. STH, 1987, p. 33. Estimate 150-250 pounds.

Berthold & Söhne. Speyer-am-Rhein, third quarter of the 19th century. Flute. Boxwood, 6 brass keys and mounts. STH, 1987, p. 34. Estimate 100-150 pounds.

Beukers, Willem. Amsterdam, [n.d.]. Voice flute. Pearwood. STH, 1994, p. 14. Estimate 6,000-8,000 pounds.

Beukers, Willem. Amsterdam, second quarter of the 18th century. Voice flute. Boxwood, no keys, no mounts. STH, 1995, p. 14. Estimate 6,000-8,000 pounds.

Billings, Friedrich. Warsaw, c.1815. Clarinet. Boxwood, 5 brass keys, horn mounts. STH, 1994, p. 12. Estimate 600-800 pounds.

Bilton, Richard. London, c.1835. Bassoon. Pearwood, 6 brass keys and mounts, salt spoon cups, pewter plugs. STH, 1990, p. 96. Estimate 700-1,000 pounds.

Bilton, Richard. London, c.1835. Flute. Rosewood, 8 silver keys and mounts, salt spoon cups, pewter plugs. STH, 1999, p. 43. Realized 350 pounds.

Bilton. London, c.1830. Clarinet. Boxwood, 13-key with ivory rings. B&B, 1998, p. 10. Estimate $1,800-2,200.

Bilton. London, c.1830. Flute. Boxwood, 1 brass key, ivory mounts. STH, 1995, p. 11. Estimate 100-150 pounds.

Blackman. London, c.1850. Flute. Cocus, 8 silver keys, the C and C sharp keys pewter plugs, silver mounts. STH, 1987, p. 22. Estimate 200-300 pounds.

Blume, Johann Christian. London, c.1790. Flute. Boxwood, 1 silver key, ivory mounts. STH, 1994, p. 14. Estimate 400-600 pounds.

Boehm, Theobald & Carl Mendler. Munich, c.1870. 1847 Boehm-system flute. Boxwood, brass keys and mounts. STH, 1992, p. 200. Estimate 2,500-3,500 pounds.

Boosey & Co. London, [n.d.]. Bassoon. Rosewood, plated keys, mounts. PHI, 1991, p. 6. Estimate 300-400 pounds.

Boosey & Co. London, [n.d.]. Clarinet in B flat. Nickel silver mounts. CHR, March 1994, p. 15. Estimate 100-150 pounds.

Boosey & Co. London, third quarter of the 19th century. Siccama system flute. Ebonite, thinned cocus head joint by Rudall, Carte & Co. STH, 1987, p. 30. Estimate 70-100 pounds.

Boosey & Hawkes. England, [n.d.]. Clarinet. Ebonite, white metal mounts. SCR, 1994, p. 16. Estimate 100-200 pounds.

Boosey & Sons. London, c.1865. Flute. Cocus, 8 nickel keys, the C and C sharp keys with pewter plugs, nickel mounts. STH, 1987, p. 65. Estimate 250-350 pounds.

Bormann, Carl Gottlob. Dresden, c.1810. Oboe. Boxwood, 8 brass keys, ivory mounts. STH, 2001, p. 134. Estimate 3,500-5,000 pounds.

Braun, Georg. Mannheim, c.1825. Flute. Ebony, 4 silver keys, 1 partly missing, ivory mounts. STH, 1987, p. 40. Estimate 80-100 pounds.

Braun, Johann Georg. Mannheim, c.1825. Mannheim, c.1825. Oboe. Boxwood, 11 brass keys, ivory mounts. STH, 1987, p. 40. Estimate 2,000-3,000 pounds.

Browne, William. London, 1941. Band flute. Ebony, 6 G.S. keys, mounts. STH, 1987, p. 10. Estimate 10-20 pounds.

Buffet, [probably Jean Louis]. Paris, c.1830. Oboe. Boxwood, 10 brass keys on post and pillars, ivory mounts. STH, 1997, p. 36. Estimate 700-1,000 pounds.

Buffet-Crampon. Paris, c.1863. Boehm system clarinet in C. Boxwood, brass key work, brass mounts, 1 ivory replacement, 3 missing, shortened barrel joint. STH, 1987, p. 33. Estimate 150-250 pounds.

Bühner & Keller. Strasbourg, c.1810. Flute. Boxwood, 1 later silver key (replacement), ivory mounts, and 3 corps de rechange. STH, 1994, p. 32. Estimate 1,800-2,500 pounds.

Buisson, F. [n.l., n.d.]. Clarinet. Metal body. CHR, March 1994, p. 15. Estimate 100-200 pounds.

Bürger, Julius Max. Strausburg, late 19th century. Conical bore Boehm system flute. Cocus, silver plated keys and mounts, 5 ring keys. STH, 1987, p. 36. Estimate 150-250 pounds.

Buthold & Thibouville. Paris, c.1860. French flageolet. Boxwood, 2 brass keys, ivory mounts. STH, 1997, p. 36. Estimate 500-1,000 pounds.

Butler, George. London, c.1860. Flute. Black wood, 8 nickel salt spoon keys and mounts, pewter plugs. STH, 1997, p. 30. Estimate 30-60 pounds.

Butler, George. London, c.1870. Clarinet in C. Boxwood, 13 brass keys on pillar and pillars, ivory mounts. STH, 1995, p. 41. Estimate 100-200 pounds.

Butler, George. London, c.1880. Alto flute. Black wood, [?] nickel keys, mounts, bent head joint, ebonite lip barrel. STH, 1994, p. 11. Estimate 600-800 pounds.

Button & Co. London, c.1815. Flute. Boxwood, 4 silver keys, ivory mounts. STH, 1987, p. 18. Estimate 200-300 pounds.

Cabart. France, [n.d., 1842-present].Clarinet. Includes case. BSL, 1992, p. 3. Estimate 80-120.

Cahusac, Thomas (elder/younger?). London, c.1775. Flute. Stained boxwood, 1 silver key, ivory mounts. STH, 1987, p. 10. Estimate 800-1,200 pounds.

Cahusac, Thomas (probably The younger). London, between 1800-1805. Flute. Boxwood, 1 silver key, ivory mounts. STH, 1994, p. 12. Estimate 700-1,000 pounds.

Cahusac, Thomas (probably The younger). London, between 1800-1805. Flute. Boxwood, 1 silver key, ivory mounts. STH, 1995, p. 46. Estimate 400-600 pounds.

Cahusac, Thomas (The elder). London, last quarter of the 18th century. Flute. Ivory, 1 silver key, 3 later keys in silver saddle mounts, 6 silver engraved mounts (later). STH, 1987, p. 13. Estimate 700-900 pounds.

Cahusac, Thomas (The elder). London, late 18th century. Oboe. Boxwood, 2 brass keys, straight topped, ivory mounts, STH, 2001, p. 132. Estimate 1,500-2,000 pounds.

Cahusac, Thomas (The elder). London, late 18th century. Oboe. Boxwood, 2 silver keys, no mounts. STH, 1995, p. 14. Estimate 2,000-3,000 pounds.

Cahusac, Thomas (The elder). London, late 18th century. Oboe. Boxwood, 2 brass keys, no mounts. STH, 1994, p. 30. Estimate 500-1,000 pounds.

Cahusac, Thomas. London, c.1775. Oboe. Boxwood, 3 brass keys, 1 ivory mount, oval finial, period bell by unknown maker. STH, 1987. p. 49. Estimate 2,000-3,000 pounds.

Cahusac, Thomas. London, c.1800. Flute. Ivory, 4 silver keys, no mounts. STH, 1987. p. 49. Estimate 1,200-1,500 pounds.

Camp, William. London, c.1838. Single flageolet. Rosewood, 8 nickel salt spoon keys, ivory mounts. STH, 1994, p. 32. Estimate 350-500 pounds.

Camus, Paul Hippolyte. Paris, c.1800. Flute. Ebony, 1 silver key, 2 later keys on pillar mounts for F and B flat and a third for G sharp now missing, ivory mounts, end cap replacement. STH, 1987, p. 32. Estimate 150-200 pounds.

Card, William. London, c.1850. Conical flute. Silver plate, 9 metal keys, the high C key missing, extra touch piece for the left thumb remains. STH, 1987, p. 58. Estimate 300-500 pounds.

Carlsson, P.A. Carlskrona, c.1830. Flute. Ebony, 6 or 8 silver keys, ivory mounts, 3 corps de rechange, 2 foot joints, 1 with a single key, the other with 3 keys. STH, 1994, p. 12. Estimate 800-1,200 pounds.

Clementi & Co. London, c.1810. Flute. Boxwood, 1 silver key, ivory mounts. STH, 1987, p. 42. Estimate 300-500 pounds.

Clementi & Co. London, c.1810. Flute. Boxwood, 6 silver keys with pewter plugs throughout, ivory mounts. STH, 1987, p. 29. Estimate 250-350 pounds.

Clementi & Co. London, c.1820. Flute. Boxwood, 1 brass key, ivory mounts. STH, 1994, p. 16. Estimate 250-350 pounds.

Clementi & Co. London, c.1830. Clarinet in B flat. Boxwood, 10 brass keys, ivory mounts. STH, 1995, p. 16. Estimate 300-400 pounds.

Clementi & Co. London, early 19th century. Flute. Boxwood, 7 keys, ivory mounts. STH 1985, number 149. Estimate $400-600.

Clementi & Co. London, first quarter of the 19th century. Flute. Boxwood, 4 silver keys, salt spoon cups, ivory mounts. STH, 1987, p. 57. Estimate 300-500 pounds.

Clementi & Co. London, first quarter of the 19th century. Flute. Rosewood, 4 silver keys, ivory mounts. STH, 1987, p. 21. Estimate 300-400 pounds.

Clinton & Co. London, c.1865. Equisonant flute. Cocus, silver key work and mounts. STH, 1987, p. 65. Estimate 300-400 pounds.

Clinton & Co. London, c.1865. Equisonant flute. Cocus, silver key work and mounts. STH, 1987, p. 34. Estimate 300-400 pounds.

Collard & Collard. London, c.1834. Flute. Cocus, 8 silver keys, salt spoon cups, the C and C sharp keys with pewter plugs, silver mounts. STH, 1987, p. 52. Estimate 200-300 pounds.

Collard, A. & Co. London, c.1885. Boehm/Carte system flute. Ebonite. STH, 1992, p. 194. Estimate 250-350 pounds.

Collier, Thomas. London, c.1790. Straight topped oboe. Stained boxwood, 2 brass keys, no mounts. STH, 1995, p. 14. Estimate 800-1,200 pounds.

Cortellini. Turnin, first quarter of the 19th century. Flute. Boxwood, 6 brass keys with pewter plugs, horn mounts. STH, 1994, p. 11. Estimate 400-600 pounds.

Couesnon & Cie. Paris, [n.d.]. Alto saxophone. CHR, March 1994, p. 16. Estimate 300-400 pounds.

Couesnon & Co. Paris, late 19th century. Boehm system flute. Silver plated, perforated plates, closed G sharp key. STH, 1987, p. 40. Estimate 200-400 pounds.

Cramer, John Baptist. London c.1800. Bassoon. Pearwood, 6 brass keys and mounts. STH, 1992, p. 200. Estimate 1,000-1,200 pounds.

Crone, Johann August. Leipzig, late 18th century. Flute. Boxwood, 1 brass key, 2 corps de rechange (1 reconstructed around G hole), later horn mount. STH, 1992, p. 196. Estimate 3,000-5,000 pounds.

Crone, Johann August. Leipzig late 18th century. Oboe. Boxwood, 2 brass keys, no mounts. STH, 1995, p. 14. Estimate 800-1,200 pounds.

Cuvillier. France, late 19th century. Bassoon. Maple, 10 brass keys. STH, 1985, number 142. Estimate $1,500-2,000.

D'Almaine & Co. London, [n.d.]. Flute. Boxwood, 1 brass key, bone mounts. B&B 1998, number 16. Estimate 80-120 pounds.

D'Almaine & Co. London, c.1840. Double flageolet. Boxwood, silver keys, 3 on the left pipe, 4 on the right pipe, the right pipe has a wind cutter key. STH, 1987, p. 38. Estimate 350-450 pounds.

D'Almaine & Co. London, c.1840. Flute. Boxwood, 1 brass key, ivory mounts. STH 1992, p. 194. Estimate 300-500 pounds.

D'Almaine & Co. London, c.1840. Flute. Rosewood, 6 nickel keys and mounts, salt spoon cups, and pewter plugs. STH, 1999, p. 43. Realized 400 pounds.

D'Almaine, & Co., late Goulding & D'Almaine. London. C.1795. Clarinet. Boxwood, 6 brass keys, ivory mounts. CHR, March 1994, p. 15. Estimate 200-300 pounds.

Delusse, Christophe. Paris, c.1780. Oboe. Cocus, 2 silver keys, ivory mounts. STH, 1997, p. 33. Estimate 3,500-5,500 pounds.

Delusse, Christophe. Paris, c.1785. Oboe. Rosewood, 2 brass keys, converted to 3 brass keys, ivory mounts. STH, 1997, p. 34. Estimate 2,000-3,000 pounds.

Denner, Johann Christoph. Nuremberg, first quarter of the 18th century. Tenor recorder. Boxwood, 1 brass key, later horn mounts. STH, 1995, p. 18. Estimate 25,000-30,000 pounds.

Denner, Johann Christoph. Nuremberg, first quarter of the 18th century. Treble (alto) recorder. Boxwood, no keys, no mounts. STH, 1995, p. 18. Estimate 12,000-18,000 pounds.

Doelling. Potsdam, c.1850. Oboe. Stained boxwood, 11 silver keys, ivory mounts. STH, 1990, p. 93. Estimate 350-500 pounds.

Doke. Lintz, first quarter of the 19th century. Flute. Ebony, 6 G.S. keys, ivory mounts. STH, 1987, p. 26. Estimate 200-300 pounds.

Doleisch. Clarinet. Boxwood, 5 brass keys, horn mounts. STH, 1987, p. 66 Estimate 800-1,000 pounds.

Dollard, John or Matthew. Dublin, c.1830. Flute. Rosewood, 1 brass key, ivory mounts. STH, 1994, p. 16. Estimate 500-800 pounds.

Dolmetsch, Arnold. Haslemere, 1919. Alto recorder. Baroque-style, rosewood, no keys or mounts. Includes serial number 1. STH, 1994, p. 30. Estimate 2,000-3,000 pounds.

Douglas, H.D. & Son. Glasgow. [n.d.]. Flute. Rosewood, nickel silver mounts. CHR, March 1994, p. 16. Estimate 100-200 pounds.

Dressler, Rafael. London, c.1833. Flute. Cocus, 9 silver keys, salt spoon cups, the low B, C and C sharp keys with pewter plugs, alternative touch piece for the short F key for the left thumb, silver mounts. STH, 1987, p. 26. Estimate 200-300 pounds.

Drouet, Louis Francois Philippe. London, 1820. Flute. Ebony, 8 silver keys and mounts, and salt spoon cups. STH, 1999, p. 39. Realized 360 pounds.

Drouet, Louis Francois Philippe. London, 1820. Flute. Ivory, 8 brass keys, silver mounts decorated with engine tuning. STH, 1994, p. 30. Estimate 1,200-1,800 pounds.

Dupeyrat, E. France, c.1900. Musette. Fruitwood, 2 joints, nickel silver keys. HVN, 1998, number 534. Estimate 500-800 Francs.

Elkhart Band Instrument Co. Elkhart, c.1930. Alto saxophone. Brass body and keys, low pitch. STH, 1995, p. 41. Estimate 300-400 pounds.

Embach, Ludwig. Adorf, c.1815. Flute. Boxwood, 1 brass key, ivory mounts. STH, 1995, p. 12. Estimate 400-600 pounds.

Embach, Ludwig. Amsterdam, c.1825. Flute. Stained boxwood, converted from 1 key to 4 key. Brass keys, ivory mounts. STH, 1999, p. 43. Realized 280 pounds.

Engelhard, Johann Friedrich. Nuremberg, c.1775. Oboe, Boxwood, 2 brass keys, 1 ivory ring. STH, 1997, p. 34. Estimate 3,000-5,000 pounds.

Euler, August. Frankfurt, c.1850. Flute. Rosewood, 8 nickel silver keys, salt spoon cups, nickel silver mounts. STH, 1995, p. 20. Estimate 200-300 pounds.

Felchin, Charles. Berne, c.1830. Flute. Ebony, 6 silver keys, on silver saddle mounts, ivory mounts. STH, 1987, p. 37. Estimate 80-120 pounds.

Felchuin, Charles. Berne, c.1830. Walking stick clarinet in B flat. Boxwood, simple system. STH, 1992, p. 196. Estimate 2,500-4,000 pounds.

Fentum, Henry. London, c.1850. Flute. Black wood, 8 nickel silver salt spoon keys, pewter plugs with nickel silver mounts. STH, 1992, p. 191. Estimate 400-600 pounds.

Fentum, Henry. London, c.1850. Flute. Cocus, 8 silver keys, salt spoon cups, the C and C sharp keys with pewter plugs, silver mounts. STH, 1987, p. 36. Estimate 300-400 pounds.

Firth, Hall & Pond. New York, c.1840. Flute. Boxwood, 1 brass key, no mounts. STH, 1987, p. 18. Estimate 300-500 pounds.

Fischer. Eger, c.1830. Clarinet in B flat. Ebony, 13 silver keys, 1 cover missing, ivory mounts. STH, 1987, p. 33. Estimate 250-350 pounds.

Fischer. German, c.1840. Flute. Boxwood, 4 brass keys, horn mounts. STH, 1987, p. 40. Estimate 250-350 pounds.

Florio, Grassi. London, last quarter of the 18th century. Fife in B flat. Boxwood, no keys, brass mounts. STH, 1987, p. 40. Estimate 80-120 pounds.

Florio, Pietro Brassi. London, third quarter of the 18th century. Flute. Boxwood, 1 brass key, no mounts. STH, 1987, p. 18. Estimate 800-1,000 pounds.

Florio, Pietro Grassi. London, 1771. Flute. Boxwood, 6 silver keys and mounts, 3 corps de rechange. STH, 1990, p. 90. Estimate 1,500-2,000 pounds.

Florio, Pietro Grassi. London, c.1775. Flute. Boxwood, 6 silver keys, ivory mounts, the C sharp trill with the maker's mark of John Hale, applied silver plaque engraved "W. Collins". STH, 1987, p. 29. Estimate 120-180 pounds.

Fornari, Andrea. Venice, 1794. Flute d'amore. Boxwood, 1 brass key (later). STH, 1994, p. 14. Estimate 6,000-8,000 pounds.

Fornari. Venice, c.1800. English horn. Boxwood, leather-bound, 2 ivory keys, 1 brass key, ivory mounts. STH, 1990, p. 93. Estimate 4,000-6,000 pounds.

Franklin, Charles. London, early 19th century. Bassoon. Maple, 8 brass keys, brass mounts, brass crook. STH, 1987, p. 57. Estimate 1,200-1,500 pounds.

Gahn, Johann Benedict. Nuremberg, c.1700. Treble recorder. Ivory, no mounts or keys. STH, 1994, p. 14. Estimate 10,000-15,000 pounds.

Gahn, Johann Benedict. Nuremberg, early 18th century. Recorder in G. Ivory, no keys or mounts. STH, 1995, p. 12. Estimate 8,000-10,000 pounds.

Garrett, Richard. London, c.1840. Clarinet in C. Boxwood, 6 brass keys, ivory mounts. STH, 1995, p. 41. Estimate 250-350 pounds.

Gautrot Aîné. Paris, c.1850. Clarinet in B flat. Boxwood, 6 brass keys, horn mounts. STH, 1995, p. 18. Estimate 500-700 pounds.

Gautrot, (aîné). Paris, c.1860. Flute. Boxwood, 5 bass keys and mounts. STH, 1987, p. 40. Estimate 70-100 pounds.

Gedney, Caleb. London, mid-18th century. Flute. Boxwood, 1 silver key, ivory mounts. STH, 1995, p. 18. Estimate 3,000-5,000 pounds.

Geib, U.S. 1818-1829. Flute. Cocus, 4 nickel salt spoon keys, ivory mounts. SKI, 1993, p. 8. Estimate $300-400.

Gerock, Christopher. London, c.1805. Flute. Boxwood, 1 silver key, ivory mounts, end cap missing. STH, 1987. p. 46. Estimate 250-350 pounds.

Gerock, Christopher. London, c.1810. Flute. Boxwood, 4 silver keys, ivory mounts. STH, 1987, p. 30. Estimate 200-300 pounds.

Gerock, Christopher. London, c.1810. Flute. Ivory, 4 silver keys and mounts. STH, 1994, p. 32. Estimate 1,200-1,800 pounds.

Gerock, Christopher. London, c.1825. Single flageolet. Boxwood, 1 brass key, unmounted. STH, 1987, p. 40. Estimate 70-100 pounds.

Gerock, Christopher. London, early 19th century. Flute. Boxwood, 1 key (later), horn mounts. STH, 1994, p. 11. Estimate 250-350 pounds.

Gerock, Christopher. London, early 19th century. Flute. Ivory, 4 keys (3 original nickel, later 1 is silver), converted from 1 key to 4 key flute shortly after construction, no mounts. STH, 1995, p. 16. Estimate 600-800 pounds.

Gerock, Christopher. London, first quarter of the 19th century. Flute. Boxwood, 1 brass key, nickel mount on the foot joint (later addition). STH, 1995, p. 16. Estimate 250-350 pounds.

Godefroy, Clair aîné. Paris, c.1860. Boehm system flute. Cocus, G.S. keys and mounts. STH, 1987, p. 33. Estimate 200-300 pounds.

Godefroy, Clair. Paris, c.1830. Flute. Cocus, 5 silver keys. STH, 1987, p. 30. Estimate 100-200 pounds.

Godefroy, Clair. Paris, c.1830. Rosewood, 5 nickel keys, ivory mounts. STH, 1987, p. 38. Estimate 300-500 pounds.

Godet, Theodore. Rheims, c.1800. Flute. Boxwood, 1 silver key, ivory mounts, 1 missing. STH, 1987, p. 29. Estimate 300-500 pounds.

Godet, Theodore. Rheims, c.1830. Flute. Ebony, 5 silver keys on pillar mounts, ivory mounts. STH, 1987, p. 37. Estimate 300-500 pounds.

Godfroy Fils. France, 19th century. Flute. 1 brass key, ivory mounts. STH, 1985, number 162. Estimate $400-600.

Godfroy, Clair Aîné. Paris, c.1825. Flute. Rosewood, 6 silver keys, ivory mounts. STH, 1997, p. 40. Estimate 400-600 pounds.

Godfroy, Clair Aîné. Paris, c.1850. Flute. Rosewood,10 silver keys, mounts. Plays to B natural. STH, 1992, p. 195. Estimate 800-1,200 pounds.

Godfroy, Clair Aîné. Paris, c.1860. Conical Boehm system flute. Black wood, silver mounts and keys. STH, 1995, p. 46. Estimate 1,800-2,200 pounds

Goodlad & Co. U.K., 1826-1838. Flute. Boxwood, 6 silver salt spoon keys, ivory mounts. BSL 1992, p. 3. Estimate 500-700 pounds.

Goodlad, John Dunkin. London, 1832. Flute. Rosewood, 8 silver salt spoon keys, silver mounts. STH, 1995, p. 48. Estimate 200-300 pounds.

Goudling & D'Almaine. London, c.1825. Flute. Boxwood, 1 brass key (cover missing), ivory mounts. STH, 1999, p. 40. Realized 120 pounds.

Goulding & Co. London, c.1825. Clarinet in C. Boxwood, 6 brass keys with detachable circular covers, ivory mounts (1 missing). STH, 1987, p. 13. Estimate 200-300 pounds.

Goulding & Co. London, early 19th century. Clarinet in B flat. Boxwood, 5 brass keys, a later 6th key removed, ivory mounts. STH, 1987, p. 33. Estimate 150-200 pounds.

Goulding & Co. London, early 19th century. Fife in C. Boxwood, no keys, brass mounts. STH, 1987, p. 41. Estimate 60-80 pounds.

Goulding & Co. London, early 19th century. Straight topped oboe. Boxwood, 2 brass keys, ivory mounts. STH, 2001, p. 134. Estimate 1,000-1,500 pounds.

Goulding & Co. London, late 18th century. Flute. Boxwood, 4 silver keys, ivory mounts. STH, 1995, p. 48. Estimate 350-500 pounds.

Goulding & D'Almaine. London, c.1820. Clarinet in C. Boxwood, 5 brass keys, ivory mounts. STH, 2001, p. 131. Estimate 500-700 pounds.

Goulding & D'Almaine. London, c.1825. London, c.1825. Clarinet in B flat. Boxwood, 6 brass keys, ivory mounts, later speaker key. STH, 1987, p. 58. Estimate 200-300 pounds.

Goulding, D'Almaine, Potter & Co. London, c.1815. Flute. Boxwood, 6 silver keys with pewter plugs throughout. STH, 1987, p. 9. Estimate 250-350 pounds.

Goulding, D'Almaine, Potter & Co. London, c.1815. Flute. Boxwood, 8 silver keys with pewter plugs throughout. STH, 1987, p. 9. Estimate 300-400 pounds.

Goulding, D'Almaine, Potter & Co. London, c.1815. Flute. Stained boxwood, 6 silver keys with pewter plugs, ivory mounts. STH, 1987, p. 36. Estimate 200-300 pounds.

Goulding, D'Almaine, Potter & Co. London, c.1820. Flute. Boxwood, 1 silver key, ivory mounts. STH, 1995, p. 18. Estimate 250-350 pounds.

Goulding, D'Almaine, Potter & Co. London, c.1820. Flute. Ivory, 6 silver keys with pewter plugs. STH, 1994, p. 11. Estimate 500-700 pounds.

Grenser, (Johann) Heinrich (Wilhelm). Dresden, c.1800. Bassoon. Stained maple, 6 brass keys with brass mounts. STH, 2001, p. 134. Estimate 400-600 pounds.

Grenser, (Johann) Heinrich (Wilhelm). Dresden, c.1810. Bassoon. Figured maple, 8 brass keys and mounts. STH, 1990, p. 94. Estimate 4,000-5,000 pounds.

Grenser, (Johann) Heinrich (Wilhelm). Dresden, c.1810. Oboe. Boxwood, 10 brass keys, onion and cotton reel finial, originally no mounts, 3 of the keys added later with brass mounts. STH, 2001, p. 132. Estimate 3,000-5,000 pounds.

Grenser, (Johann) Heinrich (Wilhelm). Dresden, early 19th century. Basset horn in F. Boxwood,15 brass keys, ivory mounts, 1 lacking and mouthpiece, brass bell. STH, 1992, p. 200. Estimate 4,000-5,000 pounds.

Grenser, (Johann) Heinrich (Wilhelm). Dresden, early 19th century. Flute. Ebony, 4 silver keys, ivory mounts. STH, 1992, p. 196. Estimate 2,500-3,500 pounds.

Grenser, (Johann) Heinrich (Wilhelm). Dresden, early 19th century. Pearwood, 6 brass keys and mounts. STH, 1992, p. 200. Estimate 2,000-3,000 pounds.

Grenser, Carl August [sic]. Dresden, 1789. Flute. Boxwood, 1 silver key, ivory mounts, end cap absent. No indication in the catalog if this was Carl Augustin I (the father) or Carl Augustin II the son. STH, 1987, p. 3. Estimate 2,000-3,000 pounds.

Grenser, Carl Augustin I. Dresden, 1778. Oboe. Boxwood, 2 brass keys, ivory mounts. 1 of 3 dated oboes by this maker. STH, 1997, p. 33. Estimate 10,000-15,000 pounds.

Grenser, Carl Augustin I. Dresden, c.1790. Flute. Boxwood, 4 silver keys, ivory mounts. STH, 1995, p. 12. Estimate 1,200-1,600 pounds.

Grenser, Carl Augustin I. Dresden, c.1800. Oboe. Boxwood, 2 brass keys, horn mounts, onion and cotton reel finial. Later bell by Steinke & Hoeprich. STH, 1995, p. 14. Estimate 3,000-5,000 pounds.

Grenser, Carl Augustin I. Dresden, third quarter of the 18th century. Flute. Boxwood, 1 silver key, horn mounts, and 3 corps de rechange. STH, 1995, p. 42. Estimate 6,000-8,000 pounds.

Grenser, Carl Augustin I. Dresden, third quarter of the 18th century. Flute. Rosewood, 1 silver key, ivory mounts, 7 corps de rechange and 2 foot joints. Lacking head joint and possibly 2 other corps de rechange. STH, 1995, p. 42. Estimate 4,000-5,000 pounds.

Grenser, H. & Wiesner. Dresden. c.1820. Flute in F. Black wood, 7 silver keys and ivory mounts. STH, 1999, p. 43. Realized 600 pounds.

Grenser, H. & Wiesner. Dresden, c.1820. Oboe. Boxwood, 7 brass keys, ivory mounts. STH, 2001, p. 134. Estimate 2,000-3,000 pounds.

Greve. Mannheim, first quarter of the 19th century. Flute. Ebony, 5 silver keys, ivory mounts. STH, 1987, p. 10. Estimate 700-1,000 pounds.

Griesling & Schlott. Berlin, c.1825. Angled basset horn. Boxwood, 16 brass keys, ivory knee joint, 2 barrel joint mounts, the lower mount of brass, brass bell. STH, 1987, p. 52. Estimate 5,000-7,000 pounds.

Griesling & Schlott. Berlin, first quarter of the 19th century. Flute. Ebony, 4 silver keys, the F key with 2 touch pieces, 3 corps de rechange, later ebony head joint, ivory mounts. STH, 1987, p. 36. Estimate 300-400 pounds.

Grundemann & Flot. Dresden, c.1800. Oboe. Boxwood, 2 silver keys, ivory mounts. Later converted to 10 key oboe. STH, 1997, p. 33. Estimate 400-600 pounds.

Grundmann, Jakob Frederick. Dresden, 1768. Oboe. Boxwood, 2 silver keys, wood mounts, third nickel G# key added later. STH, 1992, p. 196. Estimate 5,000-7,000 pounds.

Guenot, René. Paris, [n.d.]. Alto saxophone. Brass. CHR, March 1994, p. 17. Estimate 150-250 pounds.

Guerini. Mantua, c.1820. Oboe. Boxwood, 9 brass keys, ivory mounts. STH, 1997, p. 36. Estimate 3,000-4,000 pounds.

Gulik, D. Van. [probably Netherlands], last quarter of the 18th century. Flute. Boxwood, 1 brass key, horn mounts. STH, 1995, p. 14. Estimate 600-800 pounds.

Gyssens. France c.1850. Flageolet. Boehm system. GSL 1992, p. 3. Estimate 100-200 pounds.

Halary: see Asté, Jean-Hilaire.

Hammerschmidt, K. Bad Brambach, late 19th century. Piccolo. Ebony, 7 G.S. keys and mounts, metal head joint. STH, 1987, p. 10. Estimate 20-30 pounds.

Hammig, August Richerd. Markneukirchen, c.1900. Flute. Ebony, 14 G.S. keys and mounts, metal head joint. STH, 1987, p. 8. Estimate 80-100 pounds.

Hardie, R.G. & Co. Glasgow, c.1960. Bagpipe. Palisander wood, ivory mounts. STH, 1994, p. 32. Estimate 600-800 pounds.

Hastrick. London, c.1840. Double flageolet. Boxwood, brass keys (4 on left pipe, 6 on right), ivory mounts. STH, 1995, p. 11. Estimate 500-700 pounds.

Hastrick. London, c.1845. Single flageolet. Cocus, 5 silver keys with salt spoon cups, later sponge chamber, ivory mounts, bone mouthpiece. STH, 1987, p. 41. Estimate 60-80 pounds.

Hastrick. London, c. 1830. Boxwood, nickel silver keys (5 on left pipe, 5 on right pipe), 2 wind cutter keys, ivory mounts. STH, 1995, p. 41. Estimate 400-600 pounds.

Haynes, W.S. & Co. Boston, [late 19th or early 20th century]. Boehm system flute. 14 carat gold [plated over?], perforated plates, B foot. STH, 1987, p. 10. Estimate 10,000-12,000 pounds.

Heckel, Wilhelm. Biebrich, 1905. Bassoon. PHI, 1991, p. 6. Estimate 4,000-5,000 pounds.

Heckel. Biebrich, c.1880. Bassoon. Rosewood, nickel silver keys and mounts, ivory bell ring. STH, 1995, p. 17. Estimate 1,000-1,500 pounds.

Heckel. Biebrich, c.1880. Bassoon. Rosewood, nickel silver keys, ivory bell ring, crook. STH, 1994, p. 11. Estimate 2,500-3,000 pounds.

Heckel. Biebrich, c.1900. Bassoon. Figured maple, G.S. keys and mounts. STH, 1990, p. 94. Estimate 2,000-3,000 pounds.

Heckel. Biebrich, c.1910. Bassoon. Pearwood, nickel silver keys and mounts, 2 crooks. STH, 1995, p. 42. Estimate 5,000-7,000 pounds.

Heckel. Biebrich, c.1940. Bassoon. Rosewood, nickel silver keys and mounts, includes 3 later key guards. STH, 1994, p. 32. Estimate 2,000-3,000 pounds.

Helwert, Jacob David. Stuttgart, c.1835. Flute. Boxwood, 8 brass keys, the B flat and F keys with duplicate touch pieces, ivory mounts. STH, 1987, p. 69. Estimate 500-700 pounds.

Helwert, Jacob David. Stuttgart, c.1850. Flute. Boxwood, 5 brass keys, the F key with both short and long touch pieces, horn mounts, 1 replaced with horn and 1 replaced with brass. STH, 1987, p. 9. Estimate 150-200 pounds.

Hess, W. Munich, third quarter of the 19th century. Clarinet in B flat. Boxwood, 9 brass keys, 1 missing, horn mounts. STH, 1987, p. 66. Estimate 200-250 pounds.

Hess, W. Senior. Munich c.1840. Flute in E flat. Boxwood, 5 brass keys (duplicate F key), horn mounts. STH, 1992, p. 202. Estimate 200-300 pounds.

Higham, Joseph. Manchester, c.1875. Piccolo. Ebony, 6 G.S. keys. STH, 1987, p. 10. Estimate 20-30 pounds.

Hodsoll, William. London, c.1820. Terz flute. Boxwood, 1 nickel key, ivory mounts. STH, 1994, p. 14. Estimate 200-250 pounds.

Horák, Johann Wenzel. Prague, c.1860. Bassoon. Maple, 16 brass keys, metal bell. STH, 1994, p. 16. Estimate 2,000-3,000 pounds.

Hudson, John. London, c.1853. Flute. Cocus, 11 silver keys and mounts, 3 extra keys are duplicate G sharp, B flat and C keys, engraved decoration and with silver shield engraved containing dedicatory remarks, dated 1853. STH, 1987, p. 34. Estimate 500-700 pounds.

Hudson, John. London, c.1855. Flute. Palisander, 8 silver keys, salt spoon cups, the C and C sharp keys with pewter plugs, silver mounts. STH, 1987, p. 69. Estimate 400-600 pounds.

Husson & Buthold. Paris, c.1850. Flute. Black wood, 8 nickel silver keys, post and pillar, and mounts. STH, 1997, p. 39. Estimate 600-800 pounds.

Husson & Duchême. Paris, second quarter of the 19th century. Piccolo. Ebony, 1 silver key, ivory mounts. STH, 1987, p. 64. Estimate 50-70 pounds.

Ingram, Thomas William. London, c.1845. Flute. Rosewood, 8 nickel keys, salt spoon keys and pewter plugs, nickel mounts. STH, 1995, p. 14. Estimate 1,200-1,500 pounds.

Jehring. Adorf, 1810. Clarinet in C. Boxwood, 5 brass keys, 1 ivory mount replacement. STH, 1987, p. 33. Estimate 200-400 pounds.

Journet, H. London, last quarter of the 19th century. Flute. Cocus, 8 nickel keys, the C and C sharp keys with pewter plugs, nickel mounts. STH, 1987, p. 66. Estimate 100-150 pounds.

Julliot, Djalma. France, 1905. Boehm system flute. Silver, open holes, closed G sharp. Playing condition. B&B, 1998, p. 14-15. Estimate $1,600-2,000.

Keith, Prowse & Co. London, c.1830. Flute. Cocus, 8 silver keys, salt spoon cups, the C and C sharp keys with pewter plugs, silver mounts, embouchure bushed with mother-of-pearl and with a silver lip plated engraved dedication information. STH, 1987, p. 37. Estimate 180-200 pounds.

Key, Thomas, c.1840. Bassoon. Pearwood, 8 brass keys and mounts. STH, 1994, p. 16. Estimate 300-500 pounds.

Key, Thomas. London, c.1830. Clarinet in E flat. Boxwood, 8 brass keys, ivory mounts. STH, 1995, p. 16. Estimate 300-400 pounds.

Key, Thomas. London, early 19th century. Vox humana (oboe variant). Boxwood, 2 brass keys, ivory mounts. STH, 2001, p. 132. Estimate 2,500-3,500 pounds.

Kirst, Friedrich Gabriel A. Potsdam, last quarter of the 18th century. Flute. Boxwood, 5 brass keys, ivory mounts. STH, 1987, p. 29. Estimate 500-700 pounds.

Kirst, Friedrich Gabriel August. Potsdam, late 18th century. Flute. Boxwood, 1 silver key, ivory mounts, 4 corps de rechange. STH, 1994, p. 30. Estimate 15,000-20,000 pounds.

Kirst, Friedrich Gabriel August. Potsdam, late 18th century. Flute. Stained boxwood, 2 silver key, ivory mounts, short F key (later), 4 corps de rechange, 1 with later B flat key. STH, 1987, p. 16. Estimate 2,500-3,500 pounds.

Klemm and Brother. Germany c.1830. Clarinet. Boxwood, 6-key, ivory mounts, sold in Philadelphia by Klemm & Bro. B&B, 1998, p. 10. Estimate $900-1,200.

Knochenhauer, August T.A. Berlin, c.1830. Flute. Boxwood, 8 brass keys, ivory mounts. STH, 1995, p. 46. Estimate 1,500-2,000 pounds.

Koch, Franz. Vienna, 1842. Flute. Ebony, 9 silver keys, silver mounts. STH, 1995, p. 11. Estimate 700-1,000 pounds.

Koch, Stephan. Flute. Black wood, 8 silver keys with circular covers, ivory mounts. STH, 1987, p. 23. Estimate 300-500 pounds.

Koch, Stephan. Vienna, c.1820. Flute. Boxwood, 8 silver keys, 5 with circular covers, the F with duplicate touch piece, the C, D sharp, low B with pewter plugs. STH, 1987, p. 8. Estimate 500-600 pounds.

Koch, Stephan. Vienna, c.1825. Flute. Boxwood, 6 brass keys on pillars, ivory mounts. STH, 1987, p. 52. Estimate 300-500 pounds.

Kohler, I.C. Klingenthal, c.1800. Flute. Boxwood, 1 brass key, horn mounts. STH, 1987, p. 40. Estimate 300-500 pounds.

Kohler, John August. London, c.1860. Bassoon. Pearwood, 13 brass keys. STH, 1992, p. 193. Estimate 700-1,000 pounds.

Kohler, John I. London, late 18th century. Flute. Boxwood, 8 brass keys, ivory mounts. STH, 1997, p. 39. Estimate 300-400 pounds.

Kohlert, V & Sons. Graslitz, c.1920. Flute. Ebony, 9 G.S. keys and mounts. STH, 1987, p. 28. Estimate 70-100 pounds.

Kohlert, Vincenz. Graslitz, late 19th century. Piccolo. Ebony, 6 G.S. keys and mounts. STH, 1987, p. 10. Estimate 20-30 pounds.

Korzenberger. Neukirchen, c.1800. Clarinet in B flat. Boxwood, 5 brass keys, horn mounts. STH, 1987, p. 66. Estimate 500-700 pounds.

Krause, A. Augsburg, c.1850. Clarinet in E flat. Boxwood, 9 brass keys, horn mounts, 1 missing. STH, 1987, p. 38. Estimate 400-600 pounds.

Kruspe, C. Erfurt, late 19th century. Clarinet in E flat. Boxwood, 10 brass keys, horn mounts. STH, 1999, p. 42. Realized 180 pounds.

Kruspe, Carl. Erfurt, c.1920. Flute. Ebony, 19 G.S. keys and mounts, B foot, ivory head joint with raised lip guide. STH, 1987, p. 8. Estimate 80-120 pounds.

Kruspe, Carl. Erfurt, early 20th century. Flute. Ebony, 13 G.S. keys and mounts, 1 missing, B foot, ivory head joint with raised lip guide. STH, 1987, p. 28. Estimate 80-120 pounds.

Kruspe, Carl. Leipzig, c.1900. Schwedler-Kruspe flute. Conical bore, G.S. keys and mounts, to low B. STH, 1987, p. 3. Estimate 100-200 pounds.

Kusder, Henry. London, late 18th century. Flute. Ivory, 1 silver key. STH, 1992, p. 196. Estimate 3,000-4,000 pounds.

Kusder. London, late 18th century. Flute. Boxwood, 1 silver key, ivory mounts. STH, 1987, p. 69. Estimate 300-500 pounds.

Labor. Toulouse, c.1810. Flute. Ebony, 1 silver key, ivory mounts. STH, 1987, p. 37. Estimate 300-500 pounds.

Lafleur, J.R. & Son. French of Belgium, circa 1920. Flute. Rosewood, [?] nickel keys and mounts. STH, 1995, p. 48. Estimate 250-300 pounds.

Langlois, A.M. London, early 20th century. Boehm system flute. Ebonite. STH, 1995, p. 48. Estimate 100-200 pounds.

Laurent, Claude. France, 1838. Flute. Glass, silver keys and mounts. STH, 1984, [p. 2]. Estimate $4,000-$6,000.

Laurent, Claude. France, 1838. Flute. Glass, silver keys and mounts. STH, 1990, p. 90. Estimate 7,000-10,000 pounds.

Laussedat. France, third quarter of the 19th century. Flageolet. Boxwood, 5 nickel keys with domed circular covers, nickel mounts, mother-of-pearl mouthpiece. STH, 1995, p. 44. Estimate 200-300 pounds.

Lawson. London, c.1800. Flute. Boxwood, 1 silver key, ivory mounts. STH, 1994, p. 14. Estimate 150-250 pounds.

Leblanc. Paris, [n.d.] Pair of Boehm system clarinets. Wood, silver mounts. CHR, March 1994, p. 15. Estimate 1,000-1,500 pounds.

Lebrect, Louis Léon. Paris, first quarter of the 20th century. Boehm system flute. Silver plated body and keys, perforated plates. STH, 1995, p. 46. Estimate 700-1,000 pounds.

Lecomte, Arsène Zoë. France, 1859-1910? Flageolet. Ebony, 5 nickel silver keys, ivory beak. HVN, 1998, number 522. Estimate 800-1,000 Francs.

Ledere, K. Schönecki, late 19th century. Piccolo. Ebony, 7 G.S. keys, metal head joint. STH, 1987, p. 10. Estimate 20-30 pounds.

Lefêvre. Paris, c.1850. Clarinet in B flat. Boxwood, 13 brass keys, ivory mounts, 1 missing. STH, 1987, p. 33. Estimate 250-350 pounds.

Lefêvre. Paris, c.1870. Romero system clarinet. Boxwood, nickel silver keys and mounts. CHR, March 1994, p. 15. Estimate 300-500 pounds.

Lehnhold, Gottfried August. Leipzig, first quarter of the 19th century. Flute. Boxwood, 1 brass key, horn mounts. STH, 1995, p. 16. Estimate 200-400 pounds.

Leonhardt. [n.l.], c.1800. Flute. Boxwood, 5 brass keys, horn mounts, 1 missing. STH, 1987, p. 28. Estimate 250-350 pounds.

Leroux Aîné. Paris, mid 19th century. Flute. Boxwood, 4 brass keys, ivory mounts. STH, 1995, p. 11. Estimate 300-500 pounds.

Leroux, A. Paris, third quarter of the 19th century. Flute. Silver, 8 keys. STH, 1987, p. 34. Estimate 100-200 pounds.

Lewisch, M. Vienna, c.1830. Flute. Boxwood, 1 brass key, horn mounts. STH, 1995. p. 41. Estimate 300-500 pounds.

Lohner, J.A. Nuremberg, 18th century. Flute. Boxwood, 1 silver key, ivory mounts, 1 missing. STH, 1987, p. 9. Estimate 600-800 pounds.

Loree, François. Paris, c.1885. Simple system oboe. Rosewood, nickel silver keys and mounts. STH, 1997, p. 36. Estimate 1,000-2,000 pounds.

Loree, François. Paris, c.1900. Oboe. Grenadilla, 3 joints, nickel silver keys, based upon the Trièbert system. HVN, 1998, item 533. Estimate 2,500-3,000 Francs.

Lot, Louis. Paris, [n.d.] Boehm system flute. Silver. STH 1990, p. 90. Estimate 1,000-1,200 pounds.

Lot, Louis. Paris, [n.d.] Boehm system flute. Silver. STH 1990, p. 94. Estimate 800-1,000 pounds.

Lot, Louis. Paris, [n.d.]. Boehm system piccolo. Silver. STH, 1990, p. 92. Estimate 800-1,200 pounds.

Lot, Louis. Paris, c.1875. Boehm system piccolo. Cocus, silver keys and mounts, closed G sharp. STH, 1987, p. 10. Estimate 100-150 pounds.

Lot, Louis. Paris, first quarter of the 20th century. Piccolo. Black wood, silver plated keys and mounts. STH, 1995, p. 20. Estimate 300-500 pounds.

Lot, Louis. Paris, later 19th century. Boehm system piccolo. Body made of unidentified material, silver keywork and mounts, closed G sharp. STH, 1987, p. 64. Estimate 150-200 pounds.

Lot, Louis. Paris, third quarter of the 19th century. Boehm system flute. Silver, perforated plates, closed G sharp key. STH, 1987, p. 40. Estimate 800-1,000 pounds.

Luvoni, Ubaldo. Milan, c.1840. Flute. Black wood, 8 silver keys, silver mounts. STH, 1995, p. 16. Estimate 500-700 pounds.

Mahillon & Co. London, c.1890. Flute. Cocus, 8 G.S. keys and mounts. STH, 1987, p. 9. Estimate 70-100 pounds.

Mahillon. [Belgium, n.d.] Bassoon. Rosewood, nickel mounts. CHR, March 1994, p. 16. Estimate 100-200 pounds.

Mahillon. Brussels, c.1800. Müller system clarinet in B flat. Cocus, G.S. keys and mounts, 1 missing. STH, 1987, p. 33. Estimate 100-200 pounds.

Maino et Orsi. Italy, 1865-1880. Flute. Palissader wood, 11 nickel silver keys. HVN, 1998, number 524. Estimate 1,000 Francs.

Martin frères. France, c.1860. Clarinet in E flat. Boxwood, 8 brass keys on post and pillars, ivory mounts. STH, 1995, p. 16. Estimate 250-300 pounds.

Martin frères. France, c.1860. Clarinet. Boxwood, 8 brass salt spoon keys, bone ferrules. SKI, 1993. Estimate $600-800.

Martin frères. France, c.1860. Flute. Boxwood, 10 nickel silver keys, ivory ferrules, pillar and ring mounting, G.S. keys, salt-spoon cups. B&B, 1998, p. 10. Estimate $600-800.

Martin frères. France, c.1870. Flute. Cocus, nickel silver keys and mounts. B&B, 1998, p. 10. Estimate $700-900.

Martin, Adam. London, late 18th century. Flute. Boxwood, 1 brass key, ivory mounts. STH, 1995, p. 48. Estimate 300-500 pounds.

Martin, Jean-Francois. Paris, c.1830. Flute. Boxwood, 5 brass keys, horn mounts. STH, 1995, p. 20. Estimate 300-500 pounds.

Member of Jehring family. Adorf or Mainz, second quarter of the 19th century. Clarinet in B flat. Boxwood, 8 brass keys, ivory mounts. STH, 1995, p. 42. Estimate 400-600 pounds.

Metzler & Co. London, second quarter of the 19th century. Piccolo. Ebony, 6 silver keys and mounts. STH, 1987, p. 27. Estimate 150-200 pounds.

Metzler, G. & Co. London, c.1820. Flute. Boxwood, 1 brass key. STH, 1995, p. 11. Estimate 300-500 pounds.

Metzler, G. & Co. London, c.1830. Flute. Rosewood, 8 silver keys, ivory mounts. STH, 1997, p. 30. Estimate 1,000-1,500.

Metzler, Martin. London, c.1800. Flute. Ivory, 5 silver keys and mounts. Possibly made in London by Martin Metzler of Carlsruhe, and modified by Valentin Metzler of London. STH, 1987, p. 34. Estimate 700-1,000 pounds.

Metzler, Valentin. London, c.1800. Flute. Boxwood, 1 brass key, ivory mounts. STH, 1994, p. 16. Estimate 300-500 pounds.

Metzler. U.K. [n.d.] Clarinet. Boxwood, simple system. 6 brass keys, ivory mounts. BSL, 1992, p. 3. Estimate 100-150 pounds.

Meyer, H.F. Hanover, mid-19th century. Flute. Ebony 10 G.S. keys and mounts, finger holes bushed with G.S. B foot, ivory head joint. STH, 1987, p. 28. Estimate 40-50 pounds.

Meyer, Heinrich Friedrich. Hanover, c.1890. Flute. Black wood, 9 G.S. keys and mounts, B foot. STH, 1987, p. 8. Estimate 40-50 pounds.

Meyer, Heinrich Friedrich. Hanover, c.1890. Flute. Black wood, 10 G.S. keys and mounts, B foot. STH, 1987, p. 8. Estimate 60-80 pounds.

Michl, Johann & Sohn. Graslitz, c.1928. Flute. Black wood, 9 G.S. keys and mounts. STH, 1987, p. 3. Estimate 60-80 pounds.

Milhouse, possibly Richard. London, c.1805. Clarinet in C. Boxwood, 5 brass keys, ivory mounts. STH, 1999, p. 40. Realized 1,400 pounds.

Milhouse, William. London, [n.d.]. 1 piece flute. Boxwood, 1 brass key (missing), brass mounts. CHR, March 1994, p. 16. Estimate 200-300 pounds.

Milhouse, William. London, [n.d.]. Flute. Boxwood, 4 keys (2 of silver, 1 of brass, 1 missing), ivory mounts. CHR, March 1994, p. 15. Estimate 150-250 pounds.

Milhouse, William. London, c.1790. Flute. Boxwood, 1 brass key with ivory mounts. STH, 1992, p. 193. Estimate 300-500 pounds.

Milhouse, William. London, c.1800. Oboe. Boxwood, 2 silver keys, no mounts. STH, 1990, p. 90. Estimate 1,200-1,500 pounds.

Milhouse, William. London, c.1800. Oboe. Boxwood, 2 silver keys, no mounts. STH, 1999, p. 40. Realized 1,700 pounds.

Milhouse, William. London, c.1810. Flute. Stained boxwood, 1 silver key, ivory mounts. STH, 1994, p. 12. Estimate 400-600 pounds.

Milhouse, William. London, c.1835. Flute. Rosewood, 7 silver salt spoon keys, silver mounts. STH, 1995, p. 49. Estimate 200-300 pounds.

Milhouse, William. London, early 19th century. Bassoon. Pearwood, 8 brass keys (1 later) and mounts. STH, 1994, p. 30. Estimate 500-700 pounds.

Milhouse, William. London, early 19th century. Oboe. Stained boxwood, 2 silver keys, ivory mounts with later brass ferrule on the upper joint, straight toped. STH, 1995, p. 12. Estimate 600-800 pounds.

Milhouse, William. London, first quarter of the 19th century. Bassoon. Maple, 6 brass keys and mounts. STH, 1990, p. 94. Estimate 800-1,200 pounds.

Milhouse, William. London, first quarter of the 19th century. Bassoon. Pearwood, 8 brass keys and mounts. STH, 1990, p. 94. Estimate 1,200-2,000 pounds.

Milhouse, William. London, first quarter of the 19th century. Flute. Boxwood, 7 silver keys, 2 corps de rechange, ivory mounts. STH, 1987, p. 30. Estimate 1,200-1,800 pounds.

Milhouse, William. London, last quarter of the 18th century. Flute. Boxwood, 1 brass key, ivory mounts. STH, 1995, p. 41. Estimate 250-300 pounds.

Milhouse, William. London, late 18th century. Bassoon, 6 brass keys. STH, 1992, p. 200. Estimate 1, 200-1,800 pounds.

Milhouse. London, c.1800. Oboe. Boxwood. 2 silver keys, ivory mounts. STH, 1990, p. 96. Estimate 1,000-1,500 pounds.

Milligan. London, early 19th century. Flute in F. Boxwood, 1 brass key. STH, 1987, p. 34. Estimate 100-150 pounds.

Moennig, Otto. Leipzig, c.1890. Simple system oboe. Stained boxwood, nickel silver keys and mounts. STH, 1997, p. 34. Estimate 600-800 pounds.

Mogyorossy, G.Y. Budapest, early 20th century. Tarogota. Rosewood, nickel silver keys and mounts. STH, 1999, p. 42. Realized 360 pounds.

Mollenhauer, J. & Sohne. Fulda, c.1850. Flute. Boxwood, 9 G.S. keys, ivory mounts. STH, 1987, p. 29. Estimate 300-500 pounds.

Mollenhauer. Fulda, c.1850. Flute. Ebony, 8 silver keys, the 8th key for high E, ivory mounts. STH, 1987, p. 29. Estimate 300-500 pounds.

Monzani & Co. London, 1810. Flute. Ebony, 8 silver keys and mounts. STH, 1994, p. 12. Estimate 500-700 pounds.

Monzani & Co. London, 1814. Flute. Rosewood, 8 silver keys, silver mounts, second head. STH, 2001, p. 134. Estimate 1,000-1,500 pounds.

Monzani & Co. London, 1815-1820. Flute. Rosewood, 7 silver keys, silver mounts, 2 head joints, original mahogany case, grease pot, key axle tool and cleaning rod. STH, 1994, p. 32. Estimate 500-700 pounds.

Monzani & Co. London, 1816. Flute. Rosewood, 1 silver key, silver mounts. STH, 1992, p. 191. Estimate 1,200-1,800 pounds.

Monzani & Co. London, 1818. Flute. Rosewood, 7 silver keys, silver mounts. STH, 1995, p. 17. Estimate 350-550 pounds.

Monzani & Co. London, 1825-26. Flute. Rosewood, 8 silver keys and mounts. STH, 1999, p. 39. Realized 280 pounds.

Monzani & Co. London, c.1810. Flute. Rosewood, 10 silver keys and mounts. STH, 1995, p. 44. Estimate 300-500 pounds.

Monzani & Co. London, c.1815. Flute. Ivory, 7 silver keys and mounts. In original brass-bound mahogany case, ivory cleaning device, grease pot and keywork adjusters. STH, 1999, p. 40. Realized 1,800 pounds.

Monzani & Co. London, c.1825. Flute d'amore. Stained boxwood, 4 brass keys, ivory mounts. STH, 1995, p. 12. Estimate 700-1,000 pounds.

Monzani & Co. London, c.1825. Flute. Cocus, 8 silver keys and mounts. STH, 1987, p. 37. Estimate 250-300 pounds.

Monzani & Co. London, c.1825. Flute. Ebony, 4 silver keys, ivory mounts. STH, 1987, p. 32. Estimate 100-150 pounds.

Monzani & Co. London, c.1827. Flute. Cocus, 10 silver keys, including low B key, fluted head joint, silver mounts with turned decoration. STH, 1987, p. 69. Estimate 180-220 pounds.

Monzani & Co. London, c.1835. Flute. Rosewood, 10 silver keys and mounts. STH, 1994, p. 11. Estimate 500-700 pounds.

Monzani & Co. London, c.1835. Pair of flutes in A and F. Rosewood, 5 silver keys, ivory mounts. The instruments have consecutive serial numbers. STH, 1987, p. 57. Estimate 700-900 pounds.

Monzani, Tebaldo. London, c.1805. Flute d'amore. Rosewood, 4 silver keys, ivory mounts. STH, 1995, p. 12. Estimate 600-800 pounds.

Monzani, Tebaldo. London, c.1807. Flute. Ivory, 8 silver keys and mounts. 3 joints. PHI, 1991, p. 6. Estimate 2,000-3,000 pounds.

Monzani, Tebaldo. London, c.1809. Flute. Rosewood, 7 silver keys, silver mounts, ivory-bushed embouchure. STH, 1995, p. 16. Estimate 300-400 pounds.

Monzani, Teboldo. London, c.1805. Flute. Cocus, 7 silver keys, ivory mounts. STH, 1987, p. 29. Estimate 180-220 pounds.

Nicholson. London, first quarter of the 19th century. Flute. Boxwood, 4 silver keys, salt spoon cups, ivory mounts. STH, 1987, p. 36. Estimate 120-180 pounds.

Noblet. France, 19th century. Piccolo. Grenadilla, 4 silver keys, ivory mounts. HVN, 1998, p. 33. Estimate 1,000-1,5000 Francs.

Nonon, Jacques. Paris, c.1860. Flute. Cocus, 13 silver keys and mounts. STH, 1987, p. 30. Estimate 400-600 pounds.

Oberlender, Johann Wilhelm I. Nuremberg, c.1725. Oboe d'amore. Boxwood, 3 brass keys, no mounts. Excellent condition, only second known oboes d'amore by this maker. STH, 1999, p. 39. Realized 25,000 pounds.

Oberlender, Johann Wilhelm I. Nuremberg, first quarter of the 18th century. Treble (alto) recorder. Boxwood, no keys, ivory mounts. STH, 1997, p. 40. Estimate 7,000-10,000 pounds.

Oberlender, Johann Wilhelm I. Nuremberg, mid 18th century. Oboe. Boxwood, 3 brass keys, no mounts. STH, 2001, p. 134. Estimate 2,000-3,000 pounds.

Orsi, Romeo. Milan, c.1885. Baritone sarrusophone in E flat. Silverplate over brass. STH, 1992, p. 200. Estimate 4,000-5,000 pounds.

Osterried & Gerlach. Munich, c.1900. Müller system clarinets in B flat and A. Ebony, G.S. keys, 5 ring keys, thumb levers for F/C and E/B. STH, 1987, p. 33. Estimate 400-600 pounds.

Pace, Charles. London, c.1840. Bassoon. Unidentified wood, 12 brass keys, brass mounts, 3 later crooks. Instrument has been modified from a 6 key bassoon by the maker. STH, 1987, p. 56. Estimate 1,000-1,500 pounds.

Panormo, Vncenzo. [Either Palermo or London], second half of the 18th century. Straight topped oboe. Boxwood, 2 silver keys, ivory mounts. STH, 1997, p. 34. Estimate 3,000-6,000 pounds.

Parker, John. London, c.1800. Oboe. Stained boxwood, 2 brass keys, ivory mounts, reed socket mount added later. STH, 1992, p. 196. Estimate 1,000-1,5000 pounds.

Parker, John. London, early 19th century. Clarinet in B flat. Boxwood, 6 brass keys, ivory mounts, bell ring missing. STH, 1987, p. 58. Estimate 200-300 pounds.

Phillips, William Henry. London, c.1800. Piccolo. Ebony, 1 brass key, ivory mounts. STH, 1992, p. 195. Estimate 200-300 pounds.

Phipps & Co. England, early 19th century. Flute. Boxwood, 4 silver keys, ivory mounts. STH, 1995, p. 12. Estimate 250-350 pounds.

Phipps & Co. London, ca 1815. Piccolo. Boxwood, 1 silver key, ivory mounts. STH, 1987, p. 27. Estimate 300-500 pounds.

Piana, P. Milan, mid 19th century. Flute. Boxwood, 12 nickel keys with pewter plugs down to low A, ivory mounts. STH, 1987, p. 69. Estimate 200-300 pounds.

Ponte, C. France, [n.d]. Bass clarinet. Ebony. HNV, 1998, number 541. Estimate 6,000-8,000 Francs.

Potter, [William Henry?]. London, c.1800. Flute. Black wood, 1 silver key, ivory mounts. STH, 1994, p. 32. Estimate 100-200 pounds.

Potter, [William Henry?]. London, c.1820. Flute in G. Boxwood, 1 brass key. STH, 1994, p. 11. Estimate 80-120 pounds.

Potter, Richard. London, 1782. Flute. Boxwood, 5 silver keys, ivory mounts. Dated on foot. STH, 1999, p. 40. Realized 650 pounds.

Potter, Richard. London, c.1800. Flute. Boxwood, 6 silver keys, pewter plugs, ivory mounts. STH, 1987, p. 18. Estimate 200-300 pounds.

Potter, Richard. London, late 18th century. Flute. Boxwood, 6 silver keys, pewter plugs throughout, ivory mounts. STH, 1987, p. 18. Estimate 200-300 pounds.

Potter, Richard. London, late 18th century. Flute. Boxwood, 1 silver key, pewter plug, ivory mounts. STH, 1987, p. 13. Estimate 350-400 pounds.

Potter, Richard. London, late 18th century. Flute. Boxwood, 6 silver keys, pewter plugs, ivory mounts. STH, 1987, p. 18. Estimate 200-300 pounds.

Potter, Richard. London, late 18th century. Flute. Ivory, 4 silver keys, pewter plugs. Includes provenance information. STH, 1995, p. 12. Estimate 700-1,000 pounds.

Potter, William Henry. London, c.1800. Flute. Boxwood, 6 silver keys, pewter plugs, ivory mounts. STH, 1992, p. 195. Estimate 200-300 pounds.

Potter, William Henry. London, c.1800. Flute. Ivory, 8 keys, converted from a 16 keyed flute, silver keys and mounts, pewter plugs throughout, the long F and upper C keys later additions on applied ivory bosses, the B flat key with later additional touch piece. STH 1995, p. 3. Estimate 500-700 pounds.

Potter, William Henry. London, c.1810. Flute. Boxwood, 6 silver keys, ivory mounts, and pewter plugs. STH, 1999, p. 43. Realized 360 pounds.

Potter, William Henry. London, c.1810. Flute. Boxwood, 7 silver keys, pewter plugs, ivory mounts. STH, 1994, p. 32. Estimate 350-500 pounds.

Potter, William Henry. London, c.1810. Flute. Boxwood, 7 silver keys, pewter plugs, ivory mounts. PHI, 1991, p. 6. Estimate 200-300 pounds.

Potter, William Henry. London, c.1815. Flute. Boxwood, 6 silver keys, pewter plugs, ivory mounts. STH, 1987, p. 29. Estimate 50-70 pounds.

Potter, William Henry. London, c.1815. Flute. Boxwood. 6 silver keys, pewter plugs, ivory mounts. STH, 1990, p. 93. Estimate 350-450 pounds.

Potter, William Henry. London, c.1830. Flute. Rosewood, 8-key, ivory ferrules and salt-spoon key cups pewter plugs for C# and C. B&B, 1998, p. 10. Estimate $900-1,300.

Potter, William Henry. London, early 19th century. Flute. Black wood, 8 silver keys, ivory mounts. STH, 1997, p. 31. Estimate 60-80 pounds.

Potter, William Henry. London, first quarter of the 18th century. Flute. Ivory, 6 silver keys. STH, 1994, p. 12. Estimate 800-1,200 pounds.

Potter, William Henry. London, late 18th century, Flute. Boxwood, 4 silver keys, pewter plugs, ivory mounts. STH, 2001, p. 131. Estimate 400-600 pounds.

Preston & Son. London, c.1830. Clarinet. Boxwood, 8 brass keys, ivory mounts. STH, 1992, p. 194. Estimate 350-450 pounds.

Printemps, Jacques. France. 1847. Clarinet in A. HVN, 1998, number 539. Estimate 5,000-6,000 Francs.

Proser. London, last quarter of the 18th century. Flute. Boxwood, 1 silver key, ivory mounts. STH, 1987, p. 16. Estimate 800-1,000 pounds.

Proser. London, last quarter of the 18th century. Flute. Boxwood, 1 silver key, ivory mounts. STH, 1987, p. 16. Estimate 800-1,000 pounds.

Prowse, T. London, c.1830. Flute. Boxwood, 1 brass key. STH, 1994, p. 30. Estimate 200-300 pounds.

Prowse, T. London, c.1830. Flute. Boxwood, 4 brass keys. STH, 1997, p. 30. Estimate 150-200 pounds.

Prowse, T. London, c.1840. Flute. Nicholson model, rosewood, 8-key. Serial number 4472. B&B, 1998, p. 10. Estimate $800-1,200.

Prowse, T. London, c.1845. Flute. Rosewood, 8 nickel salt spoon keys and mounts. STH, 1997, p. 30. Estimate 400-600 pounds.

Prowse, T. London, c.1845. Flute. Rosewood, 8 silver salt spoon keys and mounts. STH, 1995, p. 41. Estimate 200-400 pounds.

Prowse, T. London, c.1850. Nicholson model flute. Black wood, 8-key. STH, 1994, p. 30. Estimate 200-300 pounds.

Reid, Robert. Horth Shields, c.1830 or later. Set of union pipes. Black wood stocks, blowpipe and 4 drones with brass mounts, later ivory mounts. STH, 1999, p. 42. Realized 550 pounds.

Reist, H. [no location], 1750. Oboe. Boxwood, 3 brass keys and mounts. STH, 1999, p. 39. Realized 2,200 pounds.

Reist, H. [Swiss?], 18th century. Oboe. Boxwood, 3 brass keys, the C with fishtail touch piece, later upper joint, later brass mounts. STH, 1987, p. 66 Estimate 1,200-1,500 pounds.

Richters, Hendrik. Amsterdam, c.1720. Oboe. Ebony, 3 silver keys, highly engraved ivory mounts. STH, 1997, p. 33. Estimate 12,000-16,000 pounds.

Riley, E. London, c.1800. Flute. Boxwood, 1 silver key, ivory mounts, later foot joint, silver key. STH, 1987, p. 30. Estimate 250-350 pounds.

Rippert, Jean Jacques. Paris, early 18th century. Treble recorder in G. Ivory, no keys or mounts. STH, 1997, p. 40. Estimate 10,000-15,000 pounds.

Rittershauen, Emil. Berlin, early 20th century. Boehm system flute. Ebony, silver plated keywork, mounts. STH, 1987, p. 33. Estimate 80-120 pounds.

Rödel, Johann. Bremen, c.1835. Flute. Boxwood, 9 brass keys with domed circular covers, the C and DC sharp keys with rollers, ivory mounts. STH, 1987, p. 3. Estimate 600-800 pounds.

Rottenburgh, Joannes Hyacinthus I. Brussels, first quarter of the 18th century. Oboe. Boxwood, 3 brass keys, ivory mounts. STH, 1997, p. 33. Estimate 13,000-16,000 pounds.

Rudall & Rose. London, [n.d.]. Flute. Boxwood, 6 silver keys, pewter plugs, ivory mounts. CHR, March 1994, p. 16. Estimate 500-800 pounds.

Rudall & Rose. London, c.1825. Flute. Silver salt spoon keys, pewter plugs, silver mounts. STH 1992, p. 202. Estimate 800-1,000 pounds.

Rudall & Rose. London, c.1830. Flute. Black wood, 8 silver salt spoon keys pewter plugs, silver mounts. STH, 1997, p. 39. Estimate 250-400 pounds.

Rudall & Rose. London, c.1830. Flute. Boxwood, 8 brass salt spoon keys, pewter plugs, silver mounts. STH, 1994, p. 30. Estimate 1,200-1,600 pounds.

Rudall & Rose. London, c.1830. Flute. Boxwood, 8 brass salt spoon keys, pewter plugs, silver mounts. STH, 1997, p. 39. Estimate 800-1,000 pounds.

Rudall & Rose. London, c.1830. Flute. Boxwood, 8 brass salt spoon keys, pewter plugs, silver mounts. STH, 1994, p. 32. Estimate 1,000-1,500 pounds.

Rudall & Rose. London, c.1830. Flute. Boxwood, 8 silver salt spoon keys and mounts. STH, 1994, p. 12. Estimate 1,200-1,600 pounds.

Rudall & Rose. London, c.1830. Flute. Cocus, 8 silver keys, salt spoon keys and mounts, the C and C sharp keys with pewter plugs [evidently better condition than above example]. STH, 1987, p. 16. Estimate 400-600 pounds.

Rudall & Rose. London, c.1830. Flute. Cocus, 8 silver keys, salt spoon cups, the C and C sharp keys with pewter plugs. STH, 1987, p. 16. Estimate 400-600 pounds.

Rudall & Rose. London, c.1830. Flute. Cocus, 8 silver salt spoon keys and mounts, the C and C sharp keys with pewter plugs. STH, 1987, p. 13. Estimate 250-350 pounds.

Rudall & Rose. London, c.1840. Flute. Rosewood, 8 silver salt spoon keys with pewter plugs, ivory mounts. STH, 1995, p. 16. Estimate 1,500-2,000 pounds.

Rudall & Rose. London, c.1840. Flute. Rosewood, 8 silver salt spoon keys with pewter plugs, silver mounts. STH, 1995, p. 16. Estimate 300-400 pounds.

Rudall & Rose. London, c.1840. Large hole model flute. Boxwood, 8 silver keys, the C and C sharp keys with pewter plugs, ivory mounts, fine state of preservation. STH, 1987, p. 18. Estimate 700-900 pounds.

Rudall, Carte & Co. London, c.1875. Boehm system flute, heavily modified Radcliffe model. Silver, gold mounts and 6 gold finger pads, gold barrel embouchure. STH, 1987, p. 10. Estimate 700-1,000 pounds.

Rudall, Carte & Co. London, c.1875. Boehm system flute. Silver, with B foot, the key work modified to allow for a D sharp with either little finger, open G sharp. STH, 1987, p. 3. Estimate 600-800 pounds.

Rudall, Carte & Co. London, c.1875. Flute. Rosewood, 8 nickel-silver salt spoon keys with pewter plugs, silver mounts. STH, 1999, p. 40. Realized 2,000 pounds.

Rudall, Carte & Co. London, first quarter of the 20th century. Carte and Boehm system flute. Ebonite, silver keys and mounts. STH, 1997, p. 39. Estimate 50-70 pounds.

Rudall, Carte & Co. London, first quarter of the 20th century. Radcliffe system flute. rosewood, silver keys and mounts. STH, 1997, p. 31. Estimate 400-600 pounds.

Rudall, Carte & Co. London, last quarter of the 19th century. Boehm system piccolo. Silver body and key work, open G sharp key, later silver plated head joint by another maker with raised ebonite lip plate. STH, 1987, p. 21. Estimate 200-250 pounds.

Rudall, Carte & Co. London, last quarter of the 19th century. 1867 patent Boehm system flute. Ebonite, silver key work and mounts, open G sharp. STH, 1987, p. 30. Estimate 80-120 pounds.

Rudall, Carte & Co. London, late 19th century. 1867 Boehm system Radcliff model flute. Silver body and keys. STH, 1995, p. 48. Estimate 200-300 pounds.

Rudall, Carte & Co. London, late 19th century. Alto flute. Ebony, 13 nickel keys, silver plated brass head joint, nickel mounts, closed G sharp. STH, 1987, p. 65. Estimate 150-250 pounds.

Rudall, Carte & Co. London, late 19th/early 20th century. Full Boehm system flute, Rostro model. Ebonite, silver keys and mounts. STH, 1995. p. 20. Estimate 200-300 pounds.

Rudall, Carte & Co. London. C.1876. Flute in the manner of the rare and unusual "Chrysostom" system flute. Silver, 1 piece body, 20 square or rectangular tone holes with similarly shaped covers, 23 controlling keys, 2 head joints with square embouchure holes, 1 with ivory lip plate, sold with 2 original working drawings of the flute. The instrument is sheared across below the 4th tone hole from the top, and the instrument is incomplete. STH, 1987, p. 42. Estimate 1,500-2,000 pounds.

Rudall, George. London, c.1820. Flute. Cocus, 8 silver keys and mounts. Includes alternate head-joint. Head joint made by Willis. STH, 1990, p. 90. Estimate 400-600 pounds.

Rudall, George. London, c.1820. Flute. Ebony, 7 silver keys and mounts. STH, 1987, p. 34. Estimate 300-400 pounds.

Rudall, Rose, Carte & Co. London, c.1855. Clarinet. Unidentified wood, 13 brass keys, ivory mounts. STH, 1994, p. 16. Estimate 250-350 pounds.

Rudall, Rose, Carte & Co. London, c.1855. Flute. Rosewood, 8 silver salt spoon keys and mounts, and pewter plugs. STH, 1997, p. 30. Estimate 1,500-2,000 pounds.

Rudall, Rose, Carte & Co. London, c.1860. Boehm system flute, 1831 patent model. Silver body and key work, embouchure barrel and mounts with chased decoration, open G sharp. STH, 1987, p. 30. Estimate 100-200 pounds.

Rudall, Rose, Carte & Co. London, c.1860. Flute. Hybrid Boehm system (1832), open tone hole with rings except the G hole, silver body and keys. STH, 1995, p. 41. Estimate 400-600 pounds.

Rudall, Rose, Carte & Co. London, c.1865. Boehm system flute. Silver, open G sharp, duplicate head joints. STH, 1995, p. 46. Estimate 200-400 pounds.

Rudall, Rose, Carte & Co. London, c.1870. Combined Boehm/Carte system flute. Rosewood, silver keys and mounts. STH, 1995, p. 20. Estimate 300-400 pounds.

Sattler, Carl Wilhelm. Leipzig, third quarter of the 18th century. Oboe. Boxwood, 2 brass keys, no mounts. STH, 1997, p. 34. Estimate 4,000-6,000 pounds.

Savary (jeune). Paris, c.1825. Bassoon. Maple, 8 brass keys and mounts, 1 later, later bell joint, later crook. STH, 1987, p. 58. Estimate 1,000-1,500 pounds.

Sax, Adolphe. France 1814-1894. Saxophone. Nickel plate. HVN, 1998, number 549. Estimate 12,000-15,000 Francs.

Sax, Charles Joseph. Bruxelles, c.1830. Flute. Rosewood, 8 silver keys and mounts, B foot. STH, 1995, p. 46. Estimate 600-800 pounds.

Scherer, Johann. Butzbach, c.1750. Flute. Ivory, 1 brass key (replaced), missing end cap, no cracks, embouchure and finger holes evidently not altered. STH, 1987, p. 10. Estimate 15,000-20,000 pounds.

Schetelig, Julius. Berlin, early 20th century. Flute. Cocus. 12 G.S. keys and mounts, metal lined ivory head joint, the embouchure with lip guides. STH, 1987, p. 8. Estimate 20-30 pounds.

Schlegel, Jeremias. Basel, third quarter of the 18th century. Oboe. Boxwood, 2 brass keys. STH, 1997, p. 34. Estimate 1,000-2,000 pounds.

Schöffl, Eustach. Munich, c.1820. Flute. Boxwood, 3 joints, 6 brass keys, the F key with duplicate touch piece, ivory mounts. STH, 1987, p. 37. Estimate 600-800 pounds.

Schöffl, Eustach. Munich, c.1820. Flute. Boxwood, 7 brass keys, the F key with duplicate touch pieces, horn mounts. STH, 1987, p. 69. Estimate 600-800 pounds.

Schöllnast, Franz. Pressburg, c.1830. Walking stick flageolet. Pearwood, 1 silver key, 4 silver keys with pewter plugs, 1 bone mount, brass ferrule, mouthpiece replaced. STH, 1987, p. 6. Estimate 800-1,000 pounds.

School of Denner. Germany, late 17early 18th century. Bassoon. Fruitwood, 4 brass keys and mounts, wing joint by Rainer Weber, replacement crook. STH, 1995, p. 17. Estimate 6,000-8,000 pounds.

Schott, B. Mainz, first quarter of the 19th century. Clarinet in B flat. Boxwood, 6 brass keys, ivory mounts. STH, 1987, p. 56. Estimate 300-500 pounds.

Schuchart, Charles. London, mid-18th century. Flute. Boxwood, 1 silver key, ivory mounts. STH, 1987, p. 49. Estimate 1,500-2,000 pounds.

Schuchart, John Just. London, mid-18th century or later. Bassoon. Pearwood, 8 brass keys and mounts. Overstamped by Charles Schuchart, who evidently modernized a 4 key bassoon. STH, 1992, p. 200. Estimate 1,500-2,500 pounds.

Schuchart, John Just. London, second quarter of the 18th century. Flute. Boxwood, 4 keys (missing), ivory mounts. STH, 1997, p. 39. Estimate 250-350 pounds.

Schuster, Carl Gottlob. Markneukirchen, early 20th century. Flute. Black wood, 8 G.S. keys and mounts. STH, 1987, p. 8. Estimate 30-50 pounds.

Schuster. Markneukirchen, mid 19th century. Flute. Boxwood, 9 brass keys, ivory mounts, 1 brass ferrule replaced. STH, 1987, p. 3. Estimate 60-80 pounds.

Selmer, Henri. Paris, [n.d.]. Tenor saxophone. Silver plated. CHR, March 1994, p. 17. Estimate 500-700 pounds.

Selmer, Henri. Paris, 1922. Alto saxophone. Silver plated. CHR, March 1994, p. 17. Estimate 350-450 pounds.

Selmer. Paris, 1986. Tenor saxophone, Super action, series 11. Brass lacquer finish with simulated mother of pearl keys. CHR, March 1994, p. 17. Estimate 550-650 pounds.

Siccama, Abel. London, c.1850. Flute. Cocus, 11 silver keys, 2 ring keys, silver mounts. STH, 1987, p. 37. Estimate 100-150 pounds.

Siccama, Abel. London, c.1850. Siccama "diatonic" flute. Rosewood, 8 silver keys and mounts. STH, 1997, p. 30. Estimate 600-800 pounds.

Simpson, John or Ann. London, c.1750. Flute. Ivory, 1 silver key and mounts, 3 corps de rechange. [Catalog describes the Simpsons as probably only a dealer.] STH, 1994, p. 14. Estimate 3,000-4,000 pounds.

Simpson, John. London, c.1830. Double flageolet. Boxwood, 8 silver keys, 2 wind cutters, ivory mounts. STH, 2001, p. 134. Estimate 500-700 pounds.

Simpson, John. London, c.1835. Flute. Rosewood, 8 silver salt spoon keys and mounts. STH, 1994, p. 16. Estimate 700-1,000 pounds.

Skousboe, Hennig Andersen. Copenhagen, early 19th century. Piccolo. Ebony, 1 brass key, ivory mounts. STH, 1995, p. 14. Estimate 300-500 pounds.

Stanesby, Thomas Junior. London, c.1720. Flute. Ivory, 1 silver key, mounts. STH, 1987, p. 41. Estimate 15,000-20,000 pounds.

Stanesby, Thomas, Jr. England, early 18th century. Flute. Ivory, silver keys and mounts, some replaced. STH, 1984, [p. 2]. Estimate $3,000-5,000.

Stanesby, Thomas, Jr. London, second quarter of the 18th century. Flute. Rosewood, 1 silver key, ivory mounts. STH, 1995, p. 18. Estimate 8,000-12,000 pounds.

Stanesby, Thomas, Junior. England, [n.d.]. Flute. Boxwood, 1 brass key, ivory mounts. CHR, March 1994, p. 16. Estimate 150-200 pounds.

Stanesby, Thomas, Junior. London, third quarter of the 17th century. Treble recorder. Stained boxwood, no keys or mounts. STH, 1997, p. 40. Estimate 10,000-15,000 pounds.

Stanesby, Thomas, Senior. London. Third decade of the 18th century. Oboe. Boxwood, 3 brass keys, no mounts. STH, 1997, p. 33. Estimate 4,000-6,000 pounds.

Stanesby, Thomas. London, second quarter of the 18th century. Flute. Rosewood, 1 silver key, heavy ivory mounts. STH, 1987. p. 49. Estimate 10,000-15,000 pounds.

Staub, N. Nuremberg, first quarter of the 18th century. [Alto?] recorder. Ivory, no keys, no mounts. Deeply carved head and foot joints, with undulating bands. STH, 1987. p. 49. Estimate 8,000-12,000 pounds.

Stecher, Vienna, c.1880. Flute. Ebony, 12 G.S. keys and mounts, B foot, ivory head joint. STH, 1987, p. 28. Estimate 80-120 pounds.

Stowasser, Jonas. Budapest, c.1900. Tarogato. Rosewood, 15 nickel keys. STH, 1990, p. 94. Estimate 800-1,200 pounds.

Streitwolf, Hohann Heinrich Gottlieb. Göttingen, c.1825. Flute. Boxwood, 7 brass keys, horn mounts. STH, 1987, p. 29. Estimate 80-120 pounds.

Stümple, Heinrich Conrad. Minden, c.1900. Flute. Cocus, 10 G.S. keys, alternate head joint for vertical blowing by Everhard Wünnenberg of Cologne. STH, 1987, p. 23. Estimate 150-200 pounds.

Taylor, Richard. England, circa 1780. Bassoon. Pearwood, 4 brass keys and mounts, wing joint replaced. STH, 1995, p. 16. Estimate 500-700 pounds.

Thibouville, Martin. Paris, c.1870. Flute. Rosewood, 10 silver keys and mounts, the C and C sharp keys with rollers. STH, 1987. p. 46. Estimate 250-350 pounds.

Thibouville-Herouard. France, 19th century. Flute. 5 keys, some restoration. HVN, 1998, number 521. Estimate 1,200-1,500 Francs.

Thurgood. London, c.1820. Single flageolet. Boxwood, 1 brass key, unmounted, later ivory mouthpiece. STH, 1987, p. 64. Estimate 50-70 pounds.

Tichentopf, Johann Heinrich. Leipzig, c.1725. Treble (alto) recorder. Unidentified wood, no keys or mounts. Only 1 of 2 known alto recorders identified in Phillip Young "4,900 Historical Woodwind Instruments." STH, 1997, p. 40. Estimate 7,000-10,000 pounds.

Tomschik, Martin. Brün, c.1860. Clarinet. Boxwood, 8 brass keys and mounts. STH, 1995, p. 11. Estimate 600-800 pounds.

Triébert /Couesnon. Paris, mid 20th century. Conservatoire system oboe. Silver-plated keys and mounts, stamped "Brevete, Triébert a Paris" and "Monopole" (a trademark used by Couesnon for instruments imported into the USA by Fred Gretsch Mfg. Co.). STH, 1995, p. 17. Estimate 800-1,200 pounds.

Triébert, Guillaume & Sons. Paris, c.1830. Curved English horn. Leather bound wood with gilding, 9 brass keys on post and pillars, pearwood bell, original brass crook. STH, 1997, p. 38. Estimate 5,000-7,000 pounds.

Triébert, Guillaume & Sons. Paris, early 19th century. Curved English horn. Leather bound wood with gilding, 2/10 brass keys (later keys on post and pillars), original brass crook. STH, 1997, p. 38. Estimate 4,000-6,000 pounds.

Triebert, Guillaume & Sons. Paris, last quarter of the 19th century. Boehm system oboe. [No material given], nickel-silver keys and mounts. STH, 1997, p. 31. Estimate 800-1,200 pounds.

Triébert, Guillaume. Paris, second quarter of the 19th century. Curved English horn. Leather-bound wood, 11 silver keys, ivory mounts. STH, 1987, p. 52. Estimate 2,000-3,000 pounds.

Triébert, Guillaume. Paris, second quarter of the 19th century. Oboe. Boxwood, 13 silver keys, ivory mounts. STH, 1987, p. 18. Estimate 1,000-1,500 pounds.

Triébert. [n.l., n.d.] Bassoon. Rosewood, nickel mounted. Stamped Triébert. CHR, March 1994, p. 15. Estimate 100-200 pounds.

Triébert. Paris, c.1870. Oboe. Cocus. STH, 1995, p. 3. Estimate 150-250 pounds.

Uhlmann, Johann Tobias. Vienna, third quarter of the 19th century. Flute. Black wood, 12 G.S. keys and mounts, the C, C sharp and low B with pewter plugs, metal lined ivory head joint. STH, 1987, p. 8. Estimate 30-50 pounds.

Wallis, Joseph & So. London, c.1900. Giorgi system flute. Ebonite body 3 nickel keys. STH, 1987, p. 70. Estimate 180-250 pounds.

Wallis, Joseph & Son Ltd. London, early 20th century. Giorgi model flute. Ebonite, no keys, or mounts. STH, 1995, p. 20. Estimate 200-300 pounds.

Wallis, Joseph & Son. London, c.1900. Giorgi system flute. Ebonite, 1 nickel key. STH, 1987, p. 42. Estimate 180-250 pounds.

Wallis, Joseph. London, c.1850. Flute. Cocus, 1 G.S. key, salt spoon cup and mounts, 1 missing. STH, 1987, p. 33. Estimate 100-150 pounds.

Wallis, Joseph. London, c.1850. Piccolo. Black wood, 4 silver salt spoon keys, and mounts. STH, 1997, p. 40. Estimate 250-350 pounds.

Wallis, Joseph. London, c.1860. Fife in B flat. Boxwood, 1 brass key and mounts. STH, 1987, p. 21. Estimate 150-250 pounds.

Wallis, Joseph. London, c.1860. Single flageolet. Boxwood, 1 brass key, unmounted. STH, 1987, p. 40. Estimate 150-250 pounds.

Wallis. London, c.1860. Clarinet. Boxwood, 8 brass keys (1 unattached), ivory mounts. CHR, March 1994, p. 16. Estimate 100-200 pounds.

Waylett, Henry. England, mid-18th century. Flute. Ivory, 1 silver key. STH, 1994, p. 12. Estimate 1,500-2,500 pounds.

Weisse, Johann Wendelinus. Berlin, c.1820. Flute. Ebony, 6 silver keys, ivory mounts, 3 corps de rechange. STH, 1994, p. 12. Estimate 800-1,500 pounds.

Welsh, Thomas. London, c.1830. Flute. Boxwood, 1 brass key and mounts. STH, 1997, p. 40. Estimate 200-300 pounds.

Whitaker. London, c.1825. Flute. Boxwood, 1 brass key, ivory mounts. STH, 1987, p. 34. Estimate 200-300 pounds.

Whitaker. London, first quarter of the 19th century. Flute. Boxwood, 1 brass key, salt spoon cup, ivory mounts. STH, 1987, p. 18. Estimate 200-300 pounds.

Whitaker. London, first quarter of the 19th century. Flute. Boxwood, 1 brass salt spoon key, ivory mounts (1 missing). STH, 1987, p. 18. Estimate 200-300 pounds.

Whitely. U.S. c.1820. Clarinet. Boxwood, 5 keys, ivory ferrules, ring mounted keys. B&B, 1998, p. 10. Estimate $800-1,000.

Wild, Heinrich. Flute. Cocus, 8 silver keys and mounts, 1 missing. STH, 1987, p. 69. Estimate 200-300 pounds.

Williams, E.G. London, c.1820. Clarinet in B flat. Boxwood, 5 brass keys. STH, 1987, p. 49. Estimate 250-350 pounds.

Willis, John. London, 1820. Flute. Boxwood, 6 silver keys, pewter plugs, ivory and silver mounts, stamped Geo. Rudall on head

and middle joint, Geo. Rudall, Willis on foot joint. STH, 1997, p. 30. Estimate 800-1,200 pounds.

Willis. London, second quarter of the 19th century. Flute. Cocus, 8 silver keys, salt spoon cups, the C and C sharp keys with pewter plugs, silver mounts. STH, 1987, p. 37. Estimate 200-300 pounds.

Wolf, Fr. Bohemia, late 19th century. Clarinet in E flat. Boxwood, 12 brass keys and mounts. STH, 1987, p. 33. Estimate 200-300 pounds.

Wood & Ivy. London, c.1840. Clarinet in C. Boxwood, 8 brass keys, ivory mounts. STH, 1987, p. 38. Estimate 250-350 pounds.

Wood & Ivy. London, c.1840. Flute. Cocus, 8 silver keys, salt spoon cups, silver mounts. STH, 1987, p. 70. Estimate 70-100 pounds.

Wood & Ivy. U.K. c.1840. Clarinet. Boxwood, 8 keys, ivory ferrules, metal lined barrel and upper joint, and large touch for B with roller on C#. B&B, 1998, p. 10. Estimate $1,400-1,800.

Wood, James. London, c.1810. Flute. Ebony, 8 silver keys with shell motif and pewter plugs, silver mounts turned and engraved. STH, 1994, p. 32. Estimate 1,000-1,500 pounds.

Wood, James. London, c.1820. Flute. Rosewood, 7 silver keys, the C, C sharp, and E flat keys with pewter plugs, the low C key bearing the maker's mark, ivory mounts. STH, 1987, p. 52. Estimate 250-350 pounds.

Wrede, Hermann. London, c.1820. Piccolo. Boxwood, 1 silver key, ivory mounts. STH, 2001, p. 132. Estimate 400-600 pounds.

Wrede. London, c.1820. Clarinet in E flat. Boxwood, 5 brass keys, ivory mounts, 1 missing, 1 horn replacement. STH, 1987, p. 52. Estimate 200-300 pounds.

Wunderlich, C.A. Siebenbrunn, c.1920. Conical bore flute. Black wood, to low B. STH, 1987, p. 3. Estimate 60-80 pounds.

Wunderlich, C.A. Siebenbrunn, Vogtland, c.1900. Müller system clarinet in B flat. Ebony, G.S. keys and 4 rink keys, 1 missing, G.S. mounts. STH, 1987, p. 33. Estimate 100-200 pounds.

Wünnenberg, Everhardt. Cologne, c.1880. Flute. Cocus, 10 silver keys and mounts, rollers on the C and C sharp keys. STH, 1987, p. 3. Estimate 250-350 pounds.

Wünnenberg. Cologne, late 19th century. Flute. Ebony, 9 G.S. keys and mounts. STH, 1987, p. 10. Estimate 60-80 pounds.

Wylde, Henry & Son. London, c.1845. Flute. Cocus, 8 silver keys, salt spoon cups, the C and C sharp keys with pewter plugs, silver mounts. STH, 1987, p. 36. Estimate 300-400 pounds.

Wylde, Henry. London, 1853-1855. Flute. Rosewood, 8 silver salt spoon keys with pewter plugs, silver mounts. STH, 1995, p. 17. Estimate 1,000-1,500 pounds.

Wylde, Henry. London, c.1835. Flute. Cocus, 8 silver keys, salt spoon cups, the C and C sharp keys with pewter plugs. STH, 1987, p. 36. Estimate 150-200 pounds.

Wylde, Henry. London, c.1840. Flute. Rosewood, 8 nickel silver salt spoon keys and pewter plugs, nickel silver mounts. Sold in period mahogany case. STH, 1992, p. 191. Estimate 700-1,000 pounds.

Ziegler. Vienna, second quarter of the 19th century. Flute. Boxwood, 11 nickel keys, the low B, C, and C sharp keys with pewter plugs, ivory mounts. STH, 1987, p. 69. Estimate 300-400 pounds.

Zimmermann, Julius Heinrich. Leipzig, c.1900. Flute. Ebony, 12 G.S. keys and mounts, B foot, ivory head joint with raised lip guide. STH, 1987, p. 28. Estimate 70-100 pounds.

Zuleger, Hermann. Vienna, c.1900. Flute. Ebony, 15 G.S. keys and mounts, B foot. STH, 1987, p. 9. Estimate 300-400 pounds.

Zuleger, Hermann. Vienna, early 20th century. Flute. Ebony, 13 G.S. keys and mounts, B foot. STH, 1987, p. 34. Estimate 100-150 pounds.

Societies, Museums, Auction Houses, and Websites

Non-Scholarly Societies

The following brief list of non-scholarly societies is provided simply as an example of a few societies that can, on occasion, be of value for researching musical instruments. More importantly, they contain links to other websites. At present, although some museums still seem to have no significant web presence, that will surely change, thereby making this list somewhat obsolete. Refer to the AMIS website for links to new websites.

International Double Reed Society maintains a website that includes a list of dissertations, a few of which discuss the history of the oboe and bassoon. Access to most of the pages in this website requires joining the society.

The International Clarinet Association maintains a website that includes links to abstracts of papers and articles. This is a very useful website.

The British Flute Society maintains a rather cumbersome website for people looking for information about historic examples of flutes and related instruments.

The National Flute Association is a U.S.-based society whose website is designed for current information only, and is of very limited value for researching historic flutes, but is otherwise an important resource.

The International Saxophone Society's website includes an archive of a very short list of articles that, though not scholarly, occasionally include information about the history of the instrument, makers, etc.

Smithsonian Institution, Division of Cultural History (americanhistory.si.edu/csr/cadch.htm). The collection is one of the major research collections for the U.S. piano and American reed organ industry. The website is disappointing as it includes no contents list. Information about the collection can be obtained by directly contacting the curators listed on the website.

Scholarly Societies and Related Topics

The American Musical Instrument Society (AMIS) (www.amis.org). This society publishes a scholarly journal, and a newsletter. Both publications include advertisements from professional dealers in antique musical instruments. This society's publication is available in many research libraries. The society's website contains important links to most of the important musical instrument museums throughout the world.

The International Committee of Musical Instrument Museums and Collections (www.music.ed.ac.uk/euchmi/cimcim) "aims to promote high professional standards in the use and conservation of musical instruments in museums and collections" (quoted from website). It is a member of the International Council of Museums. This is the most scholarly of the listed societies. This society's publication is not generally available in libraries.

The Galpin Society (www.music.ed.ac.uk/euchmi/galpin), based in England, is the oldest existing scholarly society dedicated to musical instrument research. It publishes a periodical that also includes advertisements from professional dealers in antique musical instruments. This society's publication is available in many research libraries.

The Fellowship of Makers & Researchers of Historical Instruments (aka Fomrhi) (www.nrinstruments.demon.co.uk/fomrhi.html). "Its aim is to promote authenticity in the preservation of original instruments, in making reproductions of such instruments, and in their use" (quoted from website). This society is the least scholarly of the listed societies, but articles in its publication can be very informative. This society's publication is not generally available in libraries.

Museums

The following list consists of websites for musical instrument museums and also museums with musical instrument divisions. Though this list is not complete, it represents some of the most useful websites available online as of August 2004. Ideally, a website should include a complete list of instruments in the museum, a good-quality photograph of the instrument, a description of the instrument and its history if available, whether the instrument is on display at the museum or must be viewed by special arrangement, and links to museum staff. For an updated list of websites, consult www.amis.org.

Bate Collection (www.ashmol.ox.ac.uk/ BCMIPage.html). Excellent collection, part of the Ashmolean Museum.

Boston Museum of Fine Arts (www.mfa.org). Extensive website with photographs and description on same page. Very useful website.

Deutsches Museum (www.deutsches-museum.de/ ausstell/dauer/musik/musik.htm). Text in German.

Edinburgh University Collection of Historic Musical Instruments (www.music.ed.ac.uk/euchmi).

Fiske Museum; Claremont, California (www.cuc.claremont.edu/fiske). The only musical instrument museum on the west coast dedicated to antique musical instrumets.

Kunsthistorisches Museum Vienna (www.khm.at/ homeE3.html). The oldest surviving collection of instruments in Europe. One of the largest collections of Renaissance and early Baroque instruments.

Library of Congress, Music Division, Dayton C. Miller Flute Collection (www.memory.loc.gov/ammem/dcmhtml/ dmhome.html). Though a small collection of wind instruments, this collection is especially strong in flutes made by Theobold Boehm, and Boehm/Mendler. Excellent website. Photographs of instruments and descriptions on the same page.

Metropolitan Museum of Art (www.metmuseum.org/collections/department.asp?dep=18). One of the most important museums in the United States.

Shrine to Music Museum. Name recently changed to National Music Museum (www.usd.edu/smm). Excellent website, excellent collection of instruments. An absolute must for anyone interested in musical instruments.

Yale University Collection of Musical Instruments (www.yale.edu/musicalinstruments). One of the first musical instrument collections in the U.S. Small but very important collection of keyboard instruments.

Additional Websites

The United States Patent Office website to search for musical instrument patents is http://www.uspto.gov/patft/index.html. This website requires some above-average skills to use. Patents from 1790 through 1975 are searchable only by Patent Number and Current US Classification. Locating the Current US Classification numbers is also daunting, but can be found online. If one has the patent number, use the following website: http://patft.uspto.gov/ netahtml/srchnum.htm. Do not include commas in the patent number search.

Auction Houses

Below is a list of auction houses that have held auctions of musical instruments.

W & F C Bonhams & Sons Ltd. U.K.
Bonham & Butterfields. San Francisco and Los Angeles, California, U.S.
Christie's. UK.
Hotel des Ventes de Neuilly. France.
Phillips. U.K.
Sotheby's. UK, US, etc.
Skinner Inc. Boston, Massachusetts, U.S.

Index

This index provides page numbers for information found within the Gallery of Instruments section, the makers' sections, and the Price List of Instruments. Within the Price List, all instruments are listed under the instrument type. No makers are listed in the index as the Price List is alphabetical by maker. As catalogs and auction catalogs described flutes and piccolos as "simple system" and "Meyer system" without much discrimination, readers will need to check both terms in this index. Readers are also directed to the appendices in this book, especially pages 143-156, which consists of auction prices of instruments listed by maker.